D0213581

How Women Legislate

How Women Legislate

SUE THOMAS

New York   Oxford
OXFORD UNIVERSITY PRESS
1994

Oxford University Press

Oxford   New York   Toronto
Delhi   Bombay   Calcutta   Madras   Karachi
Kuala Lumpur   Singapore   Hong Kong   Tokyo
Nairobi   Dar es Salaam   Cape Town
Melbourne   Auckland   Madrid

and associated companies in
Berlin   Ibadan

Copyright © 1994 by Oxford University Press, Inc.

Published by Oxford University Press, Inc.,
200 Madison Avenue, New York, New York 10016

Oxford is a registered trademark of Oxford University Press

All rights reserved. No part of this publication may be reproduced,
stored in a retrieval system, or transmitted, in any form or by any means,
electronic, mechanical, photocopying, recording, or otherwise,
without the prior permission of Oxford University Press.

Library of Congress Cataloging-in-Publication Data
Thomas, Sue, 1957–
How women legislate / Sue Thomas.
p. cm.   Includes bibliographical references and index.
ISBN 0–19–508507–8
ISBN 0–19–508508–6 (pbk)
1. Women in politics—United States.
2. Women legislators—United States.   I. Title.
HQ1236.5.U6T493 1994   320'.082—dc20   93–4264

1 3 5 7 9 8 6 4 2
Printed in the United States of America
on acid-free paper

LIBRARY
ALMA COLLEGE
ALMA, MICHIGAN

Acknowledgments

The first group of people I wish to thank for helping me turn the dream of this book into a reality is my teachers and friends from the University of Nebraska. On the top of this list of people who taught me the art and science of the study of politics is my adviser Susan Welch. No graduate student could have a more supportive and helpful guide. I am deeply grateful to her. Thanks also go to John Hibbing, who, at every step of the way, encouraged my efforts to learn substance, style, technique . . . and the confidence in my abilities necessary to master them. Finally, John Gruhl, Robert Sittig, Robert Miewald, and Lynn White were all helpful and encouraging at various points in the process. Thank you all.

Many people at Georgetown University were helpful in my efforts to complete this book. Advice and encouragement were provided along the way by my colleagues, Clyde Wilcox, Mark Warren, William Gormley, John Bailey, and, our department chair, Robert Lieber. Additionally, a large contingent of our graduate students offered crucial morale boosting and support when my spirits flagged. Many thanks to Anne Cammisa, April Morgan, Suzanne Dovi, Alexandra Carter, Lisa Ferrari, Carolyn Jesky, Lara Hewitt, Katherine Naff, John O'Donnell, and Jaime Weinberg. From among that list, I owe another debt of gratitude to three who worked on various research and editing tasks: Jaime Weinberg, John O'Donnell, and Lara Hewitt are responsible for helping me turn haphazard word-processing habits into readable, accurate, and correctly formatted prose. They spared me from endless numbers of errors, which was a monumental job. Of course, some errors remain, but it is not because these three people didn't do all they could to prevent them. I need to say a special further word about Lara Hewitt, who saved the day when unexpected surgery rendered me unable to sit at my computer and enter in final revisions to the manuscript. For her tireless work in January and February of 1993, I am deeply grateful.

On every project one finds special people in the discipline who make an extra effort to encourage the direction of one's work. Several who stand out for me and to whom I owe many thanks are Lyn Kathlene, Sue Tolleson Rinehart, Donley Studlar, Robin Kolodny, Georgia Duerst-Lahti, and Ted Jelen. Related to this group of people is one whose members have always been supportive—the people with whom I attended graduate school: Rebekah Herrick, Michael Moore, Jay Ovsiovitch, Jerry Stubben, Margery Ambrosius, Don Beahm, and Margaret Gust.

I also wish to thank David Roll, and Ruth Sandweiss, editors at Oxford University Press. It has been a pleasure to work with them from the beginning of the process to the end. While it is hard to imagine that such an anxiety-producing event could be made smooth and tension free, David and Ruth have achieved this remarkable state. Thanks also go to copyeditor, Grace Buonocore. On a related note, I wish to thank anonymous reviewers who worked with Oxford on this text.

Since some of the material from three of the chapters of this book appeared in different form in both *Journal of Politics* and *Western Political Quarterly,* thanks are in order for permission to use the material here.

This project would not have been started, much less completed, had it not been for funding from the Center for the American Woman and Politics, Eagleton Institute, Rutgers University, and the National Science Foundation, which provided funding through Grant No. SES–872221472.

Finally, I want to thank my spouse, Charles R. Tremper. It is enormously difficult to address all the ways in which his support was offered and gratefully accepted. Perhaps the most important has been his unflagging confidence that I could take this task to completion. From my earliest efforts in graduate school until today, he has believed in me and my ability to make a contribution to this field. On the days I was ready to give up hope or effort, he was always there to make sure I revived my spirits and renewed my endeavors. There are no words sufficient to convey my gratitude. To Chuck and to all the others named in this acknowledgment, thank you so much.

Contents

Tables

How Women Legislate

Introduction

Have women in legislative office had an impact on political processes and products? And, if so, is that impact similar to or different from the impact of men? Whatever the impact, how should it be judged or evaluated? What information about the political, social, and cultural environment helps us to understand why and how women participate as they do? This series of questions served as the impetus for this book. The answers are important because we cannot fully appreciate the influence of gender in the political realm without them. They are also important because no comprehensive understanding of legislative behavior is possible if they are absent.[1] Finally, the answers to these questions are increasingly important because women are running for and winning a greater share of public offices than ever before. In the 1992 election, the number of women in the U.S. Senate tripled, and the number of women in the U.S. House of Representatives nearly doubled. Currently, women hold 20 percent of state legislative seats and 10 percent of congressional seats. The latest comprehensive data for women's share of local-level office come from 1985, when women held 14 percent of mayoral offices and municipal or township governing boards. With more women in office, any impact they have is likely to have meaningful effects on legislative life. Until these effects are illuminated and understood, no theory of legislative behavior is sufficient.

The literature of political science and gender politics provides only a small amount of guidance about how to study the impact of women in office. Because women have so rarely been among the political elite, most political science research, when it considered the role of women, assumed that the male norm extended to them. Separate investigations were not common. Even the gender politics literature concentrated on the gender gap between women and men voters or their levels of participation in various political activities.[2] In recent years, as more and more women have waged campaigns for elective office, a great deal of work assessing their levels of success and its correlates has been undertaken.[3] But little research has been devoted to how women behave when they win office. Gradually, as women officeholders have taken their place beside men, scholars have turned their attention to this topic. What we have learned from their endeavors comprises essentially three stages of exploration.

In the first stage of research on women officeholders, we learned about the sociological characteristics of women in office compared with those of men. For example) women tended to enter politics from a background as a civic worker or community volunteer. Men, on the other hand, tended to enter politics from a professional base, usually some sort of business career. We also learned that women often entered politics at a later stage of life than did men, because women often fulfilled responsibilities as wives and mothers first.

The second stage of research about women in office provided insight into, among other things, women's attitudes about their role in the political world, their attitudes toward a variety of issues, and their voting records. We learned that women officeholders tended to perceive themselves as hardworking and responsible contributors to the process but also as people who often had a harder time proving themselves as capable contributors. Women in office also had somewhat different issue positions than did their male colleagues: they were more supportive of women's issues of both a traditional and feminist nature. For example, more women than men supported state-sponsored child care, and a much higher proportion of women than men (on the state and federal level) supported the Equal Rights Amendment (ERA). Their voting records were also more liberal than men's, indicating a consistency between issue position and voting behavior.

The third stage of research on women officeholders is just beginning to take shape. The overarching questions concern the impact women have had on the political realm. While past work indicated that differences existed between how women and men in office felt and behaved, it offered little indication of what kind of contribution women have made to politics or how to assess that contribution.

This book is meant to stretch the boundaries of this third stage of research on women among the political elite. Its overarching goal is to discover what difference, if any, women's presence has made to the political process or to legislation. Further, if women have made a contribution to the process, under what conditions is it enhanced and how best can we judge that contribution? The following section outlines the contents of each chapter and reveals the major themes of the book.

Plan for Analysis

The search for insight into the impact of women in political office begins in Chapter 1 with a journey through the literature (both scholarly and journalistic) about women politicians. What I rapidly discovered was that a variety of often unstated assumptions underlie the writings about women in politics. Because the assumptions were often contradictory, the conclusions reached by researchers offered little guidance into explanations of why women officeholders behaved as they did, how their attitudes and actions could be interpreted, or how changes in their behavior could be explained. If any of the questions that prompted my research in the first place were to be answered, I had to overcome the distortion of these assumptions and develop a new framework for understanding the ways in which women could have an impact in legislative office.

Undertaking this task of deconstruction and reconstruction was accomplished in stages. In order to sort the various assumptions about the behavior of political women, I first developed a typology of expectations—essentially a fourfold categorization that presents their essential components in stark relief. One dimension of the typology consists of attention to legislative procedures and legislative products. The other dimension concerns whether women ought to, do, or will seek to adapt to existing standards or reform them.

With typology in hand, knowledge of the reasons for its multiple and conflicting assumptions was my second focus. Of the three reasons uncovered, only one, societal indecision about the proper role of women in the public sphere, illuminates individual choices and collective action of modern political women. The extent to which women in the public sphere are accorded leeway in their actions has the best potential to explain their behavior over time. Moreover, this explanation is the only one with the capability of predicting future actions of women officeholders. Following this central argument about societal attitudes toward women's role in the public sphere, the journey to discover and to assess the impact of women officeholders moves from theoretical to empirical concerns.

The empirical exploration of the attitudes, actions, and motivations of women in legislative office begins with Chapter 2, which focuses on women in the legislative process. My central question is whether women alter the way legislative work is conducted or whether they work within existing procedural modes. Analysis of women state legislators' backgrounds, attitudes toward the political realm, and legislative activities currently and over time is the basis for my conclusions.

Early on, women state representatives were reticent about speaking out in the legislative setting and were reluctant to jump forcefully into the political fray. Their participation levels in typical legislative activities, such as speaking on the floor and in committee, working with their colleagues, and bargaining with lobbyists, were much lower than men's, and they seemed to focus on solving problems for constituents rather than on legislative battle. Their backgrounds in community activities, the helping professions, and family management, combined with the discrimination they felt in the legislative arena, appear to have contributed to this style of activity. Women's dissatisfaction and discomfort with existing norms of operation did not lead them to alter conventional legislative procedures; instead, they withdrew from active participation in them.

As women legislators gained more individual and collective experience in the political world, their levels of participation in the range of typical legislative activities rose sharply. Again, however, the end of that participation was not revolution but adaptation. Currently, women's and men's activity levels do not differ in any significant way. Although women and men still bring somewhat different types of backgrounds to their legislative position, and while discrimination based on sex has not been eliminated, progress has been made on both counts. The result is that women have increasingly chosen to participate in all aspects of legislative life.

These changes over time suggest that the wider societal debate about women's place in the public sphere has affected the way women have behaved in the political arena. As society expands its view about the extent to which women ought to participate, women themselves have responded by extending their range of involvement. However, it is too early to say whether bringing women into the legislative arena will transform its mode of operation. Before women could begin to change the way in which legislative work is done, they first had to feel comfortable with existing procedures, to master them, and to overcome the effects of discrimination. If women's participation in legislative life does bring procedural change, it is a change that will have to occur in the future.

In Chapter 3, I turn from the legislative process to the legislative *product*. Do women work to alter the kinds of legislation emerging from their statehouses, or do they pursue legislative agendas similar to those of men (or do they withdraw from the process in another way)? Voting records, issue attitudes, committee assignments, and policy priorities are the focus here.

Early women legislators had different attitudes than men toward political issues, had distinctive voting records, and sat on committees that coincided with women's traditional areas of expertise, such as education. Despite this, they did not withdraw from attention to bill introduction and passage, nor did they exhibit different sorts of policy priorities than men. However, current women legislators, despite pursuing the spectrum of political issues and sitting on the range of available committees, have developed their own distinctive set of concerns and priorities. Today, women legislators embrace priorities dealing with issues of women, and children and the family. Men do not share this priority list.

Once again, as societal views about the proper role of women in politics expanded, women began to embrace new possibilities for participation and contribution. Women legislators today successfully and expertly use the tools available to them to create public policy. What may be most interesting about their participation, however, is that while women use these tools to address the same public policy concerns as men, increased latitude in defining their roles has allowed them to go beyond those efforts and create distinctive priorities.

In light of the ongoing debate about women's proper role in the public sphere, it is not surprising that women representatives concentrate on legislation dealing with issues of women, and children and the family. Even though women have joined the public arena in increasing numbers and in all manner of occupations, and even though societal acceptance of women in these roles has grown, the debate is far from resolved. Society as a whole has not reached a consensus about how public and private spheres ought to be integrated and, in particular, about the extent of women's responsibilities to each. Women legislators face these questions at least as acutely as other women (if not more so), and they deal with those concerns by transforming them into public policy issues. Their efforts are ways to ensure their full and continuing role in legislative life.

Chapters 4 and 5 shift our focus from changes in the attitudes and behaviors of women legislators to how institutional factors interact with sociocultural variables to determine the type of contribution legislative women are able to make. First, the percentage of women in the state legislatures is linked to the extent to which female officeholders pursue distinctive policy priorities. Next, I examine why women have not altered legislative processes and have, rather, adopted existing tactics in light of institutional constraints on procedural and structural change.

More specifically, in Chapter 4, I further examine the argument that women legislators display distinctive policy priorities as their leeway to do so expands. In Chapter 3, I offered longitudinal evidence to support this argument; in Chapter 4, I use a cross-sectional approach, exploring whether the proportion of women in state legislatures is related to the extent to which they pursue distinctive policy priorities. Evidence suggests that support for female officeholders and their unique perspectives is related to women reaching a critical mass in any given legislature. Once that critical mass is reached, not only are women more likely to pursue their distinctive priorities, but they also begin to influence male colleagues to pursue similar interests in the places where women are most numerous and most organized.

In Chapter 5, I explore additional reasons why women's initial resistance to or distance from routine legislative activities resulted in their gradual adaptation to the process rather than reform of it. Even when individuals or groups within organizations have goals for change (even very clear-cut or strongly advocated goals), institutional factors condition whether and how those goals will be accomplished. As the recent history of reform of the U.S. Congress illustrates, efforts to modify or transform structures and rules are particularly vulnerable to institutional resistance, and only concerted effort by a core of the institution is likely to result in any level of success. Under these circumstances, it is easy to understand why women's behavior changed in the direction it did. Their adoption of existing procedures reflects, at the very least, the odds against any successful reform effort and the costs of launching one. This analysis does not suggest, however, that procedural reform is not part of women legislators' plans for the future.

In Chapter 6, I return to the overarching, guiding questions of this research study: what is the impact of women legislators on policy and process, and how should we evaluate their contributions to legislative life? I argue that, based on their fulfillment of many individual, group-based, policy, and procedural goals, women have had both a substantial and distinctive impact on the political arena. Indeed, the fact that women have been able to make an impact so significant in a relatively short period of time and under difficult conditions may be viewed as heartening to those who wish to see women's contributions as substantive as well as symbolic.

The conclusion to the book, Chapter 7, moves beyond what we currently know about the attitudes and actions of women legislators to muse about their future and the challenges that face them. Whether women join the mainstream of legislative politics depends first on how they transform it.

1

Expectations and Nature

The basic discovery about any people is the discovery of the relationship between its men and women.

PEARL S. BUCK

The current state of our knowledge about women in office is limited and inconclusive. What has been written—by both social scientists and journalists—is for the most part unsystematic, and a great deal of it is contradictory. Underlying the findings of most articles or books on the subject are a number of assumptions, usually unstated, about how the influence of femaleness impels women to act in the political realm. The problem is that no two authors agree about what this impact is, nor do most of them acknowledge possibilities other than those that formed the basis of their own work. Little if any analysis testing various assumptions or predictions has been offered.

The principal conflict is whether the perspective of women politicians will, for whatever reasons, be similar to or different from that of men. If different, bringing women into politics has the potential to usher in new ways of doing things or new things to do. If not, politics, with the increased inclusion of women, proceeds as usual. Without agreement by researchers about the nature or direction of the impact of women on the political realm, and without the testing of alternative hypotheses or the development of concrete theoretical arguments from which to base predictions or analyze results, the literature sends mixed messages about the behavior and motivations of women in office.

Some of the writing starts with the presumption that, as a result of bringing more women into political office, the very process by which business is conducted will be altered. Invariably, these articles suggest that women will reform political procedures to make them more humane, more cooperative, less cutthroat. Other writing about women in politics suggests that women keep their eyes trained on different sorts of legislative goals than men, either traditional goals, such as a focus on education or health and welfare, or feminist concerns, such as comparable worth or government-sponsored child care. Finally, a much smaller group of writings adamantly asserts that any expectations that women, as they move into the mainstream of political life, will be any different from men are naive and ill-considered. Women are required to operate within the boundaries of legislative norms in order to succeed and prosper, and they will, out of necessity and desire, meet these requirements.

Given the diversity of expectations about political women, it is not surprising that the literature on women officeholders is contradictory and lacks a clear set of conclusions about their attitudes and actions. My first step, therefore, is to organize the often tacit assumptions about how women behave in political environments and search for what is behind them. Only then can we develop a theoretical and empirical framework from which to launch a fresh investigation of the political impact of women.

Expectations about political women can be organized along two principal dimensions (see Table 1.1). The first is whether women adapt to existing political practices or reform them. The other dimension focuses on legislative products or outcomes—the bills that emerge from the process and whether they ought to reflect different concerns or maintain existing legislative agendas.[1]

The procedural half of the typology contains two opposing perspectives about how women react to existing legislative practices. Interestingly, both sides rely on the fact that women collectively have little elite-level political experience. One side consists of those who argue that women, accustomed to the nurturant life of home and hearth, abjure the coarser aspects of legislative life, such as arm-twisting and logrolling, and seek a reformed process. As Barbara Ehrenreich put it, "We imagined women storming male strongholds and, once inside, becoming change agents, role models, whistle-blowers. The hand that rocks the cradle was sure to rock the boat."[2]

TABLE 1.1.   Typology of Expectations

	Reformist	*Adaptive*
Procedures	Reformist Procedural	Adaptive Procedural
Products	Reformist Productive	Adaptive Productive

A second perspective concerning women's reactions to the messy game of politics comes from researchers who stress that socialization into existing norms and folkways of legislatures leads women to value success and to learn how to achieve it. While women may be initially uncomfortable with practices unfamiliar to them, they will come to see the wisdom of adapting to existing practices as they gain sufficient individual and collective experience in politics. With increased levels of sophistication and savvy, women learn that they can use the process for their benefit rather than risking their position by railing against it.

The second half of the typology focuses not on women's contribution to the process by which legislative work occurs but on the specific products that result from it. The writing on this subject is also notable for its contradictory impulses. First, commentators assert that women, owing to either their separate life experience or some form of natural sex difference, bring a distinctive focus to their political work. That is, they concentrate on reaching different goals than those of primary interest to men. Depending on which observer is consulted, legislators are said to focus on issues of either traditional interest to women or feminist interests. Women legislators, in this view, are expected to pursue legislation to create what Gloria Steinem called "a kinder, gentler, less rigidly gendered world."[3]

In the final section of the typology, writers argue that women politicians are no different from men in terms of the kinds of legislative products they pursue. Both must concentrate on the needs of their constituents in order both to fulfill their promises and to get reelected. To ignore these necessities would result in breaking one's contract with voters and ensuring the end of a political career. The main obligation an elected officeholder has is to devise legislative solutions to primary constituency needs. Any efforts beyond that are at the margins. In short, those supporting this perspective maintain that expecting anything else from women would be denying the realities of political life.

Why the Variety?

Why are there so many opposing assumptions about how women do and will behave? Only by understanding the reasons behind the variety can we organize a study of the behavior of women officeholders and try to explain what motivates it.

I see three interrelated reasons for the diversity of assumptions about political women. The first concerns societal indecision about women's proper role within the public arena and what women can or should contribute to this sphere. At its most fundamental level, the indecision reflects a society in transition. Women are still primarily responsible for private sphere matters and have yet to be fully integrated into the public sphere. The in-between status yields philosophical and political conflict about whether it is better to move ahead or to attempt to return to older patterns. Until there is a greater acceptance in society at large of women's full integration into the public sphere, women in those roles will be accorded less leeway to inhabit them fully. Those arrayed on either side of this debate usually base predictions about the attitudes and activities of political women on their preferred outcome.

On another level, indecision about women's role in the public sphere is also dependent upon one's vision of an ideal political atmosphere. This constitutes the second reason for the multiplicity of assumptions. For example, many participants and observers of legislative life decry its perpetuation of values that reward individual achievement above collective benefit. Because women have traditionally been associated with nurturant, less individualistic values, some people assume that they will transform the political arena along "kinder, gentler" lines. On the other hand, those who hold existing political processes and policy alternatives in high regard predict that women's contributions to the legislative arena will parallel men's contributions.

A third way to understand the conflicting assumptions about women in political office is to explore a deeper disagreement in society about women's "nature." Behind differences of opinion about whether private sphere values will guide the choices of political women or whether women will relinquish their private sphere perspectives when they assume public sphere duties are several questions about women's "true" character. Each of the questions are enduring and universal—and unknowable, at least at the present time, because each is essentialist. The first is, "Are women fundamentally different from men?" If so, how does that affect their public abilities, limits, and decisions? If women are not fundamentally different from men, ought they be treated exactly the same as men—even given the fact that in one sense, the reproductive sense, this is not possible? Even if women are not fundamentally different from men, how does their distinctive life experience as primary conductors of life in the private sphere affect their political attitudes and behaviors?

Of course we have no realistic way to answer these questions fully. But the problem runs even deeper: often those who agree on the answers disagree about what they mean for women in politics. Take, for example, the belief that women are fundamentally different from men. That is, the ability to bear children also means that women have certain natural capacities for caretaking and nurturing. On the one hand, many people who embrace this viewpoint insist that biological uniqueness translates into an imperative to confine women to caretaking functions. Forcing women to take on an "unnatural" role will destroy the unique abilities they possess.[4]

Others who believe that women and men are fundamentally different maintain that the differences are exactly the reason why women must not be locked out of the public sphere. This group maintains that women's natural capacities for compassion, cooperation, mediation, patience, and diligence are exactly the qualities that ought to be brought to the political realm. In fact, bringing women into politics in far greater numbers is the key to rescuing politics from a rampant individualism that results in deadlock or inadequate policy-making.[5]

Those who embrace the opposite point of view, that women and men, apart from reproductive purposes, are fundamentally similar, are not much better at agreeing what this means for how women ought to be treated and what their public sphere role should be. Both sides agree that women belong in the public arena. But the agreement breaks down when the discussion turns to how women are to be treated the same as men in situations in which equality is a meaningless concept. I am referring, of course, to reproductive differences. Many (although certainly not all) feminists support a different-but-equal position in which women are treated legally the same as men except in the reproductive sphere. That is, women's role in reproduction should be given special dispensation within the law. This will allow them to maintain their roles in the public sphere without being sanctioned because of time out of the work force due to maternity leaves or health problems.[6]

On the other hand, many who believe women to be fundamentally similar to men advocate absolutely equal legal treatment. Women's pregnancy and maternity absences should be treated no differently than any other disability regardless of the sex of the temporarily incapacitated person. To treat women as "special" in the eyes of the law only serves to distance them from the mainstream or the generally accepted.[7] Although differences on this particular issue may not seem of great direct importance to women in public office, the underlying disagreement it reflects in strategy among feminists will become clear later in this chapter.

This illustration is but one way to gain insight into the very different sets of assumptions that have been at the heart of research on women of-

ficeholders since its inception. My purpose in deconstructing gender politics research to date—uncovering its assumptions and the reasons for
them—is to reconstruct or develop a framework for answering the questions posed in the introduction, the most important of which is, "What is
the impact of women in legislative office?" That is the task to which I next
turn.

The Link between Societal Indecision
about Women's Proper Role
and the Study of Political Women

The shape of my research was dictated by the need to illuminate the ways in
which shifting societal perceptions about women in the public sphere—
regardless of whether they are attributed to sociocultural reasons, biological
reasons, or ideological reasons—affect the actions and attitudes of political
women. (For my purposes, the reasons for these shifts are not important,
only their impact on women in public office.) To understand these changes
over time, I examined women and men in legislatures at two points in time,
the early 1970s and the late 1980s.

I studied legislators in the 1970s by using the gender politics literature of
that period to piece together portraits of women's legislative activities and
their policy priorities. To study legislators in the 1980s I examined female
and male legislators in twelve states across the nation. I sent a mail survey
to legislators in all twelve states and conducted face-to-face interviews with
women officeholders in six of those states.[8] The dual research strategy of
surveys and interviews was designed to discern both what state representatives did and what they felt. Equally important to me were the motivations
for their actions.

My explanations and arguments derive not from the typology itself but
from three broader reasons I outlined for the conflicting assumptions about
political women. To recap, the three reasons I see for these assumptions are
that society is still in a transitional phase regarding how women ought to be
integrated into the public sphere; that many commentators and scholars
project personal ideals for the political arena on women officeholders; and
that positions on biological imperatives or sociocultural influences on
women and men dictate how one expects female politicians to behave. Of
these three, the first has the greatest potential to influence the collective
behavior of women in elective office. Individual viewpoints about the ideal

political world may guide the actions of a specific person, but lack of consensus on what that ideal is means that the collective behavior of women cannot be guided by it. Similarly, whatever the answer to the nature-versus-nurture question, it is—within the current bounds of our knowledge—unknowable. Although one viewpoint or the other has been used to justify legal and political decisions at various points in history, there has rarely been widespread consensus that political actions and behavior unquestionably result from biological imperatives. Certainly, no current collective belief structure on one side or the other of the question of women's "true" nature is dominant.

On the other hand, societal viewpoints about the proper role of women in the public sphere unquestionably have an impact on the individual and collective behavior of women officeholders. We are all products of our culture, and we all respond in some fashion to the boundaries on behavior imposed by that culture. It is no coincidence, for example, that women were scarce in public office prior to the early 1970s; the sociocultural environment frowned upon it. As society became more accepting of women in the public sphere, the number of women in public office has grown incrementally.

Another way to illustrate the phenomenon of evolving acceptance of women in the public sphere is to provide a dramatic example from a previous generation. Recently, the *Washington Post* printed excerpts from a column appearing in the *Foreign Service Journal* in May 1942.

> Some months ago, a deputation of women called upon Mr. Eden and asked him to admit women into the Diplomatic and Consular Services on the same conditions as men. Mr. Eden, after prolonged consideration, has replied in negative terms. . . . [O]f all public functions, diplomatic functions are those for which women are least well adapted. In the first place, there are certain practical difficulties which cannot be swept aside. There is, for instance, the problem of marriage. Is perpetual maidenhood to be imposed upon these women diplomatists, and if not, what happens if they marry their colleagues, or even outsiders? I can conceive few more otiose positions than that of the ambassador's husband. . . . These practical difficulties might well be overcome were it felt that the specifically feminine qualities of zeal, sympathy and intuition were useful qualities for a diplomatist to possess. I assert that these three qualities, unless kept under the firmest control, are dangerous qualities in international affairs. . . . And intuition all too often leads diplomatists to jump to conclusions which are subsequently falsified by events. . . . [T]he ideal diplomatists should be impartial, imperturbable and a trifle inhuman. These are not feminine qualities; they are male qualities.[9]

While these remarks seem so hopelessly outdated that they are amusing, society's acceptance of women in public sphere roles has still not been fully negotiated or defined. The recent discussion in the national media about the wives of presidential candidates is illustrative of the ongoing debate. Hillary Clinton, in a speech at Wellesley College prior to her husband's election, commented about the backlash against women: "Unmarried women are considered abnormal; a married woman without children is a selfish Yuppie; working women are bad mothers; mothers who stay home have wasted their education." In reporting on what she calls the "first lady culture clash," Eleanor Clift notes:

> Two years ago Barbara Bush was criticized by Wellesley students for living in her husband's shadow. Now Hillary, a Wellesley graduate, is being criticized for overshadowing her husband. It's hard to imagine anyone voting on the basis of who will be First Lady. But the candidates' wives stand as important exemplars at a time when "a woman's role" is once again the subject of hot debate.[10]

Evolving societal perspectives of women's role in the public sphere allow women access to an ever-expanding variety of roles; they also afford women the opportunity not just to choose public roles but to redefine them. Therefore, my first hypothesis is that the activities and priorities of women officeholders will evolve over time and that they will assume a more distinctive role. As long as sociocultural perspectives about the role of women in the public sphere are circumscribed, the distinctiveness of their actions will be limited. As our sociocultural perspectives of women's roles broaden, political women will be freer to bring whatever distinctive values they possess to the art and science of politics.

In what form will this distinctiveness be evident? I expect that women legislators will devote attention to those issues and activities that will make their sustained and enhanced presence viable. There is a clear element of self-interest in this. If women are to be full and equal partners to men, they will not only have to take advantage of their opportunities, but will also have to strive to perpetuate them. One way in which women are likely to ensure their role in legislative life is to integrate private sphere issues more squarely into the public agenda. As long as women are no longer dedicated fully or primarily to home and hearth, they must ensure that those needs continue to be met and those responsibilities continue to be discharged. Bringing previously private sphere issues to the governmental agenda is one way to address these concerns. This can only happen, however, if women work to ensure their status as *full-fledged* partners in the world of legislative politics and not just "honorary men" or "exceptional women." When a male-dominated environment, political or otherwise, allows only a few (usually very few) women into its enclave, no changes in its basic outlook, structure, or work product need be pursued.

Bringing new issues to the public agenda or situating issues that were previously marginal squarely in the center of that agenda is a gradual, incremental process. To do so requires no violent attack on basic assumptions about the task of legislatures; it needs no complete overhaul of procedures or structures. Further, new issues are brought to the governmental agenda by individuals. There need not be any collective agreement about the importance of a particular bill or set of bills for them to be placed into the legislative hopper.[11] Both of these conditions should help make it possible for women in statehouses to promote initiatives that will allow them and their female colleagues to maintain their public sphere opportunities.

Even if this prediction is correct—that women, as they are freed of gender-related constraints, will pursue an increasingly distinctive legislative agenda—will they succeed in altering legislative *procedures?* After all, an entire generation of feminist activists predicted that this would occur and urged it on.

My sense is that, at this stage of women's participation in elite politics, widespread alteration of legislative processes is not possible. Structure and rules are never neutral, and any change in either is a threat to those in power. Successful change of this kind requires a sustained, *collective* effort by a large majority of people engaged in the legislative enterprise. Since women are small in number in legislatures and because they are relative newcomers to the halls of politics, they cannot yet muster the kind of effort and support it takes to effectuate widespread procedural and structural change, nor could they reasonably attempt to do so without risking their personal political futures as well as those of future women officeholders.

One final point about women legislators' accommodation to existing political procedures must be made. While I predict that the presence of women will not result in an overhaul of the system, I do not intend to imply that there have been no changes in the ways in which women deal with that system. In fact, quite the opposite is true. As women legislators pursue distinctive policy issues, they will become better masters of the existing process. If they don't, their priorities are doomed to failure and their status and effectiveness in the legislative arena will be compromised.

Women in Politics: The Historical Perspective

One last task remains to set the stage for this study of women in political office. An appreciation for the historical political situation of women in the United States is necessary to situate research findings and to create a context in which to judge the contributions and impact of modern women officeholders. It is not only contemporary expectations faced by female officeholders and the constraints under which they labor that condition their goals and their impact; history also defines the range of their possibilities.

The contradictory expectations concerning today's women have deep historical antecedents. Unresolved contradictions about women's roles and nature echo throughout our history and have divided those who ruled the United States and those who sought to influence the rulers. When the issue is seen in this light, we not only understand the difficulties today's women officeholders face, but we also gain a new perspective on why the literature on gender politics has reflected contradictory assumptions and conclusions.

The Judicial Treatment of American Women

One vantage point from which to understand the impact of the debate over the role of women vis-à-vis society is to explore the legal history of women in the United States. Throughout our early history, an essentialist viewpoint guided legal thinking. In this view, God intended women and men to inhabit separate spheres, and women had no role in the public sphere. Further, violating that "natural law" was to court disaster. Not only were women ill suited to public life, they would be damaged by attempting to enter it. As noted legal scholar Martha Minow points out, the foundations of legal theory in the United States are based upon the "tendency to treat differences as essential, rather than socially constructed." She continues, "Similarly, the assumption of autonomous individualism behind American law, economic and political theory, and bureaucratic practices rests on a picture of public and independent man rather than private—and often dependent, or interconnected—woman."[12]

Early in our nation's history, women were denied their property and even their identity, as they were assumed to be under the guidance of men. Separate spheres for women and men were given the blessing of the United States Supreme Court.[13] For example, in 1873 the Court denied Myra Bradwell the right to practice law on the grounds that a woman's "destiny and mission" were to be a wife and mother. Justice Bradley wrote:

Man is or should be woman's protector and defender. The natural and proper timidity and delicacy which belongs to the female sex evidently unfits it for many of the occupations of civil life. . . . The harmony of interests and views which belong, or should belong, to the family institution is repugnant to the idea of a woman adopting a distinct and independent career from that of her husband. The paramount destiny and mission of women are to fulfill the noble and benign offices of wife and mother. This is the law of the Creator.[14]

Apparently, housewifery was so time-consuming that women could not even take time out to register their vote for public offices. In 1875 the Court unanimously denied them the opportunity to do so.[15] To make sure that women devoted time to their families, legal restrictions were placed on the number of hours women could work outside the home. In 1908 the Court stated:

That woman's physical structure and the performance of maternal functions place her at a disadvantage in the struggle for subsistence is obvious. This is especially true when the burdens of motherhood are upon her. Even when they are not, by abundant testimony of the medical fraternity continuance for a long time on her feet at work, repeating this from day to day, tends to injurious effects upon the body, and as healthy mothers are essential to vigorous offspring, the physical well-being of woman becomes an object of public interest and care in order to preserve the strength and vigor of the race.[16]

Not only the number of hours but also the type of work women engaged in was of interest to the Court. In 1948 the Supreme Court prohibited women (except the wives and daughters of a bar owner) from bartending.[17] Finally, as another way to regulate the type of duties for which women were most fit, the Court in 1961 decided that jury selection that chose women on a different basis than men (with the effect of discouraging women from serving) was acceptable.[18] The opinion of the Court about how women's reproductive capacities should affect her responsibilities to family and indeed the whole human species shows a remarkable similarity over time.

Despite the enlightened emancipation of women from the restrictions and protections of bygone years, and their entry into many parts of community life formerly considered to be reserved for men, woman is still regarded as the center of home and family life. We cannot say that it is constitutionally impermissible for a state, acting in pursuit of the general welfare, to conclude that a woman should be relieved from the civic duty of jury service unless she herself determines that such service is consistent with her own special responsibilities.[19]

Despite the fact that biological essentialism pervaded nearly two hundred years of judicial decision making, the Supreme Court of the United States, from the 1970s on, reversed its thinking and almost universally adopted an equality perspective. In cases dealing with sex equity, the Court has accepted arguments that women are just like men and ought to be treated as such.[20] Thus, the Court struck down laws that discriminated against women in jury selection, preferred men over women as executors of wills, allowed divorced fathers to support male children until the age of 21 and females only until the age of 18, denied employment or promotion of women into professional partnerships, denied employment of women with young children, imposed arbitrary height and weight standards for employment, required women to take maternity leave, and permitted differential pension payments for women and men.[21] In 1971, in a case dealing with executors of wills, the Court held:

> To give a mandatory preference to members of either sex over members of the other, merely to accomplish the elimination of hearings on the merits, is to make the very kind of arbitrary legislative choice forbidden by the Equal Protection Clause of the Fourteenth Amendment.[22]

Thus, the judicial history of women in the United States is marked by two very distinct periods. In each, the fundamental nature of women has been seen clearly, although very differently. In the first period, women's natures were determined to be suited for private life, and the law reflected that view. In the second period, women's natures were seen to be similar to men's in every respect. The law was, accordingly, shaped to reflect this newfound reality. This standard was maintained even on the one issue in which acknowledging inherent differences seemed unavoidable, the issue of reproduction. The theoretical, ideological, and practical difficulties faced by advocates of treating women the same as men have echoed in recent pregnancy decisions of the United States Supreme Court and remain unresolved today.

General Electric Co. v. Gilbert (1976) ruled on the issue of whether employers' exclusion of pregnancy from medicaid benefits constituted sex discrimination.[23] The problem with which the Court had to grapple was how to maintain standards of equity in the face of a situation that was inherently unequal. The medical needs of women in the work force were not the same as those of men in the work force (or those of women and men outside the work force, for that matter). Was it unjust for insurance companies to cover certain kinds of voluntary conditions and not others? In keeping with its overarching theory that the sexes should be treated equally, the Court developed a surprising logic to justify allowing insurance companies to exclude pregnancy and related conditions from coverage. It asserted that pregnancy among employed women is not a condition particular to their sex but a particular condition regardless of their sex. Minow explains:

> The Court considered, both as a statutory and a constitutional question, whether discrimination in health insurance plans on the basis of pregnancy amounted to discrimination on the basis of sex. In both instances, the Court answered negatively because pregnancy marks a division between the groups of pregnant and non-pregnant persons, and women fall into both categories.[24]

The choices faced by the Court were either to maintain strict standards of equality regardless of unequal circumstances or to create equal outcomes for those unequal situations. As noted, the Court chose the former course, but that did not end the debate. Subsequent to this decision, the United States Congress passed the Pregnancy Discrimination Act of 1978, which mandated that differential treatment of women due to pregnancy or related circumstances constituted discrimination and was, therefore, illegal.[25]

This Supreme Court decision and actions by the Congress illustrate well the difficulties inherent in creating public policy in a society that has not fully accepted women in a public role as well as a private one. It also illuminates that deep-seated indecision and confusion present on a societal level about women's proper place in the public realm.

The Political History of American Women

Women's political history well illustrates the definitional struggle explored in this chapter. The efforts women have made to alter their political and legal status—from suffrage to the ERA, from Seneca Falls to the current debate on reproductive rights—have reflected conflicts about the place of women outside the private sphere.

A convenient starting point is the suffrage movement. Those who first advocated the vote for women did so on the grounds that women and men were equally capable of representing themselves and that women should not be prevented from exercising political responsibility. Those who advocated this equality strategy did so across the board, fighting for equal property rights and equal marriage and divorce laws as well as the right to vote.[26] Indeed, as Susan B. Anthony stated at a trial in her defense:

One-half of the people of this nation today are utterly powerless to blot from
the statute books an unjust law, or to write there a new and a just one. The
women, dissatisfied as they are with this form of government, that enforces
taxation without representation—that compels them to obey laws to which
they never have given their consent—that imprisons and hangs them without
a trial by a jury of their peers—that robs them, in marriage, of the custody of
their own persons, wages and children—are this half of the people who are
left wholly at the mercy of the other half, in direct violation of the spirit and
letter of the declaration of the framers of this government, every one of which
was based on the immutable principle of equal rights to all.[27]

However, this first group of suffragists competed with and were soon
superseded by those who pressed for votes for women based on the fundamental *difference* between the sexes. Women were said to have more
temperate, moral natures than men and that politics could benefit enormously from their influence. Some argued that giving women the vote
would result in a purified political realm.[28] Public policies would be more
ethically informed, issues of morality (like temperance) would gain the
upper hand, and the role of the family and its centrality to society would be
of foremost concern.[29] As Sara Evans notes:

Suffragists not only asserted that women's nature suited them to the new
social responsibilities of the state, they also claimed that female morality
would clean up corruption. Indeed, "sweeping out the scoundrels" could be
another form of civic housecleaning! Furthermore, because of their different
life experiences, women needed the vote to protect their own special interests
whether as mothers concerned for the education of their children, as working
women subjected to exploitation without protection, or as the abused wives
of drunkards.[30]

Although those pressing for women's suffrage were, because of ideological disagreements, unable to agree on a strategy, those fighting against
suffrage appeared to solidify their efforts by asserting the difference perspective. Antisuffrage advocates put a twist on the purity arguments of the
prosuffrage: women's moral sensibilities would be corrupted by participation in politics. Being part of the world of compromise, bargaining, and
negotiation would only tarnish their sweet natures. Allowing them to stray
from their natural roles would not only harm women, it would harm the
family structure that women were responsible for protecting. In the words
of Senator George Vest (uttered in 1887):

I would not, and I say it deliberately, degrade woman by giving her the right
of suffrage. I mean the word in its full signification, because I believe that

woman as she is to-day, the queen of the home and of hearts, is above the political collisions of this world, and should always be kept above them. . . . It is said that the suffrage is to be given to enlarge the sphere of woman's influence, Mr. President, it would destroy her influence. It would take her down from that pedestal where she is today, influencing as a mother the minds of her offspring, influencing by her gentle and kindly caress the action of her husband toward the good and pure.[31]

In short, women's contributions were so important to keeping society functioning and their task was so exalted that they should be considered superior to men, not inferior. It was frequently said that women should desire to remain superior, not revert to a lesser, equal status.[32] Senator Williams from Oregon well illustrated this feeling: "Women in this country by their elevated social position, can exercise more influence upon public affairs than they could coerce by the use of the ballot."[33]

This struggle for definition continues today. Indeed, it seems even more pronounced. While opponents of feminist reform rely largely on arguments of women's fundamental difference, feminists are more fragmented than ever about how their beliefs about the nature of women inform their political strategy. Opponents of modern feminist goals sound remarkably similar to the opponents of suffrage. The New Right argues not only that women should stay in the home and raise children but that public policies also ought to be developed to encourage this choice.[34] Women's special, superior place as the moral protector of society ought to be preserved, according to these political activists, best represented by Phyllis Schlafly and ERA opponents, or civilized society is in serious danger of deterioration. In the words of Connie Marshner, a leader in the "profamily" movement:

[Today's woman] is the mother of the citizens of the twenty-first century. It is she who will more than anyone else transmit civilization and humanity to future generations and by her responses to the challenges of life, determine whether America will be a strong, virtuous nation. . . . [S]he is oriented around the eternal truths of faith and family. Her values are timeless and true to human nature.[35]

Among feminists, proponents of the equality strategy, like their predecessors, want women to have all the rights, privileges, and responsibilities befitting citizens of the nation. These strategists advocate equal credit rights, equal educational opportunities, and equal marital, family, and parental responsibilities. The hope is that if legal barriers to women's full participation in all walks of life are removed, eventually cultural barriers will be overcome.[36] Much of this work has been successful. Laws passed include the Equal Pay Act of 1963, the Equal Credit Opportunity Act of 1974, and Title IX of the 1972 Educational Amendments (which mandated equal treatment for girls and women in all facets of educational experiences).

These advocates press for strategies of equality because they fervently believe that women and men are fundamentally similar. Equality advocates also support such strategies because the lesson they have learned over the years is that involving a different nature of women or providing special treatment because of their reproductive responsibilities, for example, works to the detriment of women rather than their advancement. Advocating a political strategy based on difference, they contend, has always led women to inferior status somewhat along the lines of the infamous "separate but equal" position regarding race. Every time a particular public policy has been created to protect women, women seem to have come out the worse for it.[37] This apparently has even been the case with programs designed specifically to relieve inequalities between the sexes.[38] The best example of this thinking can be found in the discussion in the previous section of this chapter about the legal treatment of pregnancy in the workplace. If women's reproductive status is seen as special or in a category by itself, then legal and political arguments can be devised to prevent women from protecting their public sphere role while fulfilling the private sphere function of pregnancy and childbirth.

But the modern women's movement also includes feminists who advocate a strategy of difference. Under the umbrella of difference are a number of factions, ranging from feminist separatists who want to abandon the corrupt world of men to those who wish to ensure that women's special characteristics are valued, protected, and, ultimately, infused into society.[39] It is nearly impossible to do justice to the variety of opinions and strategies of this section of the feminist movement, so I will only provide a couple of examples to illustrate the point that many current activists believe that women are fundamentally different from men and that this difference is politically relevant. Feminist separatists believe that the character of women impels them to value, among other things, cooperation over competition and nurturing over engaging in violence and repression. Therefore, separatists, as the name implies, want to create communities of women in which their special qualities could be encouraged and developed out of danger from aggressive men. Ultimately, society could be transformed so that these superior female qualities will prevail. Estelle Freedman well articulates the need for separatism:

At certain transitional periods, the creation of a public female sphere might be the only viable political strategy for women. . . . The creation of a separate, public female sphere helped mobilize women [in the nineteenth century] and gained political leverage in the larger society. A separatist political strategy, which I refer to as "female institution building," emerged from the middle-class women's culture of the nineteenth century. Its history suggests that in our own time, as well, women's culture can be integral to feminist politics.[40]

Another example, referred to earlier, is feminists who wish to acknowledge women's inherent differences from men and ensure that these differences are protected politically. Accordingly, these feminists advocate policy changes in current law not only to give women equal status with males in society but also to protect their special capacities and roles. In other words, it is not only equal credit laws that should be promulgated but policies such as special maternity leaves and child and elderly care time requirements that should be recognized.[41]

On a practical rather than a theoretical level, feminists who eschew equality strategies point out that there are two problems with that particular strategy. First, they claim, imposing equal treatment on a foundation of male privilege still results in women maintaining a lesser status. What good is it, for example, to remove legal barriers to a variety of educational and occupational opportunities when society is still constructed such that women are almost fully responsible for home and family life? Equally important, what good is removing those barriers if society still sees those educational institutions or jobs as best inhabited by men? In other words, removing barriers does not make the playing field equal. A second problem with equality strategies concerns failure to address the real, undisputable biological differences between women and men. These advocates maintain that it is necessary to construct differential policies for men and women at least with respect to pregnancy and childbirth. That is, differential treatment is necessary if women are to bear children and carry out a full-time public role.[42]

Perhaps Martha Minow best describes the conflicts over how best to elevate women's political status that have divided feminists:

If, at times, feminists appear contradictory, arguing both for the right of women to be included and treated like men and for the right to have special treatment (which valorizes women's differences), feminists have an explanation. The inconsistency lies in a world and set of symbolic constructs that have simultaneously used men as the norm and denigrated any departure from the norm.[43]

One final, practical illustration highlights how deeply conflicts over women's role are embedded in the public sphere and how they pervade the political strategies of women. The issue concerns how best to increase the numbers of women winning elective and appointive office. Feminist organizations dedicated to increasing the numbers of women in office have a long-standing disagreement about which tactics will be more persuasive to the public. On one side are those who assert that, to get ahead, female politicians must be viewed as being no different from male politicians. Only with little danger of women legislators altering the status quo will voters realize they have nothing to lose by electing more women.

The opposing viewpoint is that more women candidates would advance if their special attributes were played up. Voters are assumed to react positively toward the moral, ethical, humane, and compassionate attitudes of women and more likely to elect women—especially when they tire of the corruption and unethical behavior that are seen to pervade the current system. Indeed, judging by the conduct of and results of the 1992 election, this strategy has proven to be an effective one—at least at this particular time.[44]

Conclusion

This chapter's purpose was to invite readers on a journey—one designed to culminate in an understanding of the contributions of women who hold legislative office. The first step on the journey was to clear a path through the tangled and overlapping terrain of information about women representatives. Three path-clearing techniques were offered: a typology of expectations to help sort out the multiplicity of perspectives about political women's attitudes and behaviors; an exploration of the deeper social attitudes and conflicts that underly the diverse perspectives; and a survey of lessons gleaned from the legal and political treatment of women in history. The remainder of this book is devoted to empirical analysis of how legislative women have acted, where they stand today, and what that means for legislative and political life.

2

The Procedural Question:
Reform or Adapt?

In April 1987, a small political party in Iceland called the Kvennalistinn (or Women's Alliance) won enough seats in Iceland's parliamentary election to hold the balance of power in the government. The feminist Alliance, which was formed in 1983, faced a tough decision: should it join the coalition and compromise some of its primary goals or should it decline to govern jointly?

Before trying to guess the direction of the decision, consider Kvennalistinn's mode of operation and its goals. First, the Alliance had no leader, and all decisions were made by consensus. Further, all the party's officeholders pledged to serve no longer than six to eight years. Positions on issues were developed with the idea that women's experience and values differ from men's and that it is imperative to bring them into the political realm.

As you may have gathered by now, the aim of the Kvennalistinn was (and is) to work within the system to change it—both the process by which decisions are made and the decisions themselves. Members believe that competitive outlooks and careers in politics hurt both the process and the product. Not surprisingly, once in political office, they have operated in a distinctive fashion. One early officeholder from the Alliance, Sígridur Dúna Kristmundsdóttir, made her first speech in the parliament (the Althing) by telling a story about a single mother who worked in a factory by day and took in sewing at night just to hold her family together. Kristmundsdóttir noted:

> I told about her concrete life experience, what it feels like on her body. I'm not aware that anybody had done that before. It's so easy in Parliament to be

completely removed from what it is like to survive in this economy. The
reality of women could have been on the moon for them.[1]

The kinds of political products that members of the Kvennalistinn advocate include women's issues such as child care, sex education, and fair
salaries. Despite a special dedication to these issues, however, members of
the Alliance insist there is a need for a women's point of view on all
domestic and foreign issues. Its platform addresses each issue based on the
economic model of a housewife on a limited budget.

Despite, or perhaps in spite of, the unique mission and goals of Kvennalistinn, it was, as noted above, successful in the elections of April 1987.
Because no two parties together had enough seats to form a government,
Kvennalistinn was asked to join a coalition government, thus holding the
balance of power. The members of Kvennalistinn refused the offer. Because the other two potential partners in the coalition would not accede to
the party's bottom-line policy demands (most important, a minimum wage
proposal), they opted out. Said one: "We were ready to take part in the
government, but only if it would really matter. We didn't want to be
flowers to make the government look good to the world."[2] Of course, the
women in the Alliance were accused of having no acquaintance with reality
and no knowledge of politics. Said one reporter who watched the party,
"The women of Kvennalistinn agree that they're not 'real' politicians in the
traditional sense, that their intention is to change the political system and
women's lives in the process."[3]

Thus, politics as usual was not the mode of operation of the Kvennalistinn. Did it hurt the party? Did it become irrelevant? In 1988, Kvennalistinn found its support among the public at a record 31.3 percent, the
highest of Iceland's six major parties. If an election had been held at that
time, it would have had the power to establish a new government.

Although this example comes not from the United States but from Iceland, the message that we can take from it is that with a distinctive perspective, women politicians can make a difference and that it is possible to
abandon politics as usual. Has that message been heeded by the women of
United States legislatures? Have women worked, for example, to reform
legislative procedures, or have they adapted to the process? These are the
questions encapsulated in Chapter 1's typology of expectations. Contrary to
the example of Kvennalistinn, on the subject of procedural reform, I predicted that women legislators will not have sought wholesale transformation of the ways in which legislatures do their business. This type of

widespread and extensive alteration of existing procedures and practices is more than is reasonable to expect given the amount of time women have been part of legislative life, their representation in statehouses, and the leeway they, as female pioneers in the public sphere, were likely to have been accorded. Even though the women of Iceland face many (but not all) of the same circumstances, they operate in a system of proportional representation that creates an entirely different set of possibilities for them and the power they wield. The prediction that women state legislators in the United States will not have concentrated on procedural overhaul does not presuppose that their procedural activity will have remained static over time; it simply means that the change will take a different form. Just what that form has been is explored in subsequent sections.

The Study of Women Officeholders

Before moving directly into the analysis of research on women legislators, it is important to discuss the kind of research studies that are available. As you read, note that the phrase "early" work on women legislators is a relative term. In the world of gender politics scholarship, the early period took place only about fifteen to twenty years ago. The reasons the history of research in this area is so short are two: first, gender politics is a very recent addition to the topics political scientists study. With the rise of the feminist movement in the 1960s and 1970s, scholars were inspired to investigate how bringing women into the political system had an impact on the people within the system and the institutions themselves. It was not until that point that an agenda developed.

A second reason why the literature on women officeholders did not grow substantially until the 1970s has to do with numbers of women in office. There were not enough women in legislative bodies before that time to make analytical comparisons among women themselves or between women and men possible. Prior to that point, the only studies of women officeholders that were feasible were biographical sketches from which few generalizable conclusions could be constructed. Put simply, studying women as a group meant that a group had to be present in the first place.

Because of the problem of numbers, early research about women officeholders tended to concentrate on women state legislators. The federal and local levels either contained too few women or presented problems of data collection. First, on the federal level, there were so few women (in 1971, 2.8 percent of Congress consisted of women) that difficulties arose in making a comparison of women and men. It was possible to look exclusively at women, but even those kinds of studies would have been problematic. With such a small number, it would have been hard to be sure that the women under study were at all representative of any wider group whether that group was women legislators or women politicians or women among the mass public. While some studies of women at the congressional level were conducted (primarily, studies of roll call voting behavior), the bulk of the work was at the state level.

Studying women officeholders on the local level also proved problematic. Although greater numbers of women (and greater percentages per body held local offices than congressional seats), other problems arose for researchers of gender politics (in 1975, 3 percent of the members of county governing boards were women and 4 percent of mayors and municipal/township governing boards were women). While there existed a large reservoir of women, the thousands of school boards, city councils, and boards of supervisors across the nation made it difficult to gather data from each of these sources. Accurate and complete records of women in these positions were not kept at any central clearinghouse, and the cost in time and money to carry out research on each site was overwhelming.

The state level, on the other hand, afforded sufficient numbers of women to make investigation fruitful, accurate records of women in these positions were kept, and the number of locations to which one had to travel for data collection was held constant at 50. All the conditions seemed right for researchers to gather and analyze data that would be meaningful and manageable, and so it was that state legislators received the bulk of the gender politics research attention at this time (as it still does today). Our knowledge, then, of women officeholders of the 1970s is culled largely from the level of the statehouse legislator.[4]

Since the early 1970s, when a body of gender politics literature developed, the field has grown enormously and studies of women officeholders have flourished. As suggested in the Introduction, many types of analysis have been pursued, including information about the life experiences and political attitudes women bring to office, their political ideologies, how they vote compared with men, whether they embrace or reject norms and standards of action, and the type of policies they pursue. In general, the direction of the body of research now available ranges from descriptions of characteristics of women to attempts to discern their impact on the political realm. In Chapters 2 and 3, the scope and evolution of this research unfold.

Women Legislators: The Early Years

What follows is an exploration of the backgrounds women and men in state legislatures of the early 1970s brought to their jobs, the attitudes they held toward women's place in the political arena, and the extent to which women participated in the normal range of legislative activities. The backgrounds and attitudes of female officeholders contain the seeds of explanation of why they chose the paths they did relative to participation in legislative activities and how those decisions relate to procedural transformation or acceptance.[5]

Backgrounds

Research on state legislators of the 1970s provided a great deal of information about the backgrounds they brought to their jobs. The primary message to come from this body of work was that the experiences and circumstances that women and men brought to their political jobs tended to differ in meaningful ways. In particular, women legislators were more likely to have lesser levels of educational, occupational, and political experience than men. They also, not surprisingly, had much higher levels of family responsibility than men.

On the educational front, women tended, more often than men, to be college graduates. However, women achieved graduate or professional degrees less often than men. Put simply, while women legislators were by no means poorly educated, they did have fewer years of education than their male colleagues.

> Educational disparities between the sexes appear at the higher achievement levels. The majority of both sexes have not had any training beyond "some college"; however, women who continue generally stop with the college degree, whereas many men go on to obtain advanced degrees. The male legislator's occupational pattern often necessitates more educational preparation; the female legislator's occupation does not. (There is no difference in the educational achievement levels of employed and nonemployed women.)[6]

The lesser educational status of women in state legislatures corresponded to differences in their occupational experience. Not only did male officeholders work in professional occupations more often than did women, they also had a more diverse range of occupations. Women tended to be congregated in low-status, poorly paid professions.

> Occupation and employment status reflect the differing social roles of men and women. Forty-six percent of the women list their occupation as house-wife, while 53 percent of the men hold jobs in either the professions or business. The vast majority of the women currently employed outside the home hold relatively low status professions. Clerical and sales and service positions are the norm; none is an attorney; and only 5.3 percent are in the professions.[7]

These background differences between women and men meant that women, as a group, were less likely than men to inhabit occupations that could provide high status, high prestige, and high community visibility. Such occupations also provide the flexibility of time, contacts among the community, and access to politicians and donors helpful in launching and sustaining a political career. Thus, women state legislators made their way into politics from alternate routes than men.

A second category of background differences between women and men in state legislatures concerns the family responsibilities of each. Predictable and very deeply divided portraits of the family commitments of women and men were evident. Marriage rates, number of children, and age of entrance into office reflect this pattern.

While the majority of all state legislators during this era were married, slightly more men enjoyed this status than women. Presumably, it was more difficult for women to maintain a demanding professional career at the same time they fulfilled the role of wife. It was apparently even harder to maintain careers as well as the responsibilities for children. This likely accounts for the fact that female representatives tended to have fewer children than men and fewer young children. One study of the era found that "twenty-eight percent of the men had a child below the age of ten, while this was true of only 13 percent of the women."[8] Another reported that a low proportion of female statehouse representatives had young children, with only 3 percent with children under 6 years old and 47 percent with children 18 plus.

In cases where women did not forgo marriage and children to be politically active, women state legislators were more likely to postpone elective political involvement until after their children were grown. A lower entry age into the legislature for men than for women was the norm. "The age differences between the men and women also reflect societal gender roles. As expected, there are very few young women—only 7 percent of the women are under forty as compared to 21 percent of the men.''[9] Another study reported that the female statehouse legislators were predominantly middle-aged (40–49 years of age), with a higher percentage falling in the 50-plus age category than 39 and under.

These trends in marriage rates and number and ages of children illuminate the difficulty women have had in maintaining professional and private careers. Because women were responsible for home and hearth, political careers for them have often been an either-or choice—or, at least, a life cycle–dependent choice.[10]

Perhaps owing to the circumstances noted above, women officeholders of this era had different types of political experience than men before ascending to the state legislature. While both sexes were equally likely to have held public office prior to their current position, there were differences in the kinds of office occupied. A school board job was most common for women, while a city council slot was most common for men.[11] Of those women who had prior appointive experience, a majority had held a party office.[12] One particularly interesting finding was that the more recent female entrants in state legislatures in these studies had more political experience prior to their current office than women who had entered earlier in the decade.[13]

After a fairly thorough cataloging of the backgrounds women and men brought to the world of statehouses, the next important area of inquiry is whether these distinctive backgrounds contributed to women legislators' attitudes toward the political world. For example, did women's quite separate sets of experiences, ranging from the educational and occupational to the familial, contribute to their attitudes about the political process and women's place within it?

Attitudes

Research on the political attitudes of officeholders shows marked differences between female and male state legislators. The differences are apparent for every dimension explored, including perceptions about how hardworking women politicians are, their levels of effectiveness, and the advantages and disadvantages they face as a result of participation in a largely male-dominated environment. In fact, it would not be an overstatement to say that the viewpoints of female and male legislators of the 1970s displayed dramatic differences. The presentation below is structured so that the views of women legislators and men legislators are presented serially.

An area of enduring interest to researchers of gender politics has been how women see their performance on the job relative to their male colleagues. The literature is replete with comments by women officeholders indicating that they view themselves and their female colleagues as extraordinarily hardworking and dedicated to the job. Women state legislators of the 1970s conform to this widespread pattern. They perceived themselves as unquestionably harder working and more responsive to constituents than their male colleagues. The frequent comments elicited by the primary studies of this era indicate that women legislators felt they read and studied legislation and policy alternatives much more frequently and with greater attention than their male counterparts, spent more time working directly with constituents and listening to their problems, were more conscientious, had higher-quality performance in office, spent more time on official activities, had greater general knowledge and information than men, had better abilities to make relevant contacts, did more research on pending issues, and were better at developing policies. Perhaps because of these differences, women in statehouses believed that "the country would be better off if there were more women in public office."[14] The common thread among the comments reported was that women were more attentive to detail, were willing to spend time developing alternative solutions to problems, and were better at working with people.

Did all that attention and hard work translate into high levels of effectiveness? Not according to the majority of women state legislators. These women did not feel that they were as well prepared for legislative life as men and did not feel themselves to be as influential with their colleagues, despite high levels of preparation and knowledge about the bills before them. On self-ratings about their preparation for office and their effectiveness in office, more female than male officeholders rated themselves poorly on past training and experience, persuasiveness in argument, influence and prestige with colleagues, financial and economic judgment, and overall effectiveness.[15]

It is interesting to speculate about why women felt they worked harder and were more prepared than their male colleagues but did not consider themselves to be as effective. The first reason may simply have been the effects of newcomer status. Newcomers or inexperienced participants often have to expend more effort than average to catch up to their colleagues. Until the transition is made from novice to old hand, these players will likely be less effective than the experts. Until one is skilled in the rules of the game, winning it is very difficult.

Another reason why women did not consider themselves to be effective players of the political game may have had to do with the limitations society places on women in public sphere roles. Much more so than today, female legislators of this generation were very much without role models of how to do their job. Most important, conventional wisdom regarding women's inability to play hardball or to do the heavy lifting of political life had the probable effect of creating doubts about their abilities to do so as well as disincentives to step too far out of their traditional role. Thus, it is highly likely that the women themselves responded to ingrained training about sex roles suggesting that women excel at tasks involving methodical work and attention to detail but are poor at taking risks or engaging in such political staples as horse trading or logrolling. Operating within the limitations of sex stereotyping would have produced behaviors that were conducive to widespread knowledge and long hours; doing so would also have resulted in the avoidance of behavior that contributed to effectiveness in the political arena. The result of working hard but feeling of limited effectiveness is predictable given the constraints under which these women labored.

Evidence that this may have been the case is available in responses to survey questions about what women legislators saw as the advantages and disadvantages of being a woman in a male-dominated environment. As illustrated below, each of the advantages and disadvantages cited by women legislators conformed to stereotypical attitudes about women's capabilities and limitations within the public sphere. The responses suggest that both women and men either accepted or at least worked within the boundaries of these stereotypes.

First, because many men assumed that women were not savvy players of the political game, they underestimated their women colleagues. Several women said this miscalculation on the part of men resulted in advantages in getting amendments accepted or bills passed. Women also felt that traditional views about women allowed them to be more direct in seeking information without experiencing sanctions and resulted in a lesser likelihood of being undercut by colleagues. Breaking the rules of the game was also likely to have been seen as less serious for women than for men. To put it in concrete terms, one woman state legislator in Irene Diamond's study noted:

> I have a great reputation for—you know, we have these hearings, and I'm supposed to be a commissioner-hater because I put very awkward questions to them and I pin them down. And many times my colleagues have said: "You know we wouldn't dare ask the questions you do. Because you're a woman you can get away with it."[16]

Not only did colleagues make assumptions about women's capabilities and limitations, so did lobbyists. They approached women less frequently than they approached men, which might very well have contributed to decreased effectiveness. The mixed messages of the day, however, were responsible for feelings of pride over avoiding that which many women considered illegitimate.[17] One woman commented:

> I notice that the few women we have . . . (in my house) are not beholden to special lobbying interests. I say this with great pride. They will represent citizens' groups, the League of Women Voters, a citizen group that has banded together for a particular ecological purpose, the citizens' group that is truly concerned with the safety of children walking to and from school—that type of thing. But they are not paid by the lobbying interests.[18]

Women may also have considered themselves less effective in the legislative arena because constituent perceptions of their availability and ability to be of individual assistance took time from legislative tasks. For example, the women officeholders in one study indicated that constituents perceived them as ever available. As a result, they seemed to be burdened with more constituency service chores than their male colleagues.[19] Women may have been working harder and putting in longer hours, but a large portion of those hours were going to tasks not directly related to legislative matters.

Another possibility is that women did not consider themselves as effective as they considered men because of the experience of discrimination. Since women were entering a male preserve in greater numbers than ever before, uncomfortableness among men may have been widespread. One consequence of uncomfortableness is discrimination, and in this case there is substantial evidence that such conditions were fairly pervasive in statehouses in the 1970s. Women of this time period indicated that discrimination, whether subtle or overt, was rampant. In one study, 41 percent of women felt they experienced sexism, stereotyping, or being taken less seriously than men.[20] Another study reported that even when women gained acceptance as legitimate participants in the process, they were being channeled into traditionally female roles such as positions on education committees or health and welfare committees rather than finance committees or those dealing with economic development. One woman commented: "I was undecided. . . . There were several I was interested in, and I just simply couldn't take them all on, and it was kind of hard choosing. . . . It came down to a choice between Elections and Public Health, and I was urged just a little bit to take the one that would be more suitable for a woman."[21]

In the same vein, women in statehouses felt that leadership positions were much harder to obtain given similar levels of experience and seniority. In their eyes, women were simply not considered viable candidates for leadership. That few women held any kind of leadership position at that time, whether it be chairing a committee or becoming a party whip, may have been testament to these feelings. Jeane Kirkpatrick, in her pioneering study of female state legislators, noted: "In addition, almost all perceive that there are sex-specific limits on how high a woman can rise in the legislative hierarchy; certainly no woman could be speaker or majority leader."[22]

Whether because of inexperience, stereotyping, or discrimination, women during this era worked hard but felt less effective than they might have been given their level of effort. How this affected their perceptions of their political contributions and their political futures might be deduced from their levels of political ambition. At this time, women tended to be much less ambitious to seek higher office than men, whether they were at local, state, or federal levels.[23]

With a fairly detailed picture of how women legislators felt about their jobs, we are left with the question of how men in state legislative office saw the same matters. Men's perceptions of women's advantages as nontraditional job holders were markedly different from women's.[24] Men did not think women were better at constituent service, had higher visibility, or devoted more time to office. They did agree with women, however, that women had more time available because they did not have to earn a living (and apparently did not spend that time on matters relating to their public role).

Perhaps ironically, men's perceptions of women's difficulties do not coincide with women's perceptions of them. Male officeholders saw less sexism and stereotyping of women than did the women themselves, and they less often perceived that women had to exert greater effort to prove competence. It is interesting to note that men expressed less belief than women in stereotyping or sexism and then identified areas of deficiencies for women that tended to conform to stereotyping. For example, more men than women also thought female legislators were not as politically astute and possessed lesser relevant training.[25] Men also saw women as having special expertise in dealing with people owing their societal role as nurturers. Perhaps male officeholders reconciled these contradictory beliefs by attributing sexism to others. In fact, some of the evidence supports this contention. Male state legislators attributed any discrimination against women to constituent-based bias rather than to bias on their own part or their colleagues' part. On the other hand, men did acknowledge that women in office had some disadvantages that men did not have to face. These included having more family pressures, more personal difficulties, and greater likelihood of deficiencies in qualifications.[26]

Legislative Activities

As the foregoing sections tell us, women state legislators in the 1970s came from backgrounds quite different from those of their male colleagues. The experiences that shaped their perceptions were therefore distinctive. Upon arrival in statehouses across the nation, women also lived somewhat different political lives. For a variety of reasons, they felt that they worked harder than their colleagues and faced more obstacles to achievement such as discrimination and stereotyping. The latter circumstance resulted in expectations placed upon their behavior from both their constituents and their colleagues. In this section, I concentrate on the kinds of legislative activities women engaged in on a regular basis and more about how their backgrounds and attitudes might have affected their activity levels. At the heart of these inquiries is the implicit question of whether women sought to reform legislative procedures.

One way to understand how women legislators approached their jobs and met their goals is to investigate various aspects of their day-to-day lives in statehouses. Typical activity routinely required of legislators consists of participating in committee meetings and floor sessions, meeting with lobbyists and other representatives of various interests, and bargaining with lobbyists and legislative colleagues to achieve desired outcomes. How much activity did women engage in, and in what kinds of activity were they participating? How did women's participation compare with men's participation on all these measures?

Based on the research on women and men legislators of the 1970s, it is clear that women participated in the range of legislative behaviors mentioned above to a lesser degree than men. Women state legislators spoke less in committee meetings and in floor sessions, they did less bargaining than their male colleagues in order to achieved desired goals, and they met less with lobbyists and other representatives of interest groups than men did. Significantly, the activity that seemed to be the most infrequent for women was meeting with lobbyists. "The female legislator's interactions with lobbyists seem to be affected by her sex status to a greater extent than her interaction with any other of her legislative role partners."[27]

It is also instructive to explore women's relationship to another critical aspect of a representative's job—constituency work. In contrast to lesser levels of activity in the legislative hallways, in committee rooms, and on the floor, women state legislators embraced constituency service with gusto. The research on this subject includes surveys of both state and local representatives and reveals that women officeholders highly valued constituency service and engaged in it to a greater extent than men. First, in response to questions concerning the parts of their jobs that are most important, women emphasized obligation to the community or general public interest, while men emphasized status within the legislative body or bill passage.[28] Additionally, work conducted on city councilmembers across the nation suggests that women both placed a higher priority on constituency service than did men and spent more time conducting it.[29] For example, the median number of hours women spent on the job was twenty-five; for men, it was twenty. Likewise, women spent more hours doing constituency service than their male counterparts (the median for women was ten; for men, it was seven).[30]

That women officeholders of the 1970s emphasized the importance of constituency service and spent time conducting it is consistent with their perceptions about their strengths. Women state legislators perceived themselves most often as problem solvers—or "innovators," people who found new ways to deal with continuing problems. Men, on the other hand, tended to fall into broker or advertiser categories.[31] Relatedly, more women than men articulated belief in the importance of good government and government service as an avenue of legislative concern, and women more often cited the desire to enhance the welfare of the community or claimed a high interest in social problems and public service.[32]

What this adds up to is that women legislators in the 1970s appeared to shrink from activities of a legislative nature and embrace those related to their backgrounds in community service and individual problem solving. This outcome is by no means startling given that women were just beginning to enter elite-level political positions. Negotiating a role for themselves in these new circumstances and under the variety of constraints they were so clearly faced with makes the outcome more predictable than surprising.

Women of the 1970s: Reformist or Reticent?

How might the findings presented above be interpreted? How does the typology of expectations introduced in Chapter 1 apply to female representatives of this era? What do these findings tell us about women's inclinations toward reforming the political process or adapting to it?

A great deal of the gender politics literature of the period was consistent with the reformist portion of the typology with respect to procedures. The writing on this subject anticipated that women would bring a new style of operation to the legislative arena (or perhaps it lobbied for them to do so). Instead of accepting an environment in which everyone had to be out for him- or herself, one in which cutthroat competition and battles for domi- nance were the norm, women were expected to create an environment that would encourage cooperative methods of doing business. It was assumed that such an environment would encourage the emergence of better ways to craft public policy than to rely on fragmented, compromised attempts that were wrestled from competing centers of individual power or party- centered solutions. As Barbara Ehrenreich put it:

> When the feminist movement burst forth a couple of decades ago, the goal was not just to join 'em—and certainly not just to beat 'em—but to improve an imperfect world. . . . We didn't claim that women were morally supe- rior. . . . [But] the values implicit in motherhood were bound to clash with the "male values" of competitiveness and devil-may-care profiteering.[33]

Women's emphasis on activities that reflected cooperative values and their avoidance of those that required zero-sum outcomes certainly contrib- uted to predictions that bringing more women into the political process meant than the next stage would be wholesale procedural revision. But were these reasonable conclusions under the circumstances, or were they mostly projected desires to see the process transformed? Was it possible that reti- cence or withdrawal on the part of female legislators implied little more than inexperience in the system and limited options under prevailing socio- cultural standards of proper public sphere behavior? Even if the behavior of women of the 1970s signaled dissatisfaction with the system, would reform be the direct result of such dissatisfaction or would an intermediate step be necessary? The answers are to be found in the next section, which explores the attitudes and activities of women and men in the late 1980s.

The Gains of Women

Before moving directly to research on women state legislators of the current era, it is instructive to detail changes in the sociocultural and political environments from the 1970s to the 1980s. This will allow us to place the gains of political women in context. It is not only their increased numbers that I am interested in, it is any changes in the way they relate to the legislative environment. Should we find alterations in levels of activity, the direction of change may very well be connected to the extent of leeway that women, as public sphere participants, were accorded.

Many political and social changes occurred in the United States between the early 1970s and the late 1980s. Not the least of these were gains women made in expanding their participation in public life. Educational and occupational opportunities were expanding for women, and all indications were that women made use of them.

> Women students constituted 52 percent of all college students in 1984, compared to only 46 percent in 1974. Not all students in higher education earn degrees; however, women are increasing their share of degrees in every level of post-secondary education. In 1974, women were awarded 45 percent of all bachelors' degrees; in 1980, their share was up to 50 percent, and, in 1982, it reached 51 percent.[34]

> Women are earning a significantly larger share of advanced degrees than they used to. As of 1964–65, very few of the first professional degrees in dentistry, medicine, and law went to women, but in 1983–84, women received almost 20 percent of such degrees in dentistry, 28 percent in medicine and 37 percent in law.[35]

With increased educational opportunities, women began entering the workforce in increasing proportions.

> Few trends over the past 35 years have been as pronounced as the increase in female labor force participation. As of April, 1986, 51.7 million women were in the civilian labor force, an increase of 180 percent since 1950. The number of women in the labor force translated into an overall female participation rate of 54.6 percent in April 1986.[36]

Not only were women entering the work force, they were doing so in a wider range of occupations than ever before. They joined the ranks of nontraditional occupations from construction worker to engineer, from fire fighter to physician.

> Despite continuing and sometimes growing job segregation in many occupations, women's representation in a number of nontraditional jobs is on the rise. Women now [1985] account for 18 percent of all lawyers and judges, up from seven percent in 1975; 1 percent of architects, versus four percent in 1975; and 35 percent of economists, as opposed to 13 percent in 1975.[37]

The patterns that were evident for all women were, of course, repeated among women in the political arena. On many levels, women participated in politics at greater rates than they had previously. For example, 68 percent of women are now registered to vote (compared with 65 percent of men). In 1972, 72 percent of women were registered to voted compared with 73 percent of men. It was not until 1980 that women registered (and voted) at greater rates than did men.[38]

Women have also gained entry into what had been entirely male-dominated political positions. From presidential and gubernatorial cabinets to local city councils and mayoral positions, women increasingly were running for and winning these jobs. For instance, in 1991, women consti-tuted 5.6 percent of the United States Congress, held 17.8 percent of statewide elective executive offices, accounted for 18.1 percent of state legislatures, and made up 8.9 percent of county governing boards. Further, among the 100 largest cities in the United States, 19 had women mayors. As of January 1991, out of approximately 900 mayors of cities in the United States with populations over 30,000, 150 were women.[39]

There is also some evidence that as women became more visible in the world of elite politics, they have been more accepted in that role. Studies of public opinion find that citizen willingness to vote for a woman for presi-dent has risen steadily since 1972. This trend is evident in Gallup polls of the period.[40] To what extent did women legislators take advantage of decreasing constraints to influence the way in which legislatures do busi-ness or the products they produce? The following section addresses the first of those matters—whether the enhanced leeway accorded women in the ranks of public life was reproduced in the lives of political women—and if so, how life choice alternatives influenced the way in which women partici-pated in the daily life of statehouses.

Women of the 1980s: The New Research

With the lessons of research that investigated women officeholders in the 1970s in place, scholars looked toward a new generation of studies to gauge the impact of women in office. Consistent with this goal, I designed re-search to gather information about the attitudes, actions, and priorities of state legislators of the late 1980s. The results are presented in the remainder of this chapter as well as in the next two chapters.[41] First, though, it is necessary to describe the research design and its execution.

The Research Design

The primary instrument for data collection was a mail survey of women and men in state legislatures across the nation. Since it was not possible to survey people in all fifty states (because of time and money constraints), twelve states were targeted for attention: Arizona, California, Georgia, Illinois, Iowa, Mississippi, Nebraska, North Carolina, Pennsylvania, South Dakota, Vermont, and Washington. These states were chosen to account for as much diversity as possible in terms of region of the country, political culture, and proportion of women in state legislatures.[42] Capturing diversity ensures that the sample of representatives is not, in any relevant way, different from the entire group. In other words, the sample can be judged representative of the whole.

Once the states under study were settled upon, all women of the lower chambers in each state were surveyed along with a sample of men in each state. The reason that a sample of men was selected rather than all of them was because men outnumber women in all legislatures (in some by as much as 97 percent). In order to make equal comparisons, it was important to survey about equal numbers of men and women. In all, 226 women were surveyed and 375 men.[43] (See Table 2.1 for proportions of women in the legislatures.) After the work of mailing surveys and receiving responses was complete, the response rate stood at 54 percent overall.[44] Nine states had good response rates of 50 percent plus or minus 10 percent. Two states were significantly above that level: Nebraska with 64 percent and Washington with 78 percent; one was significantly below: Mississippi with 22 percent.[45]

TABLE 2.1. Women in State Legislatures[a]

State	Total Women/ Both Houses	Percent of Women	Total Women/ Lower House	Percent of Women
Arizona	21/90	23.3	15/60	25.0
California	16/120	13.3	12/80	15.0
Georgia	26/236	11.0	24/180	13.3
Illinois	32/177	18.1	20/118	16.9
Iowa	22/150	14.7	18/100	18.0
Mississippi	4/174	2.3	4/122	3.3
Nebraska[b]	9/49	18.4	—	—
North Carolina	24/170	14.1	20/120	16.7
Pennsylvania	16/253	6.3	14/203	6.9
South Dakota	18/105	17.1	13/70	18.6
Vermont	44/180	24.4	41/150	27.3
Washington	37/147	25.2	30/98	30.6

[a] This information provided by the Center for the American Woman and Politics, Eagleton Institute of Politics at Rutgers University, and reflects figures for 1987.
[b] Nebraska has a unicameral legislature.

Questions for the portion of the study dealing with backgrounds, attitudes toward women's place in the political realm, and extent of participation in routine legislative activities were geared specifically to detect changes on these variables over time. Respondents were asked to tell us about themselves with respect to their political ideology, party, marital status, number of children, educational level, age, family income, religion, prior offices held, occupation, length of tenure in office, age upon entering office, and ambitions for higher office. (Appendix C contains the complete survey instrument.)

With respect to attitudes toward women's place in the political world, respondents were asked questions about perceptions of the status of women in society and in legislative life (such as whether the respondent believes women have it easier than, harder than, or the same as men in getting jobs, advancing in politics, being accepted in professions, and getting appointed to office), and whether or not respondents are particularly interested in seeing more women run for political office.

The questions on legislative activities focused on the extent to which respondents participated in routine legislative activities including estimates of how much each respondent engaged in each type of activity in a typical week. The activities were speaking in committee meetings, speaking on the floor of the chamber, meeting with lobbyists, and bargaining with colleagues. Respondents were also asked how many pieces of legislation they introduced in the last complete legislative session and how many of those bills passed.

We now turn to the findings of this study.

The Backgrounds of Women State Legislators

The political and social changes that were reflected in the wider environment were, of course, mirrored in the political arena. One place such effects were evident was in the backgrounds these women brought to their statehouse jobs. Women state legislators of the late 1980s were more highly educated, and they came from a more diverse range of occupations than their peers of the 1970s. First, the educational levels of women state legislators increased somewhat. As Table 2.2 indicates, in the late 1980s, 43 percent of women were college graduates as compared with 29 percent of the men, and 31 percent of women obtained graduate or professional degrees compared with 42 percent of men. This is a slight increase relative to 1977 survey results, in which 37 percent of female statehouse representatives were college graduates and 26 percent held professional degrees.

TABLE 2.2. Gender Differences in Political and
Demographic Characteristics

	Male (%)	Female (%)
Married	89[a]	75[a]
Children		
One	5	10
None	9	12
Education		
College graduate	29[a]	43[a]
Grad./prof. school	42[a]	31[a]
Born since 1942	41[b]	32[b]
Family Income		
Top one-third	12[a]	18[a]
Bottom one-third	3[a]	7[a]
Prior Occupation		
Business	37[a]	25[a]
Educator	12[a]	30[a]
Housewife	0[a]	9[a]
Professional	19[a]	15[a]
Year Elected—Most Recent One-third	38[a]	49[a]
Age Entered Office—48 +	30[a]	42[a]
Constituency Type		
Urban	21[a]	30[a]
Rural	31[a]	15[a]
Party ID		
Democrat	54	60
Republican	45	40
Ideology		
Liberal	15[a]	32[a]
Conservative	48[a]	21[a]
Plan to Run for Higher Office	16	17

Note: N = 322.

[a] Gender difference significant at the .05 level.

[b] Gender difference significant at the .10 level.

Women legislators of the 1980s participated in a greater diversity of occupations than they did in the early 1970s. Twenty-five percent of women in this survey listed their occupation as business- or management-related, and 15 percent were in professional fields. Although women did not equal men in these two categories (37 percent of men were in business or management and 19 percent of men were professional workers), both represent increases from a decade ago. On the other side of the coin, fewer women listed occupations as housewives and clerical workers than in previous years. In the late 1980s, 9.3 percent of women were housewives, and only 1.4 percent were in a clerical field. Even with increasing diversity of public sphere participation, women in statehouses, like women in the general population, opted, in fairly large proportions, for positions of a traditional nature. In this survey, 30 percent of the women listed an occupation in the field of education, while only 12 percent of men did. Thus, in the late 80s women worked in more diverse categories of jobs than they did fifteen or twenty years ago, but they did not occupy nontraditional jobs in anything approaching equal proportions to men.

Perhaps as a result of increased opportunities and experience in the public sphere through educational, occupational, and political achievements such as those listed above, women state legislators of the later period more closely resembled their male colleagues with respect to levels of prior political experience. In fact, women and men were all but equal in this characteristic. About 40 percent of men and women held an office prior to winning a seat in the state legislature. Perhaps more significantly, there were no differences in the type of office previously held. Women permeated a wide variety of elective and appointive offices at the state and local levels and have approached the male norm in this respect.

It seems women's political and social status was changing steadily, and that fact was reflected in their desire to win elective office and their success in doing so. One explanation of the method by which this progress has been achieved is what is referred to by R. Darcy, Susan Welch, and Janet Clark as the social eligibility pool.[46] This pool can be thought of as the informal qualifications for office that exist in our society. We typically think candidates for office are "qualified" if they have professional jobs or professional educational degrees (or both) and if they have demonstrated their ability in politics by having held a prior elective or appointive political position. This eligibility pool serves as a pipeline to public office, and over time we may expect the women who seek office to possess the standard credentials. Evidence that this expectation is accurate is available from at least one recent study of female congressional candidates which found that educational differences between the female and male congressional candidates for Congress all but disappeared.[47] This suggests that women perceive that, in order to be considered as viable candidates, they must obtain the typical kind of credentials of current officeholders. It also suggests that those women who possess standard credentials are increasingly viewing a political career as viable.

In contrast to changes in educational and occupational status and extent and type of political experience, family status differences between men and women seem to be little different from the patterns found more than a decade ago. This, too, appears to reflect trends prevalent in the general population. We know that women, even when they work full- or part-time outside the home, are almost solely responsible for home and hearth. As many studies note, even in two-parent families, mothers continue to do most of the housework and child rearing.[48]

Among state legislators of the late 1980s, much like their counterparts in the seventies, fewer women than men were married (89 percent for men as compared with 75 percent for women), and fewer women tended to have families with more than one child (see Table 2.2). Women in state legislative office were still more likely to be older than their male colleagues (32 percent of the women were born since 1942, while 41 percent of the men were), and women, on average, still tended to enter office at a later age than men. Taken together, these statistics form a picture of a woman who had to make a choice between home and family or career. Not marrying or not remaining married, choosing to have only one child, or waiting until children are old enough to be responsible for themselves are all ways women seek to walk the tightrope between the public and private spheres. Although women in public life have most definitely found more freedom to pursue a variety of jobs, society's acceptance of them has not spread sufficiently to allow them to lessen their private sphere load.

The fact that women chose political officeholding when they could work it in around their other responsibilities was reflected also in their income levels. When women legislators were in a two-income situation, their portion of the income seemed to be supplementary rather than primary. The fact that more female than male respondents composed the high-income category (top one-third of respondents) is suggestive of this interpretation. Another interesting finding with respect to income is that more women than men also composed the low-income category (bottom one-third of respondents). That women had lower educational levels than men and were in female-dominated (hence lower-paid) occupations more often than men illustrates that women generally faced a harsher economic reality.[49]

In sum, several background characteristics of female state legislators of the late 1980s became more like those of men, while others remained quite similar to the pattern of the 1970s. This is so because, though women made use of the educational and occupational opportunities available to them and parlayed their credentials into political office, the changes they experienced did not translate into changes in their private sphere roles. Societal expectations regarding the female role as wife, mother, and primary homemaker (whether or not coupled with professional status) changed much more slowly than the social eligibility pool.[50]

Legislative Attitudes in the 1980s

Although there have been some changes in the backgrounds that women brought to the political world of the 1970s and the backgrounds they brought in the late 1980s, these changes were not all-encompassing. More than that, societal acceptance of women in public life, while much higher than it was in the past, did not afford them the same opportunities as men. It may not be surprising to readers, therefore, that there were very few changes over time in the attitudes of women legislators toward women's status in the political arena. Women still felt, as did their sisters in the seventies, that politics was a place that was, in many respects, hostile to women. As a result of those feelings, the modern female representative believed strongly in the need to support other women in politics and the need for male legislators to be more aware of the hardships faced by women. In a dramatic reversal, however, women of the more recent era overcame their environment and began to perceive themselves as highly effective legislators.

The hardships of women legislators are related to society at large as well as the world of politics. For example, in this survey, many more women than men indicated that it was harder for women to obtain a job suitable to their skills and accomplishments. In fact, as Table 2.3 indicates, the gender

TABLE 2.3. Gender Differences on Attitude Variables

	Male (%)	Female (%)
Harder for Women to Get:		
Suitable job	50[a]	74[a]
Ahead in politics	41[a]	73[a]
Ahead in a profession	38[a]	63[a]
Appointed to office	33[a]	65[a]
Women More Effective	6[a]	41[a]
Want More Women to Run	40[a]	92[a]

[a] Gender difference significant at the .05 level or below.

gap on this question was 24 points, with 74 percent of women agreeing with this statement compared with 50 percent of the men. Further, the overall pattern was replicated in each of the states, with more women than men agreeing that women had a harder time (see Appendix A). The majority of women legislators also believed it was harder to get ahead in the professions, whereas only a minority of men agreed with this statement (63 percent of women compared with 38 percent of men). The gender difference in agreement with two other questions was equally dramatic. More women than men believed it was harder for women to get ahead in politics (73 percent of women agreed compared with 41 percent of men). Finally, 65 percent of women believed that was harder for women to get appointed to office.[51] Only 33 percent of men agreed with that statement.[52]

Women of the late 1980s were no more likely than their counterparts in the seventies to think that the political world was an easy place for women to inhabit. However, the difference between these two time periods is that more recently women appear to have overcome unwelcoming environments. Women perceived themselves as having risen above their circumstances of the late eighties, and they prevented obstacles from blocking their effectiveness. The modern women saw themselves as being not only as effective as their male colleagues but more effective. Forty-one percent of female legislators felt that women were more effective legislators than men. Only 6 percent of men agreed with this statement. This finding stands in marked contrast to women legislators of the 1970s who saw themselves as harder working than men but less effective. Perhaps because the women in this survey felt that women were hardworking and at least as effective as men, they indicated that their ranks should contain far greater numbers of women. In fact, 92 percent of the female legislators responded yes to this question, whereas only 40 percent of men responded similarly.[53]

Evidence that women's hard work is appreciated by other women is available in public comments by two California legislators. Senator Rose Ann Vuich noted: "Women take their job as a legislator a little more seriously than men do. Women also tend to follow through more than men. That doesn't degrade men. Women just tend to look at problems differently."[54] Similarly, Assemblywoman Jackie Speier said: "The Legislature is a male bastion. Women are scrutinized closer, and we know that. So, we tend to be better prepared. We also tend to be overachievers, for good or ill."[55] The appreciation women legislators had for the hard work and effectiveness of other women and the fact that they wanted more women included in their ranks suggest a supportive subculture of "sisters" (supporters of other women) rather than "queen bees" (women who revel in their unique and special status and therefore do not work to help other women achieve similar goals).

In another rather dramatic reversal of trends over time, the level of political ambition possessed by women has increased substantially. Rather than a bimodal distribution with most women displaying little political ambition and most men displaying at least some ambition,[56] women and men in statehouses in the late 1980s exhibited almost identical levels of ambition (17 percent of women indicated such an ambition compared with 16 percent of men; this is a statistically and substantively insignificant difference).

The findings of this survey with respect to ambition are replicated by another recent work devoted entirely to this topic.[57] It deals with political ambition levels of California political party activists and leaders over a twenty-year period and concludes that the gender gap in political ambition has been closing.[58]

In sum, women's attitudes toward the hospitality they faced in the political environment have not changed much in fifteen or twenty years' time. What has changed, however, is how women responded to that environment. With increased acceptance of women in public life and the increased opportunities that flow from acceptance, women in statehouses of the 1980s became effective legislators and ambitious ones. They saw futures for themselves in politics. One would expect, therefore, that perceptions of effectiveness and enjoyment are borne out in records of activity. That is the topic to which we now turn.

Legislative Activities

In the 1970s, women state legislators concentrated more on the constituency aspect of their jobs than on the legislative one. Probably as a result of their own inclinations and areas of expertise, societal expectations, dissatisfaction with the existing process, and the discrimination women faced within the legislative process, they tended to gear their efforts toward working within the wider community rather than the legislature itself. The question of interest now is whether these patterns have remained constant or have been altered. And, if they are altered, in which direction—toward accepting and participating in the existing process or transforming it? Based on women state legislators' educational and occupational advancement, their abilities to transcend obstacles in their paths, and their rising political ambition, one would expect some type of alteration in their levels of legislative activity in the statehouse itself.

The 1988 study surveying legislatures in twelve states, introduced earlier, contained the following questions relevant here: frequency of performance of a variety of certain legislative tasks in a typical week in session (such as floor speeches, participation in committee hearings, bargaining with colleagues, and meeting with lobbyists); difficulty in bargaining for legislative goals; the total number of bills introduced in the last legislative session, and the total number passed by the legislature; and the number of priority bills passed (see Appendix C for specific question wording). While measures such as these are not the only relevant indicators of attempts at procedural transformation (indeed, others are considered in later chapters), activity levels are the first and perhaps most revealing place from which to investigate it.

The results of the survey indicate that women state legislators of the late 1980s resembled not at all their sisters of the early 1970s on these measures. While women of the seventies seemed to participate in the normal range of activity in the statehouse on a diminished basis, the women of the eighties increased that activity substantially. In fact, there was little difference between female and male state legislators on frequency of floor or committee speaking, bargaining, or meeting with lobbyists. As illustrated in Table 2.4, while women participated in each of these activities slightly less than men, the differences were neither statistically nor substantively significant.[59]

In addition to the overall levels of activity on these variables for women and men, it is instructive to explore differences among states. In at least half of the states, women participated more than men in floor and committee speaking and bargaining activities. In seven states, women found bargaining less difficult than men did. Women in six states reported fewer meetings with lobbyists than did men. (Appendix B lists each variable by state, so those interested in which states fit the general patterns and which deviate may explore them.)

Not only had women participated nearly equally in comparison with men in the range of legislative behaviors discussed above, they also had similar levels of bill introduction and passage. Comparison of activity levels extended to priority legislation as well. Women and men were equally likely to be successful in passing those bills deemed of the highest priority to individual legislators. Thus, women not only participated at levels equal to

TABLE 2.4. Gender Differences on Activity Variables

	Male (%)	Female (%)
Speaking on Floor		
(1–2 times per week)	50	60
Speaking in Committee		
(3–10 times per week)	50	48
Bargaining		
(3–10 times per week)	34	38
Meeting with Lobbyists		
(3–10 times per week)	48	42
Difficulty Bargaining		
(never)	14	17
(occasionally)	67	71
Total Bills Introduced		
(13 or above—highest one-third)	46	46
Total Bills Passed		
(7 or above—highest one-third)	48	39
Passage of Priority Bills		
(passed all of 5 top priority bills)	11	12

Notes: None of the relationships above achieves statistical significance. The categories depicted above for the floor, committee, bargaining, and meeting with lobbyist variables were selected because I wanted to present the percentages for each variable in which most legislators fell. This changed from variable to variable.

those of their male colleagues, they were not just empty actions; women also mastered the process to achieve their goals.

Women of the 1980s: Adapting to Procedural Norms

Predictions that women officeholders would use their entry into the legislative arena to transform its way of doing business do not appear to have been borne out. This does not mean that the activities of women in statehouses did not change over time; it means that the change did not result in differential levels of activity between women and men. Had women engaged in some activities to a lesser or greater extent than men, it would be possible to interpret such findings as indicative not only of dissatisfaction with the process, but efforts toward reform. But that did not occur. Does this mean that those in the adaption portion of the typology were correct about the behavior of women in political office? Only partially.

Each of the predictions—that women would reform the process and that they would simply adopt existing standards—suffer from an incomplete understanding of the incremental nature and pace of change. Women's evolution from lesser levels of participation in routine activities to equal participation could be interpreted as acceptance of the status quo. It could also be interpreted as the necessary next step in an eventual progression toward procedural reform. In other words, mastery of the process fulfilled multiple goals. Using newly available leeway to operate effectively in all aspects of legislative life allowed women to enhance individual longevity, meet legislative goals, and, not of least importance, plant seeds for future reform activity. Whether female state legislators of the more recent era harbored such goals is explored in Chapters 5 through 7.

Conclusion

In contrast to their sisters in the 1970s, women state representatives in the late 1980s participated in all aspects of legislative life. Whereas women once held themselves apart from the process and operated on its margins, they later joined in the fray and adapted to ongoing norms and procedures. Research results comparing participation levels of women and men in floor and committee activity, bargaining, meeting with lobbyists, introducing legislation and seeing it successfully through the process are all suggestive of this conclusion.

What accounts for the change from the seventies to the eighties? One part of the answer harkens back to societal debates about women's proper public sphere role. As society expanded its views concerning the extent to which women ought to participate and the ways in which that participation was acceptable, women themselves responded by extending their range of involvement. New possibilities for participation and contribution opened up as some of the barriers were reduced. Women legislators of the late 80s used successfully and expertly the tools available to them in the creation of public policy. It is easy now to see that this stage—one marked by mastery of the process rather than shunning it—was the logical next step for women as their opportunities and experience grew. What follows from this stage of mastery is open to speculation, and discussion of this matter is forthcoming later in the book. Whether women legislators in the United States pursue a philosophy closer to that of the Kvennalistinn is exciting to consider.

More immediately, we will concern ourselves with the other half of the typology of expectations: policy priorities. Did women state legislators develop distinctive policy priorities, or did they concentrate their attention in areas similar to those addressed by men? Those are the questions addressed in Chapter 3.

3

Legislative Products:
The Influence of Women

In 1964, Patsy Mink, a Democrat from Hawaii, won a seat in Congress. Believing strongly that it was important to represent the interests of the women of Hawaii and women across the nation, she was instrumental in a variety of initiatives to further the status of women. One such example of her efforts on behalf of women related to a nominee to the United States Supreme Court. Representative Mink was among the early opponents of Harrold Carswell, an appointee of President Nixon, because she believed that consent to the appointment would be an affront to the women of America. It had come to light that while Carswell was a judge on the Fifth Circuit Court of Appeals, he refused to reconsider a case in which a woman alleged that she had been rejected for a job solely because her children were of preschool age. Representative Mink charged that Carswell "demonstrated a total lack of understanding of the concept of equality . . . and the right of women to be treated equally and fairly under the law." Her early opposition is said to have created momentum for Carswell's eventual defeat.[1]

Patsy Mink's contribution to the debate about Carswell was a distinctive one. Prior to Mink's assertions, no one had come forth to question Judge Carswell's attitudes toward the equality of women. Had she not zeroed in on Judge Carswell's views, that aspect of his fitness to join the U.S. Supreme Court may have gone unquestioned. What is important to discover is whether evidence exists to suggest that Patsy Mink's inclinations to bring her experiences as a woman to her work in the Congress are shared by other women or whether they are idiosyncratic. The purpose of this chapter is to investigate these questions systematically.

"Do women emphasize different sorts of legislative products than their male counterparts?" "Have women developed a distinctive approach to political issues that is evident in issue attitudes or issue priorities?" These questions are vital because we have seen that, at least for the time being, women legislators work within existing process norms. Thus, if they are to be judged to have a distinctive impact, it is in the area of legislative product that difference must appear.

Despite two views being represented in the typology of expectations (and in the real world), the weight of opinion of those who think and write about this topic comes down on the reactive side. In fact, to most gender politics scholars (and others), it seems almost untenable that the private sphere responsibilities of women and the social and cultural training about women's strengths and weaknesses to which they are exposed will not have an impact on how women work with governmental issues. How could women not bring their experiences in the home and community to their legislative work?

A great many people who have written and do write about the effects women can have on political institutions and outcomes have harbored an outright hope that women will have a distinctive impact on legislative agendas. The chief reason is the desire to see women legislators provide substantive as well as symbolic representation. If women gain entry into the political institutions and turn out to act and react in exactly the same way as men, then their presence will provide only symbolic representation. The benefits of symbolic representation are that girls growing up in our society will have role models to emulate in deciding which careers best suit them and will assume that political careers are appropriate and available. As Texas Governor Ann Richards recently said:

> There will be a lot of little girls who open their history texts to see my picture—I hope along with Barbara Jordan's—and they will say, "If she can do it, so can I." The significance is enormous. It is sociological change, not just governmental change. It means the doors are going to be open to everyone.[2]

As this quote expresses well, symbolic representation is crucial if women are eventually to permeate all aspects of the public sphere and be represented on an equal basis with men. However, many advocates of bringing more women into politics do so with the hope that benefits in addition to symbolic ones will result from the presence of women in politics. They hope that substantive representation will also occur. With substantive representation, women will bring different kinds of public policies to the legislative agenda—they will alter the status quo. Most often the desired impact includes bringing concerns of the private sphere to the governmental one and assuring that women's place in the public sphere will be made equal to men's.

The chief area of interest of researchers concerned with the impact of women on politics, thus, has come to be the question of whether women among the political elite contribute to a political product that differs in any way from men's. My prediction is that, over time, we will see women developing distinctive policy priorities. Part of these distinctive policy interests are likely to concern private sphere issues and their legitimation on the public agenda. By bringing collective solutions to what were previously only individual responsibilities will free women to participate fully in the life of the legislature. Additional areas in which women may concentrate their legislative efforts are likely to be those that ease the entry and smooth the way for women in all types of employment situations. As societal attitudes toward the proper role of women in the public sphere become more tolerant, women legislators will have the opportunities to voice their unique concerns and will experience enough support to do so.

The sections that follow present two primary sets of research findings. The first examines policy attitudes and priorities of women of the early era, and the second concerns those of the current one.

Priorities and Positions: The First Stage

Although we know a great deal about women legislators in the 1970s, we have a relatively small amount of information about what is arguably their most important characteristic. How did these women feel about the legislative issues of their day? Did they have different issue positions than their male counterparts? Did they have different voting records? Is there any evidence that they had distinctive policy priorities?

The first important question concerns attitudes toward specific political issues and general ideological outlooks. Did women of this era resemble men on these key indicators? While the studies available are not comprehensive in that they do not cover a range of issue attitudes, what they do offer as evidence suggests that the answer is no. Several studies explored political attitudes or positions of issues related to the feminist movement.

One study found that women state legislators were more supportive than men of day care, state labor laws as they related to women, and the liberalization of abortion laws. For example, 68 percent of women supported day care for all, with each family paying what it could afford. In contrast, 47 percent of men were supportive of this concept. Fifty-six percent of women state legislators believed that state labor laws of the day benefited women, whereas 75 percent of the men agreed with that statement. Similarly, 56 percent of women in statehouses believed that abortion laws in their state (this was before *Roe* v. *Wade* had been decided) should be repealed so that abortion would be a private matter between doctor and patient. Only 35 percent of men agreed with that statement.[3]

Another study reports that a majority of women in statehouses expressed support for the ERA (but less than a majority of men did (67 percent compared 48 percent); women disagreed with a constitutional ban on abortion in larger majorities than men (71 percent versus 56 percent); and a majority of women, but not men, agreed that homemakers should get social security (62 percent versus 44 percent). Additionally, more women than men (but not a majority of either sex) thought that government should support child care (39 percent versus 32 percent) These differences remained regardless of party identification, political ideology, age, or education level.[4]

Whether attitudes toward issues and policy expertise translated into reported voting behavior is another important question. Evidence suggests that the voting behavior of women and men in statehouses did differ in meaningful ways. On roll call votes, women officeholders, on the national and state levels, voted in a more liberal fashion than their male counterparts and more often supported women's issues. For example, women in Congress were more supportive than men of the Civil Rights Act of 1964 and the Equal Rights Amendment.[5] At the state level, women in both ratified and unratified states were more supportive of the ERA than male legislators. Female members of Congress were also more supportive of social welfare legislation and less supportive of defense spending and interventionist foreign policy.[6] These voting records would lead us to believe that women legislators were generally more ideologically liberal than their male counterparts. Several studies examining this question conclude that this was the case.[7]

Another indication that women and men in state legislatures felt differently about political issues concerns information on the types of legislative issues on which women developed expertise and devoted time. These included topics of social welfare, education, and family life.[8] Virginia Sapiro captured concisely the conclusions of study after study showing that, once elected, women expressed interest in certain traditional areas of expertise and requested or were placed on committees that accorded with these interests: "Once women are in office, their committee assignments, initiation of legislation, and the topics on which they speak tend to reflect traditional women's concerns."[9] Similarly, Irene Diamond notes:

> The sexes develop different areas of policy expertise. Women most frequently cited "Education" (18 percent) as their area of expertise, while men cited "Fiscal Affairs" (17 percent). "Health and Welfare was the second most frequent area among the women (8 percent). Women were concentrated on two committees: 26 percent served on Health and Welfare, and 25 percent on Education. Men, being the majority, were not concentrated in any particular committees. Women, however, did not appear to be excluded from the important committees.[10]

We know, therefore, that women tended to feel differently about a range of issues than did men, voted in a more liberal fashion, and were placed on or chose different kinds of committee assignments than those selected by or assigned to men. That women legislators were more supportive of those traditional and feminist issues than were men is fully consistent with the expectation that women would feel strongly about advancing the status of women in the public sphere. What is not clear is whether the presence of women legislators on committees dealing with topics of traditional concern had to do with their differing voting records and stands on traditional and feminist issues or whether something else was at play. Related to evidence from Chapter 2, it may have been that women did not feel effective enough to branch out from areas in which women are stereotypically considered experts. It also may have been that legislative leaders steered women to such committees because of similar sorts of stereotypical notions of women's interests or abilities. One way to judge which of these possibilities is likely to have been true is to find out whether women legislators of the 1970s used their clear issue differences to develop a distinctive set of priorities.

The question of whether women legislators of the 1970s displayed distinctive policy priorities is a difficult one to answer given the evidence available. First of all, it is important to specify exactly what I mean by a distinctive set of legislative priorities. Research on priorities in the past (and currently) has tended to focus on that concept in two ways. The first concerns asking legislators to rate the top priority issues facing the state (or the city, region, or nation, depending on to whom one is posing the question). A second way of tapping into the concept of priorities is to ask legislators what their one (or more) top priority issue is at the moment or what it was in the last full legislative session. Unfortunately, research on the early period placed little emphasis on such questions, so we have only a small amount of evidence from which to make a determination.

With respect to the first way to measure priorities, two studies are available. Susan Mezey conducted research at the local level (representatives from communities across Connecticut) and at the state level (representatives from all sectors of elective politics in Hawaii from party leaders to members of Congress) to investigate whether women and men differed in terms of how they felt about women's issues and whether they gave such issues differing priority. Mezey found that while the women in both her studies were more supportive than men of both traditional and feminist women's issues, they did not accord those issues any higher priority ranking than men did. In fact, women's and men's rankings of all issues (such as transportation, pollution, prison facilities and rehabilitation programs, unemployment, housing, and public recreation) were almost identical. To sum up her findings, Mezey notes: "These data continue to cast doubt upon the policy impact of increasing the number of women in office."[11]

Another study, one in which women and men from all levels of elected office were surveyed, contained a question about officeholders' three most important issues. Results indicate that women and men rated similar issues as most important (the most often mentioned items by women and men were planning and development issues, finance and taxation issues, and government administration and reform). Only 1 percent of women (compared with none of the men) named status of women's issues among their three most important issues, a difference of neither substantive nor statistical significance.[12]

It appears, then, that to the best available evidence women, while they clearly had different issues attitudes and voting records than men, did not develop their own discernible set of policy priorities. As such, it seems that speculations about feelings of a lack of effectiveness and stereotypical views of those in leadership probably accounted for women's predominant presence on committees in which women's traditional issues were considered.

Women of the 1970s: Attitude Differences and Policy Similarities

Women officeholders of the early era displayed a variety of attitudinal and behavioral differences from men. These included views on a series of issues, ideological stances, and roll call voting behaviors. Additionally, women and men were concentrated on different types of committees. On the other hand, there is no evidence that women and men had different kinds of policy priorities. What does all this suggest about the typology of expectations introduced in Chapter 1? Does the evidence support an interpretation that women sought to alter legislative products or simply chose to continue pursuing bills similar to those within existing frameworks?

Once again, it appears that the dichotomous choices found in the typology of expectations do not serve well as analytical tools. The patterns displayed by women legislators of the 1970s are complex ones, and their most accurate placement is somewhere between the categories rather than squarely within one or the other. Although women's policy priorities were similar to men's, their attitudes and voting records suggest that the status quo was not the vision they held of desired policy outcomes. What reasons are there for the disjunction between issue attitudes, voting records, and policy priorities? On the one hand, it would not have been unreasonable to infer from these data that women wished to reform legislative products. On the other hand, if a legislator (or a group of legislators) wished to alter the types of products coming from legislatures, it seems one key step along the way would be to create a set of priorities to reflect the desired changes. This women officeholders of the 1970s did not do.

I argue that the best explanation of this disjuncture concerns the latitude available to public sphere women at this time. Women had just begun, in large numbers, to take on these roles. Nowhere was this as true as elective politics. Participation by women in the political elite was still at low levels, and women were just beginning to come into their own in terms of gaining their offices independently of a spouse or other male relative. The public was unused to thinking of politicians as women as well as men; hence, the latitude women were accorded was limited, and the parameters of the role were not yet clearly defined. The result: women politicians felt fairly constrained in the extent to which they could differ from mainstream opinions and actions, and the risks in doing so were high. Trepidation about whether such action would engender nearly insurmountable opposition or whether it would brand women as nonprofessional or lightweights could very likely have thwarted their efforts. In short, expressing policy distinctiveness in the form of issue attitudes and voting records was, more than likely, about as much latitude as women legislators felt was available.

One indicator that this hypothesis is a plausible one would be a finding that women legislators in the late 1980s did develop distinctive policy priorities. This is the question to which we now turn.

Women Legislators: Recent Research

From the earliest work on women in elite-level politics, the majority of writing on their impact on legislative agendas was framed within the reactive segment of the typology of expectations. Based on the combination of women's private role as chief caretaker of families and the difficulties women confronted as relative newcomers to the public arena, many observers predicted that women representatives would vote differently from their male counterparts and would give priority to legislation dealing with both traditional and feminist women's issues. Proponents of this view expected that women would, much more than men, broaden the role of government by bringing issues such as child care, elder care, domestic violence, spousal rape, teen pregnancy, and parental leave to the legislative agenda and convince their colleagues that these issues are as worthy of political attention as any other. Not only were women expected to break down the barriers between public and private, they were assumed to have an overriding interest in creating a public sphere conducive to the contributions of women. Flexible working hours, job sharing, sexual harassment, and comparable worth were all assumed to be issues that women would champion with far greater enthusiasm and attention than would their male colleagues.

Another, more subtle assumption about how female officeholders would transform legislative products has sometimes been expressed. That is, women were expected to cast a more critical eye toward all legislation, whatever the subject matter, to judge how its purposes would indirectly affect segments of constituencies usually overlooked. As Susan Carroll noted, "[R]egardless of whether the issue is foreign aid, the budget, or the environment, women are more likely than men to consider the possible impact of the policy on the lives of women and children."[13] This concept was also expressed in the discussion at the beginning of Chapter 2 concerning the Icelandic Kvennalistinn party. Its members felt that a need exists for a women's point of view on all issues and based its platform on the economic model of a housewife on a limited budget.

We have seen that the first wave of women legislators, while exhibiting some of the behaviors that would have rendered these predictions true, did not act in complete accordance with them. What was the situation of women in the 1980s? Did their behavior conform neatly to the adaptive or the reformist portions of the typology, or did some other mixed pattern develop? Did women state legislators of the late 1980s resemble their sisters in the 1970s with respect to issue attitudes, voting records, and ideologies?

Did they develop different types of policy priorities than men? F
my predictions correct—that women displayed distinctive policy pri
as their opportunities to do so expand? The next section is devoted to
answering each of these questions.

Ideologies, Attitudes, and Voting Records

Women officeholders of the late 1980s resembled their counterparts of the
1970s in three respects. They reported liberal ideological stances in greater
proportions than men, a gender gap on specific issues continued, and their
voting records reflected greater support for issues related to women, to
families, and to general social welfare concerns. Issues of defense spending
and foreign intervention typically received less support by women.

In the 1988 survey of state legislators from twelve states across the
nation, a question was asked concerning ideological stance. Respondents
were asked whether, regardless of party, they considered themselves conservative, liberal, or middle of the road (gradations of liberal and conservative were also included as possible responses). As can be seen in Table 3.1,
much higher proportions of women reported a liberal ideology than men.
Thirty-two percent of women considered themselves liberal compared with
only 15 percent of men. Conversely, 48 percent of men labeled themselves
conservative, whereas only 21 percent of women did. Even given the fact
that a greater percentage of women were Democrats (60 percent of the
women; 54 percent of the men), this difference in ideological identification
is both statistically and substantively significant.[14]

Buttressing these findings are recent studies of ideological gender gaps
conducted on political elites other than elective officeholders. This research
extends our understanding of women's response to the existing political
environment and suggests that as politically active women move into the
world of elective officeholders in increasing numbers, the patterns currently
operating are likely to continue. One such study, which analyzes caucus
participants in both parties in 1984 and 1988, illustrates this point. Results
indicate a greater gender gap on issue attitudes and candidate selection
among these political elites than exists even at the mass levels. Women
were significantly more liberal than men on foreign policy issues, women's
issues, and social welfare issues. Further, these differences transcended
party. On foreign policy and women's issues, in particular, the gender gap
was greater among Republicans than Democrats. Clearly, then, more than
party affiliation guides such attitudes.[15]

Ideological stance tells us something about the political views of women

TABLE 3.1. Gender Differences on Indirect
Indicators of Priorities

	Male (%)	Female (%)
Ideology		
Liberal	15[a]	32[a]
Conservative	48[a]	31[a]
Committee Assignments		
Health/welfare	22[a]	39[a]
Education	34	39
Business	57	46
Budget	36	35
Committee Chairs		
Health/welfare	2[a]	10[a]
Education	7	4
Business	11	5
Perceptions of Constituency		
Elderly	70	72
Business	53	47
Labor	31	38
Women	33[a]	57[a]
Party	21[a]	28[a]
Racial minorities	30	38
Pride in Accomplishments (1)		
Public interest	15	12
Business	23	12
Ed./medical/welfare	23	28
Crime	5	5
Budget	9	6
Women/children	11	16
Pride in Accomplishments (2)		
Public interests	22	19
Business	26[a]	10[a]
Ed./medical/welfare	20	20
Crime	3	3
Budget	8[a]	3
Women/children	6[a]	30[a]

Note: $N = 322$.
[a] Gender difference significant at the .05 level.

in state legislatures. What about their specific issue attitudes? A recent
national study of state legislators reports that the gender gap on issues
ranging from the ERA to child care that was alive and well in the 1970s
continues today. For example, 79 percent of women state legislators support the ERA compared with 61 percent of men. There is a wide gap on the

issue of choice in abortion decisions. Only 26 percent of women agree that abortion should be prohibited in almost all circumstances compared with 39 percent of men. Fifty-seven percent of women oppose parental consent provisions for minors to obtain abortions, whereas only 33 percent of men oppose such provisions. On issues that are not directly related to women, a gender gap exists as well. Fifty-one percent of women, compared with 67 percent of men, support the death penalty. Only 16 percent of women favor construction of more nuclear power plants to meet state energy needs; 29 percent of men favor construction of this sort. Finally, 47 percent of women agree that the private sector can solve economic problems with minimal governmental regulation, whereas 59 percent of men agree with that premise. In fact, on only two issues in the survey was there no significant gender gap. Seventy-one percent of women support providing government-sponsored child care to families on an ability-to-pay basis. Fully 68 percent of men are similarly supportive. Lastly, 61 percent of women and 59 percent of men support increasing taxes to provide social services to compensate for reduced past funding levels.[16]

Another important indicator of differences goes beyond attitude, outlook, or perspective: voting record. While there are not many recent studies available, those extant suggest that women are still more supportive than men of women's and family issues and less supportive than men on defense spending and military intervention.[17] One recent study of voting behavior concerning women's issues in the 101st Congress, conducted by the National Women's Political Caucus, shows that women legislators in the House of Representatives supported the caucus's position 71.7 percent of the time compared with men's support, which stood at 55.7 percent. When results are broken down by party, we see that the lion's share of the difference between women and men generally is attributed to differences among Republican legislators.[18] In the Senate, only two women served during that session (although six women currently serve). While one cannot make much of a comparison of ninety-eight men and two women, there was still a difference. Women averaged a 75 percent support rate for NWPC positions, whereas the men averaged a 58 percent support rate.

Committee Assignments

In the 1970s, women representatives were concentrated in a narrow set of committee assignments. Whether it was by choice or not, the participation of women was, in these respects, confined to certain kinds of topics. The good news is that the situation in the seventies no longer prevails. The 1988 survey of state legislators from twelve states reveals that women were no longer confined to certain types of committees. As Table 3.1 illustrates, women were no more likely than men to be members of education committees (39 percent of women had at least one such assignment, as did 34 percent of men—a difference that does not achieve statistical significance). This is a major change from the 1970s when women were most heavily concentrated in these assignments. Additionally, women made their way to the more traditionally male-oriented committees, as illustrated by their nearly equal likelihood with males to be members of budget committees.[19]

Having said all that, women and men were not proportionally equal on all types of committees. Most strikingly, women were significantly more likely to have an assignment on health and welfare committees than men. As Table 3.1 reveals, 39 percent of women and 22 percent of men had at least one health and welfare type of assignment. Women were also less likely than men to sit on committees dealing with business and private economic concerns. Forty-six percent of women had at least one business assignment, whereas 57 percent of men sat on at least one such committee. This pattern was replicated in committee chair assignments. Women were more likely than men to chair health and welfare committees and less likely to chair business committees. Ten percent of women and only 2 percent of the men were chairs of health and welfare committees. Conversely, 5 percent of women and 11 percent of men were chairs of business committees.[20]

For another view of the patterns in the aggregate data, Table 3.2 provides a breakdown by state. Women were found more often than men on health and welfare committees in eleven out of the twelve states. In contrast, women were found less often than men on business committees in nine of the twelve. Similarly, women were, more often than men, chairs of health and welfare committees in eight states and were less often chairs of business committees in eight of the twelve. Interestingly, women sat on education committees more often than men in ten states. The reason that aggregate figures report that women and men were essentially equal on this measure is that the margin of difference between women and men in almost all these states was so slight that they are washed out when the total is calculated.

On the one hand, then, women broadened their membership on committees and were no longer exclusively choosing or were steered toward areas traditionally of interest to women. Yet their membership on all committees as well as their leadership of these committees was not entirely similar to

TABLE 3.2. Gender Differences in Committee Assignments and Committee Chair Positions, by State

	EdCom	HWCom	BusCom	BdgtCom	HWChr	BusChr
AZ	*	*		*	*	
CA			*		*	*
GA	*	*	*			*
IL	*	*		*		
IA	*	*			*	
MS	*	*	*	*		*
NE	*	*		*	*	
NC		*		*	*	
PA	*	*				
SD	*	*		*	*	
VT	*	*			*	
WA	*	*			*	*
	10	11	3	6	8	4

* = Women are more often on committee and are more often chair of committee than men in that state.

men's assignments. There are at least two possible explanations for these findings. First, it may be that women faced discrimination in committee assignment and election or appointment to leadership of those committees. The stereotypical views about women's expertise that were likely operational in the 1970s may have persisted. Without ruling out this possibility, there is another one that is also plausible. Women may have been more concentrated than men on health and welfare committees and less on business committees because the former reflected their priority interests. In other words, women may have chosen health and welfare committees more often because of expertise in these issue areas or a desire to effect change in those areas (or both). Support for this latter explanation can be had in some recent research. A Center for the American Woman and Politics study that also surveyed women and men in state legislatures finds that the greatest gender disparity in committee assignment occurs on health and human service committees. Analysis of the data suggests that it is out of choice rather than coercion or discrimination that this occurred.[21] Further, that women no longer dominated education committees as they did in the seventies is evidence that choice is the correct explanation. Another way to evaluate whether this portrayal is accurate is to discover what sorts of priorities state legislators select. This is the next topic of interest.

Do Women Have Different Policy Priorities Than Men?

The 1988 survey of state legislators from Arizona, California, Georgia, Illinois, Iowa, Mississippi, Nebraska, North Carolina, Pennsylvania, South Dakota, Vermont, and Washington contained several questions about how women and men in statehouses think about priorities and what actions they take to define and implement them. The presentation below contains three groups of questions. The first two provide insight into the motivations that create the priorities. Legislators' attitudes toward various segments of their constituencies and the accomplishments in which they have the most pride round out our understanding of the building blocks of priority selection. I shall report on these areas first. Subsequently, a direct discussion of priorities is offered.

Attitudes toward segments of the constituency. One question in the survey asked, "There are many interests demanding attention from you as a legislator. How important is representing each of the following interests to you?" The specific selections for legislators to respond to included the elderly, business, labor, women, their party, and racial minorities. No gender differences were apparent in responses concerning the elderly (70 percent of men and 72 percent of women responded that this segment of the constituency was very important). In the categories of business interests, labor, and racial minorities, there were, as Table 3.1 indicates, differential support levels, although none were statistically significant. Only in two areas were there significant (statistically and substantively) differences between women and men. The first difference concerned the respondent's political party. Twenty-eight percent of the women considered this interest very important, whereas 21 percent of the men agreed with that formulation. It may be that women felt more tied to their party than men because the party provided them with the contacts that are so necessary for successful candidacies of their own. Traditionally, men have had larger outside networks from which to draw support than have women. Evidence for this interpretation is available in a recent study examining ambition levels of women and men over time. The study reveals that women are more committed to their party than are men. In the words of the author,

> Women respondents have been more likely than men to hold party office, to claim that they have never supported a candidate of the opposing party, to describe themselves as "one of those people who can be counted on to work for the party and in its campaigns year after year, regardless of candidates," to attribute their selection as delegation slate members to the time and energy

they have devoted to their party and to their loyalty to party leadership, and to identify their party as the most important organization to which they belong. Clearly, the women studied here are more deeply anchored in their political party than their male counterparts.

He hypothesizes that:

> For them, party activity and commitment may serve to overcome the advantages typically enjoyed by male competitors as they strive for power, for example, as the functional alternative to the prestigious occupations often used by men as a springboard for lateral movement into high office.[22]

Whatever the explanation for the gender differences in importance of representing one's party, the real story behind answers to the various components of the question is the large gender gap found in responses to the importance of representing women. Fully 57 percent of women state legislators considered representing women very important; only 33 percent of men responded similarly. This is the single largest difference between the sexes on any component of this question and is the most statistically and substantively significant. Another way to appreciate the magnitude of the difference on this indicator is to scan the breakdowns by state. In Table 3.3, women in fully nine out of twelve states in the study considered women to be a very important segment of the constituency. It is clear that women state

TABLE 3.3. Gender Differences on Perceptions of Constituency, by State

	Elderly	Business	Labor	Women	Party	Race
AZ		*	*	*	*	*
CA		*		*		
GA	*		*	*	*	*
IL				*	*	*
IA				*	*	*
MS		*		*	*	
NE	*	*	*			
NC			*	*		
PA		*	*		*	*
SD					*	
VT	*		*	*	*	*
WA			*	*		
	3	5	7	9	8	6

* = Women in that state are more supportive than men of various segments of the constituency.

legislators felt a special affinity for the status of women in society and considered representing those interests as important.[23]

Given that the majority of women state legislators were predisposed to consider the representation of women important, this leads us to expect that they took such attitudes into account when creating their legislative agendas. Before discovering whether this was the case or not, there is one more indirect indicator of the motivations for creating priorities.

Pride in accomplishments. Another survey question simply asked respondents to reflect back on their tenure as a state legislator and identify one or two of the accomplishments of which they were most proud. Naturally, there were a wide variety of answers. Other than two categories of broad answers (helping individual constituents with problems and generally being an effective legislator), each of the answers fell into accomplishments on issues. The patterns related to which issues displayed a gender difference and those in which no statistical or substantive difference appeared are interesting and provide more insight into motivations for creating legislative priorities.

The responses to the first accomplishment listed showed no gender differences on issues of crime and punishment, budget and taxation, or what I have called public interest issues (those dealing with benefits to the society as a whole rather than specific parts of it, such as clean water legislation). Table 3.1 shows that differences did appear in three telltale issue categories. First of all, there was an eleven-point difference in feelings of pride in accomplishments related to business issues. Twenty-three percent of men indicated that they were proud of accomplishments in this area compared with 12 percent of women. Conversely, women were more proud than men of accomplishments relating to bills dealing with women, and children and families and with education, medical, and welfare issues. In both categories there was a five-point difference in favor of the women.[24]

Analysis of the responses that were listed second reflected a generally similar pattern. There were no gender differences on issues of crime and punishment or public interest issues. This time there were no differences in the category of education, medical, and welfare issues. However, large differences were apparent on issues of business and issues dealing with women and children. There was a sixteen-point difference on business issues, with a greater proportion of men than women expressing pride in accomplishments related to this area. On issues of women, children and families, there was a twenty-four-point difference, with 30 percent of women expressing pride compared with only 6 percent of men. In this second set of responses, there was also a small difference between women and men with respect to budget and tax issues, with 8 percent of men expressing pride in accomplishments in this area and only 3 percent of women expressing a similar pride. Finally, in Table 3.4 we can see not the aggregate finding but the pattern by state. In ten out of twelve states, women were most proud of accomplishments dealing with women's issues, whereas women in only two states were most proud of issues dealing with business.

What do these findings suggest overall? The patterns in the data indicate that women and men display different attitudes toward their accomplishments. The constant across the responses was that women were more often proud of issues related to women, children and families and men are more proud of issues related to business. Not coincidentally, these differences mirror the differences between the sexes in committees to which they were assigned and chair positions that they held. It is important when considering this information that it not be misinterpreted. Women and men were not polarized on any of the variables we have been considering so far. Women were, for example, represented on the full range of committees and ex-

TABLE 3.4. Gender Differences in Pride of
Accomplishment, by State

	Proud W	Proud B	Proud WL	Proud C	Proud L
AZ	*				*
CA					
GA	*		*		
IL	*				*
IA	*		*	*	*
MS	*	*			*
NE	*				
NC	*		*	*	*
PA				*	*
SD	*		*	*	*
VT	*		*		*
WA	*	*			*
TOTAL	10	2	5	4	9

Notes: ProudW stands for pride of accomplishments dealing with women's issues; ProudB deals with business issues; ProudWL, with welfare issues; ProudC, with assisting constituents; and ProudL, with pride connected to being a good legislator. The stars stand for the same things as noted in earlier tables.

pressed pride in accomplishments of all sorts. In no category of responses were women absent. The correct interpretation of these data is that while women had access to and expressed interest in the range of legislative affairs, they also seemed to gain expertise in, worked on, and gained satisfaction from issues of certain sorts more often than did men. The important question to which we now turn is whether the next step was taken. Did women have distinctive legislative agendas? Do women make priority of the sorts of issues that they are connected with in other ways?

Policy priorities

> A member of Congress, whether man or woman, is responsible for the legislative interests of the district he or she serves, representing men as well as women. . . . The result is that, in the practical work of legislation, a woman member of Congress finds herself associated with or pitted against men and women similarly representing group interests. . . . Accordingly, legislation for women becomes no more important to most women members of Congress than legislation for men. They become immersed, perforce, in the general problems of the country and their respective districts.[25]

> The Congresswomen carry a special responsibility, as do all "minority" politicians. They are called upon to speak with a single voice for the cause of "women's issues." The women of America are a diverse population and the women in Congress reflect that diversity. . . . Nonetheless there are areas of mutual agreement which allow us to formulate a common legislative agenda.[26]

Which of these quotations accurately depicts the behavior of women legislators of the 1980s? In order to determine the answer, the twelve-state survey asked respondents to list their top five legislative priorities in the last complete legislative session. From their responses, eight categories of bill type were constructed for analysis. These categories included women's issues; child and family issues; issues of education and medical care; welfare; criminal justice; energy and environment; state budget and governmental efficiency; and business and transportation. In addition to the information gathered from the survey of legislators in twelve states, in the second half of 1988 and the first half of 1989, I personally interviewed women legislators in six of the twelve states: California, Georgia, Mississippi, Nebraska, Pennsylvania, and Washington. The focus of the interviews had specifically to do with policy priorities and how women differed from men in this regard.[27] The viewpoints of women state legislators on this issue are included in this discussion.

The responses of women and men in statehouses indicate that, indeed, women developed distinctive legislative agendas—women's priorities were quite different from those of men. As you scan Table 3.5, notice that I report average differences in policy priority for the state legislators. Because the survey asked for legislators' top five priorities, the most meaningful and most comprehensible summary statistic is the average. The way to interpret these figures is straightforward. To arrive at the figure for total bill introductions for men, for example, I simply added the total number of bills introduced by each man in the last legislative session and divided the resultant figure by the number of men in the sample. The same calculation was performed for the women in the sample. This having been said, the data contained in the table show that women's lists of priority bills contained more legislation pertaining to children than the lists of men. Women introduced an average of 0.35 more bills on children. This means that an increase of ten women legislators would have resulted in introduction of three or four more children's bills each session. These distinctive interests held in the wake of multivariate analysis as well. A final look at the pattern

TABLE 3.5. Average Number of Bill Introductions and Passages by Men and Women

	Male	Female
Total Bill Introductions	17.5	13.6
Total Bill Passage	8.4	6.6
(through legislature)		
Types of Priority Bill Introductions		
Women	0.03[a]	0.11[a]
Children/families	0.20[a]	0.55[a]
Business	1.1[b]	0.68[b]
Passage of Priority Bills	2.2	2.3
(through legislature)		
Passage of Priority Bills	1.8	2.1
(governor's signarure)		
Passage Rate of Bills Dealing with Women, Children and Families	11.1[a]	27.1[a]
(through legislature)		
Passage Rate of Bills Dealing with Women, Children and Families	8.0[a]	25.6[a]
(governor's signature)		

Note: For total bill introduction, legislators could enter an unlimited number; total bill passage was some portion of total bill introductions. For priority bills, legislators were held to their top five, so the range was from zero to five. Passage of priority bills also ranged from zero to five. The passage rate of bills dealing with women, and children and families is the total number of such bills introduced divided by the total number of those bills that were passed.

[a] Statistically significant at the .05 level.

[b] Significant at the .10 level.

to the data is to explore sex differences by state. As Table 3.6 reveals, women in eight of the twelve states introduced more legislation dealing with children and the family than did their male counterparts.

Another area of interest to women in statehouses is women's issues.[28] Women were, more often than men, apt to make issues of this type a priority. Indeed, while neither women nor men had large numbers of such priority bill introductions, a 0.08 average difference existed. The small number of bills that were listed by women or men on women's issues and the fact that women and men did not differ very substantially are particularly intriguing, since these findings seem to counter the multitude of others. I turned to the personal interviews to uncover possible explanations. The interviews support the fact that women legislators were more committed to women's issues than were men. Consider these comments: One legislator noted that women's legislative priorities are different from men's because "women are different in some capacity." She continued, "Women have perspective men don't have. I am introducing legislation to help women. Women must protect women. That's what I do."

A southern legislator said that women's legislative priorities are different from men's because "women in general tend to focus on women's issues. You seldom see men work on displaced homemakers' issues, etc."

One western legislator said: "Most of the women are or have been married and have kids. Since they had that experience, those issues are very important to them. They see it as their responsibility."

Another southern legislator said: "Women lean more toward compassion issues and education. Men lean toward farming, fishing and retirement issues. Also there is a totally different approach. Women are more family oriented; men are more economics."

Talking about the similarities and differences in women's and men's legislative priorities, one legislator said women's priorities were different from men's. "Women tend to look at more issues of women and children. This is not to say others aren't addressed, but they [women] carry more legislation more quickly and put in more energy and effort. Women are lead people on this type of stuff."

Finally: "Women's legislative priorities are similar to men's, but women are more attuned to issues that are family-oriented. Men do some also though men are interested in teen pregnancy and family violence, but almost all women have something in all categories [of bills of interest to women] and will support your bills of this kind with no question."

While I cannot quote all the women I interviewed on the differences in priorities between women and men in statehouses, I can tell you that almost all of them mentioned some differences along the lines suggested above. Since the figures do not represent such a large difference, it may be that women worked on these issues in large numbers but were not necessarily listing them or thinking about them as *top* priorities.

Another way to understand difference by gender is to examine the findings not just in the aggregate but by state. Table 3.6 shows that, out of the twelve states in the study, women in eight of them had a higher average priority level on bills dealing with children and families than did men. Further, women in seven of the twelve states had a higher average of policy priority on women's bills than did men.

One final way to analyze the types of priorities to which women legislators were committed is to devise a combined indicator. I calculated a figure in which all the priority bills of legislators that dealt with women, children and families were combined. Next, I calculated sex differences. The findings were both statistically and substantively significant. Forty-two percent of women had at least one priority bill dealing with issues of women, and children and families, whereas only 16 percent of men were similarly situated. The mean amount of priority legislation dealing with women, and children and families was, for women state legislators, 0.65 (out of a possible 5.0) and, for men, 0.19. This difference is statistically significant.[29]

In contrast to the types of bills that women considered high priority, notice that men placed priority, more often than did women, on bills dealing with business. In fact, men introduced an average of 0.42 more bills on business than did women. Looked at another way, men in all twelve states introduced higher numbers of business bills than did women in their states.

It would be a mistake to interpret the findings discussed above as meaning that women only cared about bills dealing with women, and children and the family, and that men only cared about bills dealing with business. That is most certainly not what was going on. Women and men were both interested in and introduced legislation on the full range of issues before legislatures. However, even allowing for wide-ranging interests by both sexes, we did find some distinctive patterns. Women did give more time, energy, and effort to bills dealing with women's, and children's and family issues. This is reflected in the kinds of committees on which they sat, the chair positions they held, the types of accomplishments about which they displayed pride, as well as the bills they pursued. Men, on the other hand, expressed more pride in accomplishments related to business, were more often on business-related committees, more often held chair positions on

Table 3.6. Gender Differences in Policy Priorities, by State

	Total Introduced	Total Passed (Leg.)	Priority Passed (Leg.)	Child Intro.	Women Intro.	Bus. Intro.	Selected Priority Pass Ratio (Leg.)	Priority Passed (Gov.)	Selected Priority Pass Ratio (Gov.)
AZ	*	*	*	*	*			*	
CA		*						*	
GA				*	*		*		*
IL			*	*	*		*	*	*
IA	*	*	*	*	*		*	*	*
MS			*					*	*
NE	*	*	*				*	*	*
NC				*	*		*	*	*
PA	*			*			*		*
SD				*			*		*
VT	*	*	*		*		*	*	*
WA	*	*	*	*	*		*		*
Total	6	6	7	8	7	0	9	8	10

* = Women have more total bill introductions and total bills passed than men, more priority bills passed, more priority bills introduced in each of the issues areas, and a higher ratio of introduction to passage of those priority bills dealing with issues of women, and children and families.

76

such committees, and introduced more bills dealing with business issues than did women. The areas of expertise of women and men were not polarized, but they were distinctive.

Success in passing policy priorities. A list of the priority bills of a particular legislator tells us something about her or his values and how those values translated into legislative action. However, the mere introduction of bills tells us nothing about whether legislators were successful in seeing those bills through the process. If women had an effect on legislative products, they had to pass, not just introduce distinctive legislation. It is true that women of the 1980s displayed distinctive priorities, but since their priorities were still not entirely mainstream, it is possible that these bills might have had a more difficult time getting through the legislative process.

Given that women of the 1980s participated in all facets of legislative life and considered themselves effective across them, the safe prediction is that the sexes were equally successful in getting their priority bills passed. If this is true, it will say a great deal about the expansion of leeway accorded women within the public sphere as well as the extent to which their concerns were brought into the mainstream of public life. One question in the survey allows us to judge the relative success levels of women and men on this measure. Respondents were asked to indicate the outcome of each bill. This made calculation of success levels a simple matter.

Table 3.5 indicates that women and men were, as predicted, substantively equal in terms of their success rates with respect to passage of priority bills through the legislature. Women passed an average of 2.3 of their top five priorities, and men averaged about 2.2. This translates into women legislators passing 46 percent of their top five priority bills compared with men's passage rate of 44 percent. To examine the pattern by state, turn to Table 3.6. Women in seven of the twelve states had higher passage rates of priority bills than did the men in those states. As Tables 3.5 and 3.6 also reveal, women and men were substantially equal in obtaining their governor's signature on bills and, therefore, seeing them become law. This evidence suggests that women were successful in the legislative arena. They introduced and placed priority on the range of topics in the governmental sphere, and they also brought a distinctive concern for issues of women, and children and families. Furthermore, they were effective in seeing their policy priorities through the process.

Success in passing selected priorities. Before making a final judgment about the effectiveness of women legislators of the late 1980s, it is important to investigate their success rates in passage of priority bills dealing with women, and children and families. Since this is the distinctive contribution that women bring to legislatures, it is important to know whether they had relatively more or less success passing these particular bills. The answer is an unequivocal yes. Table 3.5 informs us that the ratio of introduction to passage through the legislature of these types of bills was higher for women than men (27.1 for women compared with 11.1 for men). An easier way to think about these differences may be in percentages. Men in statehouses passed only 13 percent of their priority bills dealing with women, and children and the family through the legislature, whereas women had more than double that success rate, with 29 percent of their bills in these areas achieving passage. Once again, if we look at Table 3.6, we find that the overall priority passage ratio was higher for women than men in nine out of the twelve states. Similar if not more dramatic patterns are evident with respect to obtaining gubernatorial signatures on bills dealing with women, and children and families. Women legislators' average ratio of introduction to signature of these types of bills was 25.6 compared with men's average of only 8.0. Further, women in ten states had higher ratios of introduction to signature.

Together, information about priority bill introductions, priority bill passage, and priority bill passage rates for bills in the areas of women's, and children's and family issues indicates that women were bringing distinctive concerns to the legislative arena and were quite successful in passing their priorities. More than that, it appears that they put more energy than men into the priority bills that deal with women's, and children's and family issues. This conclusion is reflected in the remarks of a staff member in a western legislature who works on women's issues: "Women absolutely make a policy difference. They are more sensible, more practical, and more comprehensive. They are more willing to fight for women's and children's policies. They don't give up as easily."

While a great deal of evidence has been introduced to depict the distinctive contribution of women in terms of legislative product, one type of evidence remains unavailable. At the start of this section, I mentioned that some gender politics scholars expect that women can bring a fresh perspective to all legislation, not just legislation on which they place priority. If we can envision what the next stage of research in this area will look like, we will be able to design appropriate studies. In fact, it is not just scholars who believe that such information should be gathered. At a 1982 conference of women legislators, one of the items on legislators' wish lists was "identifying issues that are not traditionally seen as women's issues and looking at how women are differently affected by policies in these areas."[30]

In summary of the findings concerning women state legislators of the 1980s, it is clear that they resembled their counterparts in the 1970s in several respects. Women legislators of the 1980s continued to have more liberal ideological attitudes than their male colleagues and voting records that reflected greater support of women's issues and social welfare issues and less support of defense spending and foreign intervention. However, women of the 1980s were found on the range of available committees and worked on legislation from across the issue spectrum. Most significantly, women of the 1980s developed different policy priorities than men. Issues of women, and children and families went to the top of their agendas. The differentiation that was not evident between women and men in the 1970s has manifested itself in the more recent era.

Additional support for findings. Research conducted at the Center for the American Woman and Politics at Rutgers University also explores the question of whether women bring to state legislatures substantive representation as well as symbolic representation. It is encouraging that even though somewhat different questions were asked of the respondents, similar kinds of results were recorded. First, in response to a question on whether the legislators had worked on any bills dealing with women's issues, women legislators were more likely than men to have worked on such bills. In fact, "more than half the women compared with about one-third of the men, had worked on such legislation."[31] When the responses were analyzed more deeply to separate out not only women from men but feminists from nonfeminists, the results were encouraging. Among feminists, women were more likely than men to have worked on a bills to help women. Interestingly, even nonfeminist women were more likely than their male counterparts to have worked on an issue helping women.[32]

Further, there were differences in the single most important legislative priority of women and men. About three times as many women as men had a top priority bill dealing with women. (It is important to note, say the authors, that only a tiny minority of such bills dealt with antifeminist concerns.) In addition, women in statehouses, more often than men, listed as top priorities bills dealing with health and welfare issues. As with much recent research, there were no gender differences in bills dealing with education. Finally, women legislators in this study, just like the ones in my 1988 study, were just as successful as the men in getting their top priority bill passed.[33]

Two further studies dealing with the topic of women state legislators deserve comment. Each deals with only one legislature, but the results of findings are consistent with multistate studies. First, an article by Michelle Saint-Germain, which focuses on the policy priorities of women legislators in Arizona, provides one of the few available longitudinal analyses of the behavior of women officeholders. From 1969 to 1986, a clear pattern emerged with respect to the kinds of bills introduced by women and men, how successful these bills were, and how increasing proportions of women in the legislature over time were associated with women's choice of bill introductions. First, Saint-Germain found that, overall, women introduced more bills than men that dealt with women's issues. This list included bills of a feminist nature and bills that have been traditionally of interest to women (such as health and welfare issues). Significantly, women were not just equally as successful as men in shepherding these types of bills to passage, they were more successful. Finally, there was an increase over time in women state legislators' involvement in women's issues. Saint-Germain notes that this increase was concomitant with the rise in the proportion of women in the statehouse.[34]

While the increase in involvement may tell us something about women state legislators' response to greater support (due to more women colleagues), we cannot be sure that increased proportions of women alone were responsible for rising interest in issues related to women. This is because another plausible explanation may be that the women's movement, increases in educational, occupational, and political opportunities that have become available to women, and increased societal acceptance of women in the public sphere resulted in rising interest in women's issues by female state legislators. In order to tell if proportions of women representatives are associated with a greater willingness of women to introduce women's legislation, one would need a cross-sectional survey of a number of states, all with varying proportions of women. We shall explore this type of analysis in Chapter 4.

Another recent study by Lyn Kathlene, Susan Clarke, and Barbara Fox that concentrated on members of the Colorado House of Representatives found that "while the topics addressed by women's and men's bills in general were similar, the innovative bills women introduced were more likely than those of men to address education or family/children issues." Further, women, more than their male counterparts, proposed spending state money for direct services to people, whereas men concentrated on spending for government commissions and regulatory bodies. Again, the pattern is clear—the priorities of women state legislators were markedly different from those of men.[35]

Women of Today: A Distinctive Agenda

Why have women state legislators, over time, moved from failing to translate ideology, issue positions, and expertise into distinctive policy priorities
to successfully doing so? Put another way, why is it that the reformist
portion of the typology correctly characterizes the legislative efforts of
women of the 1980s whereas women legislators of the 1970s hovered between its adaptive and reformist elements? In the 1970s, the relatively
low level of acceptance of women in the public sphere resulted in depriving
them of the tools to translate issue positions into policy priorities. First,
owing in large part to societal conflicts over whether women belonged in
the public sphere, and if so, how complete their role ought to be, women
legislators did not have the sense of effectiveness and support necessary to
bring forth issues of particular interest to them. Moreover, it is likely that
women were uncomfortable risking the positions and reputations they had
acquired by bringing issues from outside the mainstream directly to the
legislative agenda and bearing responsibility for shepherding them through
the process.

It was not until society came to a somewhat greater acceptance of women
in public roles that female representatives were accorded the latitude to
work effectively in all facets of the legislative process and to push for issues
of primary importance to them. In short, past constraints about the proper
role of women that impeded their access to and desire to participate in
legislative life were lowered, and women of the late 1980s and onward have
taken advantage of changing attitudes. This explanation does not, for a
moment, argue that all barriers have been removed and that women in
politics face the same constraints and opportunities as male politicians.
Indeed, it is possible that, under such circumstances, we might see little, if
any, distinctive behavior. It merely suggests that as barriers have been
lowered, women have taken advantage of the situation to develop and
defend policies dear to them.

Moving beyond the fact that women developed distinctive policy priorities to understanding why they developed these specific ones, it is important to consider the fact that their greater access to the public arena did not
free them from their responsibilities in the private one. For most women,
their public sphere role was only half of their job; they continued to bear the
major responsibility for home and hearth. Given this dual role, it is not
surprising that women have used their latitude to participate in the legislative arena to make private sphere issues legitimate governmental concerns.
They tended to have more awareness of and more connection to the private
sphere than did most men, so their knowledge of such issues impelled

women to bring them forth. Further, if women legislators are to continue in and expand their public sphere roles, they need to devote attention to obstacles that may be in their path. Lessening the burden of being a full-time worker and a full-time homemaker is one way to address such problems—not only for themselves but for all women in public life.

There is a final reason why women legislators were more likely than men to place a greater level of emphasis on legislation dealing with issues of women, and children and families. The debate about exactly how women ought to balance their dual roles of home and office and to what extent men ought to accept responsibility for private sphere matters has yet to be resolved. Unless and until it is resolved, women will feel the tug of two worlds and will have a psychological need to have a public connection to both.

In short, women have gained latitude and the experience in legislative politics to translate ideological stance, issue positions, and voting behavior into full-fledged policy priorities. They have used these opportunities and have brought issues of women, and children and families into the center of their legislative efforts.

Conclusion

The research findings presented in Chapters 2 and 3 help us construct a portrait of women state legislators as they were in the 1970s and the late 1980s. We know that, in some respects, women of the eighties resemble their counterparts of the seventies, but that important changes have taken place. For example, women state legislators in the 1970s possessed lower levels of education than men, were primarily employed in positions that were female dominated, had relatively little political experience prior to assuming their place in the statehouse, and were not particularly interested in gaining higher political office.

Women of the late 1980s made inroads in educational and occupational opportunities, gained a great deal of individual and collective political experience, and developed political ambition at ever-increasing rates. What is particularly interesting and perhaps admirable about this latter group is that they accomplished all this with very little reduction in their responsibilities to children and home. Superwoman may be a myth, but it is one that women legislators were (and are) under some pressure to uphold.

Women state legislators in the late 1980s compared with their sisters in the 1970s were different in other respects as well. Women in both decades found that in society at large, and in politics in particular, women faced obstacles to success. Discrimination was a fact of life and a barrier to achieving effectiveness. Women in the 1970s, however, reacted to that barrier by avoiding it, whereas women of the 1980s, with additional support for a public sphere role, overcame it. In the 1970s, women state legislators, for all their acknowledged hard work and preparation, did not engage in active participation in the everyday world of legislatures. For numerous reasons, they held themselves back from speaking in committees and on the floor of their chambers. They did not negotiate and bargain with their colleagues and they found such actions difficult to engage in. Instead, women contributed to the political arena by working hard to take care of their constituents and to deal with community concerns.

In contrast, women of the 1980s, while acknowledging similar obstacles, clearly plowed through them and moved on to contribute in all areas of legislative life. They participated on equal levels with men in speaking on the floor and in committees, meeting with lobbyists, and negotiating and bargaining with their colleagues. What is more, women state legislators of the late 1980s used their participation to introduce and secure passage of distinctive legislation. While women were active on the range of legislative topics in the eighties, they placed priority, more than did men, on issues concerning women, and children and families. These efforts were success-ful ones, and women were proud that they were able to contribute in these ways.

There are some striking similarities between the women who occupied statehouses in the 1970s and those who made their contributions in the 1980s. Both sets of women officeholders were equally adamant about want-ing to see more women in public office, believing that women faced sub-stantial barriers to participation within and success in the public sphere but that those barriers could be overcome. Both were consistently more liberal than their male counterparts, more attitudinally supportive of women's issues and social welfare issues (and less supportive of defense spending and military intervention), and voted in ways that reflected these attitudes. Women state legislators were also found, more often than men, on commit-tees dealing with these concerns, such as health and welfare committees. The difference in the 1980s may have been that women selected such tasks freely, as opposed to such tasks being placed upon them because of the stereotypical attitudes of others. All of these similarities are illustrative of the fact that, although women have made progress in gaining and keeping positions and moving up in the world of the public sphere, complete inte-gration was not achieved. While society accepts women in these roles more readily than it did in the past, by no means are women or women's distinctive goals treated equally in the workplace—be it political or otherwise.

This overall portrait of women legislators reflects the evolution in their attitudes and behaviors. Structuring the investigation using the typology of expectations has helped us track the changes and understand how constraints and opportunities have influenced the ways in which women responded to them.

4

The Nature of Support

Organizations with a better balance of people would be more tolerant of the differences among them. In addition to making affirmative action a reality, there would be other benefits: a reduction in stress on the people who are "different," a reduction in conformity pressures on the dominant group. It would be more possible, in such an organization, to build the skills and utilize the competence of people who currently operate at a disadvantage, and thus to vastly enhance the value of an organization's prime resource: its people.[1]

The words of Rosabeth Moss Kanter, written about the ratio of women to men in corporate sales forces, signal that the attitudes and behaviors of people inside a given institution are influenced, in part, by the diversity of its participants. Implicit in the words is the recognition that an inverse relationship exists between balanced environments and increased conformity pressures and that bringing an institution closer to balance lessens that pressure.

Kanter's words also signal recognition that sociocultural influences on the extent to which women in the public sphere are accorded leeway to display distinctive attitudes or behaviors or, conversely, experience constraints are filtered through the mores and standards of organizational environments. The institution's norms and standards for activity or the way in which activity is pursued interacts with societal perspectives of the proper public sphere role of women to limit or enhance their opportunities and actions. Accordingly, in this chapter and the next, I concentrate on what aspects of institutions allow the emergence or repression of women's unique contributions.

Since we now know that women legislators do have a distinctive impact—at the very least, the policy priorities they bring to the agenda and successfully usher through the process are different from men's—the next important question is, "What in the institutional environment is most likely

to foster the development of or hinder women's distinctive policy priorities?'' I argue, following Kanter, that the answer is those environments in
which higher proportions of women are present. If the theory developed
throughout this book—that fuller acceptance of women in public sphere
roles increases the chances of emergence of their unique contributions—has
any validity, it follows that time frame is not the only factor contributing to
support levels. Another key variable may also be support levels for
women's concerns within the legislatures themselves. In testing this propo-
sition, longitudinal evidence of the theory's strength and explanatory power
is supplemented by cross-sectional evidence.

The specific reason for the prediction that proportionality is another
vehicle for support is that the choice of priority issues is influenced, in part,
by the calculation of whether or not the legislator will be stigmatized by her
colleagues for pursuing a controversial or marginal issue as well as what
level of support for the issue can be expected. Female representatives are
more likely to believe that their distinctive concerns, those dealing with
issues of women, and children and families, will be well received in a
legislature with higher proportions of women. The data on issue attitudes of
men and women from Chapter 2 are ample evidence of this expectation. It
stands to reason, then, that female legislators are more likely to develop
distinctive policy priorities in high-proportion environments.

The pages that follow are designed to test this hypothesis. First, I offer a
brief survey of psychological and sociological arguments about conformity
pressures inside organizations and the extent to which imbalance between
dominant and minority groups affects conformity pressures. Next, I explore
the results of existing empirical investigations based on such theories and
how they can be applied in the political context. The heart of the chapter
consists of original research testing the prediction with the survey and
interview data introduced in Chapters 2 and 3.

The Lessons of Psychology and Sociology

The literatures of psychology and sociology are replete with analyses of
how institutional environments develop norms of behavior related to the
behavior of their dominant groups. While the reasons why norms develop
and why pressures to bow to them are so strong are multivariate, whatever
sets of norms are adopted, their very existence militates against distinctive
activity. Few manage to deviate in substantial and sustained ways. Those
who do almost always pay a price, whether it be financial, psychological,

social, status related, or in terms of compromised job effectiveness.[2] Thus, even those who are most likely to have developed sensibilities distinct from the dominant perspective are likely to repress or abandon dissonant behaviors.[3]

The literature of these two disciplines also confirms that greater convergence toward existing norms and standards can be expected as exposure to and experience in any given environment increases. There are several reasons why this is likely to occur. First, the very choice of joining an organization (assuming a certain level of choice was operational) signifies that the person doing the choosing considers the organization or its goals to be generally valuable and legitimate. Moreover, the longer one is a member of an institution or organization, the more likely one is to have been rewarded by the system and feel an attachment to it. Even in the absence of significant rewards, an individual is likely to perceive time spent as valuable rather than wasted and therefore feel allegiance to the institution and its traditions.[4]

While organizational norms serve to constrain behavior within a specific range, they are not eternally static, nor do they exert the same sort of pressure on every member of the organization. Typically, groups outside the mainstream are those most severely constrained because, by definition, they are the most likely to possess distinctive attitudes and perceptions and because they are the ones most likely to be judged harshly for deviation. The constraints on those in the minority are not invariable, however. They depend, in large part, on the size of the minority group in relationship to the dominant or majority group. In situations in which the imbalance is significant, members of the minority are highly unlikely to deviate from the norms. Conversely, when the relationship between the two groups approaches balance, members of the minority are freer to display distinctive behaviors. At the intersection of balance and imbalance, alternative values or perceptions begin to be integrated into the dominant perspective.[5]

The quote that opens this chapter came from the path-breaking research of Rosabeth Moss Kanter and provides an example of how this theory applies to situations of gender balance or imbalance and precisely where those lines of demarcation lie. She argues, as noted above, that the closer the ratio between women and men (or, for that matter, any minority and majority) is to balance, the less women feel constrained in their actions and the less their behavior is unnatural. In other words, "relative numbers of socially and culturally different people in a group are seen as critical in shaping interaction dynamics."[6] In the case of a skewed group (15 percent or less of the total), women are perceived as tokens, and this status alters behavior. Rather than just blending into the mainstream, the female tokens continuously respond to their differential status—usually in some extreme fashion, such as accepting the isolation that has been thrust upon them or defining themselves as exceptions to their social category and distancing themselves from other women. As organizations develop "tilted" groupings (minority members constituting 15 to 40 percent of the total) or approach "balance" (a 60–40 split), women are less often perceived as aberrant and are more often able to respond to the environment in an unrestrained fashion.[7]

Thus, conformity pressures inside organizations are strong, they tend to exert a strong hold the longer one is in an organization, and they are the most inhibiting to those outside the dominant social group—the very people who are likely to possess a distinctive perspective on organizational goals and procedures. However, the extent of the balance or imbalance of majority to minority members does have an important effect on the emergence of distinctive behavior on the part of those in the minority.

Applications to the Political Realm

What pressures both inside the institution of legislatures and within the wider political environment impel politicians to conform? Two types of conformity pressures are operational. The first concerns the psychological need to value that which one has actively sought. Anyone who has achieved an elective office is likely to have devoted a great deal of time, effort, and expense to do so. Such individuals are unlikely to have gone through the difficulty of campaigning if they did not, on some level, perceive the political arena as legitimate and of value either to themselves personally or to a set of people or policies upon which they can have an impact. Successful candidates for elective political office are therefore people who enter their jobs with a reasonably high regard for the institution they are about to join and are people who, by virtue of winning an election, have been rewarded for their efforts. Perceptions of legitimacy and the rewards conferred mix with ever-increasing experience in the institution to exert a powerful influence on the behavior of the individual. The direction of the influence will, of course, be toward conformity with whatever standards and norms are operational in the environment.[8]

The second type of conformity pressure within legislatures concerns the best way to be effective in the pursuit of good public policy and influence within the chamber: gaining respect from one's colleagues.[9] Ample evidence exists to suggest that the primary precondition for high respect and good reputation in legislatures is playing by the rules of the game. While failure to conform to the ways of the legislative world is unlikely to result directly in job loss or ostracism, as may be the case in corporate life, it will compromise one's ability to reach goals and produce results.[10] In legislative life, unlike corporate life, the conformity pressures come less from one's direct "boss" than from one's colleagues.

Having briefly noted that conformity pressures are no less strong in the legislative arena than the corporate one (although they are enforced differently), we can proceed to the next relevant question: "How do the theories and findings of research on the concept of balanced environments translate into the world of politics?" Do women representatives feel freer to exhibit distinctive behaviors (policy priorities, for example) in places where they are more numerous or less free to do so where they are extreme tokens?

The first indicator that levels of gender balance make a big difference in the extent to which women representatives feel compelled to display or repress their distinctiveness is available in a study of county supervisors in Santa Clara County, California. In the early 1980s, the county was hailed as the feminist capital of the nation. The mayor of San Jose was a woman (Janet Gray Hayes), and the City Council of San Jose as well as the Santa Clara County Board of Supervisors had female majorities. This had two telling effects. First, the presence of supportive colleagues (other women) encouraged female representatives to speak out and participate in the process rather than exhibit the reticence to which they might otherwise have resorted. Second, the study's author suggests that women on the board felt freer to pursue issues they might have, in other circumstances, left aside for fear either that their choices would be considered deviant or that they would be poorly supported.[11] Not surprisingly, a great deal of legislation aimed at women's issues, such as comparable worth and day care, was the result.

Not only did the presence of other women in this environment give individual female officeholders the support they needed to pursue distinctive agendas and to speak out when they found that crucial viewpoints were not being articulated, it also spurred a new ethic among the women. Even those who never viewed themselves as representatives of women or women's issues became educated about their import. As one city councilmember commented:

> It was not part of my consciousness. It had to be brought to my attention. I got more philosophical about the issue. I began to realize how proud I was of the women who ran against the men. I owe a lot to those who came before me. They did a good job and made it easier for me. . . . I have shifted from seeing the feminist capital as irrelevant to seeing it as a source of pride.[12]

This finding is similar to anecdotal statements made by women legislators in other settings. The words of Geraldine Ferraro are illustrative:

> I didn't go down to Washington to represent the women of this nation. I ran, and was elected, not as a feminist, but as a lawyer. I didn't go to Washington to speak for the poor of this nation. I am not a bleeding heart, a sob sister. My campaign slogan in 1978 was "Finally, A Tough Democrat." I represent a conservative, middle class, hard working constituency, and I went to Washington to represent them.
>
> Something has happened in the years since I went to Congress. I have come to recognize how People Like Us can become People Like Them, through no fault of our own, especially if we are women.

The authors of the biography of Geraldine Ferraro from which these quotes are drawn further note:

> And she came to the cause, she has said, only after realizing the economic hardships of single women supporting families. During her first campaign, she never mentioned the word feminist.[13]

Thus, a more balanced environment affects whether people predisposed toward a certain point of view act upon those feelings. Greater balance also served to raise the consciousness of those who had not previously considered a particular perspective. This type of effect is not limited to women legislators; men also can be persuaded to consider newly defined issues, including child care and child support, domestic violence, and other issues of family law. In Santa Clara County, the presence of women on the board and the perceived clout of women voters served to raise the overall amount of legislation pertaining to women that was introduced by both women and men.

Another way to explore the effects of a skewed versus a balanced environment on the behavior of women officeholders is to use a longitudinal lens. One such study of the Arizona state legislature found that women legislators sponsored more legislation dealing with feminist issues and bills traditionally associated with female concerns than did men. Most relevant here, as the percentage of women increased, the number, subject matter, and rate of enactment of such bills tended to increase.[14]

There are, therefore, theoretical arguments as well as some preliminary empirical evidence to suggest that an environment that more nearly resembles gender balance (or at least an environment in which the proportion of women is not tiny) has an impact on the inclination of female representatives to overcome constraints. Applying those theories to the case of women in statehouses, we should also see less constrained behavior on the part of women in those places where they are more numerous. That is, women ought to exhibit their distinctive priorities in places where they have the most support. If we see these kinds of patterns are present, another dimension is added to the theoretical framework of earlier chapters. We will understand how societal expectations of the proper public sphere role of women interact with institutional circumstances to enhance or inhibit the behavior of women politicians.

The words of political theorist Mary Katzenstein highlight the subtlety of these influences:

> To understand the process by which the consciousness of gender issues is transformed, we must acknowledge the ways in which gender consciousness is reinvented, transmuted, and encouraged by women activists inside the preeminent institutions that govern American society and the American state.[15]

The Connection between Proportion of Women in Legislatures and the Pursuit of Policy Priorities

Following the lead of the psychological, sociological, and political science research detailed above, I now turn to an investigation of whether the percentage of women in twelve state legislatures is associated with the extent to which they pursue distinctive priorities. The fundamental question, then, is whether legislatures that have the highest percentages of women are also those in which women legislators pursue greater amounts of legislation dealing with women, and children and families. At issue is whether women introduce such legislation as well as see it successfully through the process. A corollary question concerns whether those legislatures with the highest percentages of women are also those in which the highest general level of legislation dealing with women, and children and families is introduced. In other words, are legislatures closest to gender balance ones in which women and men see such issues as important and legitimate?[16]

In order to test such propositions, the 1988 mail survey of legislators in twelve states across the nation is again relied upon. The questions highlighted in Chapter 3 concerning the top five legislative priorities of the last legislative session and the fate of those priorities are used to develop two separate measures of the dependent variable.[17] The first is gender differences in types of bills among women's and men's top legislative priorities. The second measure is gender differences in levels of success in passing priority bills dealing with issues of women, and children and the family.

Next, for ease of interpretation, the twelve legislatures are divided into three categories representing legislatures with less than 10 percent female membership, legislatures with 10 to 20 percent female membership, and those with 20 percent female membership or more. Mississippi and Pennsylvania compose the low category. In the middle category are California, Georgia, Illinois, Iowa, Nebraska, North Carolina, and South Dakota. Finally, Arizona, Vermont, and Washington compose the high category.[18] Legislatures were grouped rather than analyzed individually in order to conform more closely to the categories developed by Kanter.

Before we move directly to analysis of the data, it is useful to detail the various relationships between percentage of women in the legislature and policy priorities that are of interest. Thus, the following five sets of predictions are offered:

1. In the states with the highest level of female representation, women legislators will be more likely to exhibit policy priorities that are different from men's than will women legislators in states with the lowest levels of representation. The priorities of women will, more often than men, concern issues of women, and children and the family. The expectation that such issues will be enhanced where there are more women members does not assume that women have wholly different priorities than men. As we saw in the last chapter, nothing could be further from the truth. It merely assumes that women, more than men, focus on legislation dealing with issues such as child care, parental leave, domestic violence, comparable worth, and teenage pregnancy, for example.

2. Although women's and men's differing priorities on issues of women, and children and the family are expected to be evident more often in those states with higher proportions of women legislators than in states with low proportions of women, any other issue priority differences are *not* expected to be related to relative proportions of women in the statehouses. It is possible, for example, that women may place higher priority than men on education and medical issues (historically, an area of concern and expertise); however, no patterns related to the proportion of women in the legislature are expected. This is because issues apart from those dealing with women, and children and the family have long been included in mainstream legislative agendas. There is no need for women to address them in any concerted fashion for the issues to become central to the political debate. On the other hand, women's issues have been largely ignored except by

women officeholders; children's and family issues have been addressed rarely, and when approached, they have been in ways that almost exclusively benefited men. [19] Therefore, only on issues of women, and children and the family are women expected to, in a supportive environment, be impelled to reverse past inequities.

3. Not only will the proportion of women in the state legislature affect the introduction of legislation concerning women, and children and the family, it will also affect passage rates of such legislation. That is, in states with the highest proportion of women, women will be more likely to be successful in passing priority bills than will women in states with the lowest representation. This, of course, presupposes that in those legislatures with the highest percentages of women, the positive votes of men on these issues will be obtained. At this writing, there is not a single legislature in which women alone have enough votes to pass legislation.

Beyond the votes of men, I expect that under certain circumstances their commitment to legislation that is of priority to women will also be gained. Harkening back to the research of Janet Flammang and others, cited earlier, in those places in which women are the most numerous, their distinctive priorities will be legitimized and men also will champion those issues. Thus, the following two hypotheses have been developed.

4. The higher the proportion of women in office, the more likely it will be that the ethic of the legislative chamber itself will shift toward higher introduction rates of bills dealing with women, and children and the family. Thus, the more women in the legislature, the more likely it is that women's attitudes will permeate the wider legislative atmosphere. As women become more numerous and as they address these issues, men are expected to be educated about the importance of governmental action in what have heretofore been underaddressed areas. While little past research addresses this question, one study found that "in this supportive climate" (high levels of female representation on the Santa Clara County Board of Supervisors), "local male officials as well took leadership roles in women's issues."[20]

5. The final expected pattern of behavior concerns the pervasiveness with which women's, and children's and family issues are achieved. I anticipate that states with the highest levels of female representation will also tend to have the highest overall passage rates of legislation concerning women, and children and the family. The assumption, of course, is that the more supportive the climate, the more success women as well as men who introduce such legislation will have. In short, distinctive priorities of women will permeate the overall legislative environment.

The Evidence

For ease of interpretation, the data analysis that follows is divided into four categories that generally reflect the order of the hypotheses listed above. They are gender differences in the types of priority bill introductions by categories of proportion of women in legislatures; gender differences (by category) in success rates of priority bills; interlegislative differences (by category) in types of priority bill introductions; and interlegislative differences (by category) in success rates.

Gender Differences in Types of Priority Bills Introduced

One way to investigate whether bringing more women into legislatures affects policy is to measure gender-based differences in priority legislation. An important component of power is bringing issues to the agenda that have previously been suppressed or overlooked[21] because to do so results in a better representation of issues vital to all segments of society.

Table 4.1 displays the eight categories of bill types. Dealing first with issues of women, and children and the family, the level of introduction of these types of bills was related to the proportions of women in the legislatures. Although a perfect linear trend did not appear, female members in the states within the high and low categories conformed to the expectations for the data quite nicely. In Arizona, Vermont, and Washington, the states with more than 20 percent female membership, women legislators gave priority to bills dealing with these issues more often than did men. In the states with less than 10 percent felmale membership, we see a very different result. In Mississippi, women and men were equally uninterested in legislation in these two categories, as neither introduced any such bills. In Pennsylvania, with a slightly higher representation of women than Mississippi, women and men were tied, with no bills on issues relating to women. However, female legislators made priorities of bills dealing with children and the family more often than did men.[22] In short, in states within the high category with respect to percentage of women in the legislature, women introduced a greater amount of bills dealing with women, and children and the family than did men. In states in the low category, no such pattern is displayed.

Two categories encompassing areas traditionally of interest to women are education and medical issues, and welfare. With respect to education and medical legislation, women in nine of the twelve states had more priority bills in this area than the men in their states. However, no patterns

TABLE 4.1. Gender Differences in Priority Bill Introductions, by Category

	Women	Children	Business	Welfare	Educ./Med.	Crime	Budget	Environment
WA	*	*		*		*	*	
VT	*	*		*	*	*		*
AZ	*	*			*		*	
SD	†	*			*			
NE				*	*	*		*
IA	*				*	*		
IL	*	*		*	*			
NC	*	*						
CA								*
GA	*	*			*	*		
PA	†	*			*			
MS	†	†		†	*		*	*
‡	7	8	0	4	9	5	3	4
§	2	1	0	1	0	0	0	0

* = Women have more bills in this area as a priority.

† = Women and men are equal with no bills in this category listed as a priority.

‡ = Total number of states in which women had more bills in this area as a priority.

§ = Total number of states in which women and men had an equal number of bills in this area as a priority.

relating to percentage of women arose.[23] Dealing next with welfare issues, overall, women made welfare bills priorities less often than men did, and, again, no pattern based on percentage of women in the legislature emerged. In the states in which women had higher mean levels of priority welfare bills, all three categories of percentage of women in the legislature, all three political cultures,[24] and all regions of the country were represented. In short, education, medical, and welfare issues (unlike bills dealing with women, and children and the family) were not linked to the percentage of women in the legislature.

In contrast to issues of education or welfare, women have not been traditionally associated with business or fiscal matters. Given this, we would expect to find lower levels of priority interest by women legislators on issues of business or the budget. This is exactly the result on business issues—in every state. Under these circumstances, variance in the proportion of women in the legislature (or any other factor) becomes irrelevant. It may be that in states with few women, stereotypical notions about women's abilities prevent female legislators from working heavily in this area. In states with high percentages of women, it may be that women were still viewed as less capable or that they are judged capable but chose other priorities because of overriding interests elsewhere. In combination, these two explanations may account for the lack of priority placement women gave to business issues.

A similar but slightly different pattern appears in the area of budgetary legislation. As might be expected, female legislators generally made budget bills a priority less often than men. This was the case in nine out of twelve states. In the remaining three states, however, women representatives exceeded the men in placing priority status on budgetary legislation (Arizona, Washington, and Mississippi). Interestingly, these three states have no common characteristics. What does deserve mention is that, on this set of issues, neither relatively small percentages of women nor political cultures thought to adversely affect women's participation level extinguished participation even in this nontraditional area. Women's participation across the range of legislative endeavors most definitely increased.

As anticipated, the last two sets of issues, crime and environment/ energy/public land use, displayed no particular patterns. While women, overall, tended to make bills in each of these areas priorities less often than men, neither the percentage of women in the legislature nor the political culture was predictive of whether the women or men in each state placed a higher priority on each type of bill. In sum, the findings so far indicate that women did have distinctive priorities that concern issues of women, and children and the family. Further, women introduced bills based on these priorities more often in states in which they found the most support. No other area, including welfare, education and medical issues, crime, the budget, or environment, energy, and public land use, in which women gave higher priority to an issue than men. The last pattern worth special note is that women in every one of the twelve states, less often gave priority to bills dealing with business issues.

Gender Differences in Success of Legislative Priorities

Since women did indeed tend to have different policy priorities than men and since those differences were associated with the level of representation of women, the next logical questions are whether women were successful in passage of their priorities, specifically those dealing with issues of women, and children and the family, and to what extent success was related to the proportion of women in the legislature. As such, we will analyze the passage rate of those bills introduced by each legislator in his or her top five priorities for the last legislative session that delt with women's, and children's and family issues. While general priority passage rates (individually

or by states) tell us something about the success of male and female legislators on legislative activity (and, indeed, women had a higher mean percentage of passage of all priority bills than men), investigating success rates in
selected areas tells us something about levels of attention and effort devoted
to certain priorities as well as where these activities yielded success.

Table 4.2 presents differences in passage rates of these priority bills.
There was substantial gender-based difference in mean level of success of
all respondents. Almost 13 percent of men's priority bills dealing with
women, children and families passed, whereas almost 29 percent (more
than double) of comparable bills introduced by women passed. Turning to
the patterns among the states, in the low category, women in Mississippi
tied with men in that state by having none of their bills in these issues areas
pass, the worst absolute record of women in all twelve of the states.
Interestingly, women in Pennsylvania, with just 3.6 percent more women
in the lower house than Mississippi, were much more successful than men
in passing priority bills concerning women, and children and families.

A somewhat mixed picture is displayed by the states in the high category.
In Washington and Vermont, the states with the two highest percentages of
women in the legislature, women officeholders far surpassed men in passing priority bills dealing with women, and children and families. How-

TABLE 4.2. Gender Differences in Passage Rates of
Women's, and Children's and Family Legislation

	Men	Women
Washington	11.1	30.4[a]
Vermont	0.0	11.3[a]
Arizona	17.6	12.5
South Dakota	11.8	22.2[a]
Nebraska	7.1	50.0[a]
Iowa	15.0	61.7[a]
Illinois	23.1	36.9[a]
North Carolina	16.7	23.8[a]
California	51.5	37.5
Georgia	7.7	25.0[a]
Pennsylvania	0.0	20.0[a]
Mississippi	0.0	0.0
Male Mean: 12.9	Female Mean: 28.5[a]

[a]Women legislators have a higher mean ratio of passage to introduction.

ever, in Arizona, the men were more successful in passing their priority bills in this area. In fact, it is only in Arizona and California, the two states out of the twelve in which women were not more liberal than their male counterparts, that the women did not exceed the men in passage of this type of priority. Since these bills are generally categorized as liberal measures, the result is not so surprising. In short, women in all but three of the twelve states were more successful than men in passing priority bills dealing with women, and children and families. This may constitute evidence that women legislators worked especially hard on legislation not previously included in mainstream legislative agendas.

Overall, then, women tend to have higher ratios of introduction to passage of priority bills in the areas of women's, and children's and family legislation. That the fit is not perfect between the states with the highest and the lowest percentages of women, appears to be the case only because women in every state but two (the ones in which women are not more liberal than men) had lower introduction to passage ratios than men. We can now appreciate the extent to which the institutional environment does have an effect on the behavior of individual legislators. The better the balance between women and men, the more women can cast aside inhibitions related to minority status and support issues central to their lives.[25]

Interlegislative Differences in Priority Bill Introductions

Having investigated gender differences in priority legislation, I examine next whether or not women's distinctive interests permeated legislatures in places where their numbers were the greatest. In other words, did legislatures with the highest percentages of women also have higher *overall* introductions of legislation concerning women, and children and the family? The premise of this inquiry is that in those states with the highest proportions of women representatives, their distinctive concerns were legitimized and pursued by at least some of the men in the legislatures. That is, men's commitment to such legislation was gained as well as their votes.

If we find that the answer to our question is yes, a critical threshold whereby a minimum level of women can affect general legislative policy and perspective will have been identified. Since the lower house with the greatest percentage of women was in Washington (30.6 percent female), that would mean roughly 31 percent of the legislative membership had an effect on the remaining 69 percent. If the answer is no, one of two things may have been going on. First, other factors may have determined whether women's priorities influence the chamber, or a larger critical mass was necessary for pervasive influence. It may have been that Kanter was right when she predicted that an organization is balanced when at least a 60–40 ratio has been reached. Since such a balance did not exist in any state at that time (and still does not), it may be that we simply do not have the circumstances necessary to put this theory to an adequate test.

To determine whether the states with the highest percentages of women in the legislature also had the highest overall level of bills concerning women, and children and the family, regardless of whether the bills were introduced by men or women, comparisons were made of the mean number of instances in which all legislators named each type of bill among their top five priorities. Only in the case of bills dealing with either women or children and the family did any remotely relevant finding emerge. Mississippi and Pennsylvania, the states with the lowest percentage of women, scored eleventh and twelfth on both these measures. In no other instance did any pattern based on percentage of women (or, for that matter, region or political culture) emerge.

Given these results, it is clear that 25 to 30 percent female membership in legislative chambers does not constitute a critical mass able to affect overall policies and priorities. It is likely, as mentioned above, that it takes a figure closer to parity for effects such as these to diffuse. In keeping with that understanding, the results concerning Mississippi and Pennsylvania suggest that at least 10 percent female representation is necessary for women's distinctive interests to emerge. This is not surprising, since Kanter also speculated that in any group, more than 15 percent is required before any potential influence by the minority can be felt. Finally, it may be that factors other than proportional balance were also at work. In fact, this latter possibility is explored in the next section.

Interlegislative Differences in Priority Bill Passage

Is the percentage of women in legislatures positively related to the likelihood that the legislature will pass a bill concerning women or children and families? Like the results on interlegislative differences in bill introductions, the answer appears to be no. Passage of these sorts of priority bills were not related to the category in which a legislature was classified. Washington, Arizona, and Vermont, for example, were fourth, seventh, and tenth on a scale measuring the ratio of bills passed to those introduced dealing with women's, and children's and family legislation. In other words, we can be fairly confident that slightly less than one-third of women within a legislative chamber does not constitute a critical threshold for relatively assured diffusion of policy priorities.

Once again, the only relevant findings concerned states in the low category of representation. Pennsylvania and Mississippi scored eleventh and twelfth respectively on this measure. It appears that while 31 percent is not enough to assure uniform dispersion, less than 10 percent means that even women with differing priorities have little chance of passing their own bills, much less having their priorities influence others. The group is too skewed to have an effect on work output.

Speculation about explanatory factors related to passage of legislation of priority to women may include political, social, and economic indicators. One political factor testable with these data is the presence or absence of a formal women's legislative caucus within the state legislatures. While investigation of the relationship of this factor and priority bill introduction produces little of significance, examination of the relationship of states with caucuses and success levels of legislation dealing with women, and children and families produces a revealing result. The top five states in the passage of such legislation were, in order, California, Iowa, Illinois, Washington, and North Carolina. Except for Washington, these were the only states of all twelve that had formal legislative caucuses. Further, Washington was the state with the highest percentage of women in the lower house.[26] This suggests that visibility, in the form of either the presence of a formal women's caucus or relatively high percentages of women, is necessary for the passage, on a general basis, of legislation dealing with women, and children and the family. If this is the case, the finding is completely consistent with the major expectation of this chapter, which is that percentages matter. Since we already know that women have developed distinctive priorities, the question of whether they both introduced and successfully passed their priority legislation is dependent on support. A certain amount of support could be counted on from female colleagues, but this in itself would not be enough to ensure bill passage, since women were not (and still are not) a majority in any state. Thus, legitimacy within the wider legislative environment had to be a prerequisite. Higher percentages of women in the legislature are one way to achieve visibility and power. Another is the presence of a formal caucus. When a caucus bands together, it represents political clout—a weapon with the potential to overcome skewed groups.

Additional evidence of the potential power of a legislative caucus is available in the story of events in West Virginia in 1987. During that year, the women's legislative caucus supported a prenatal care bill. To ensure its success, the caucus launched a lobbying and publicity campaign focusing on the fact that West Virginia had one of the highest infant mortality rates in the nation and the second highest rate of teenage pregnancy. For a time, the campaign seemed to be very successful, and the bills soon cleared the lower chamber. The victory was short-lived, however, as trouble developed at the bill's first stop on the Senate side, in the Health Committee. The chair of Senate Health, who opposed the legislation, manipulated a vote to kill it. It appeared that the battle was over. But the women legislators made up their minds that defeat on this issue was unacceptable and, in retaliation, threatened to filibuster both chambers until reconsideration was initiated. The power of organized efforts became evident to the legislative leadership, and soon Senate Health voted out the bill unanimously. The story does not end here, however; the drama continued. Despite the high-visibility issue and high visibility action taken by the women's legislative caucus, the governor of West Virginia vetoed the bill. In a last, all-out effort, the women of both chambers orchestrated a successful veto override. The bill that would not die finally became law in West Virginia.[27]

Higher percentages of women in legislatures, therefore, create an environment of support for the concerns of women, but do higher percentages affect the behavior of men in legislatures? Findings of interlegislative differences indicate that, even in states in which women legislators constituted nearly one-third of the membership, the fact that women had different priorities than men did not have a direct, consistent effect on the diffusion of such policies throughout the chamber. The states with the highest overall levels of successful legislation concerning women, and children and families did not conform to patterns based on percentage of women in the legislature, except in the cases of those states in the low category. One further result of this research is that there are factors in addition to proportionality that can affect the extent to which women's distinctive concerns gain the commitment of men. Either a relatively high percentage of women or the presence of a formal women's legislative caucus accounted for the highest overall success levels of women's, and children's and family legislation. This confirms that support is a key issue with respect to whether female legislators' distinctive priorities permeate the general environment.

There is one important caveat to these findings that must be offered. At the present time, we have not had a legislature in which balance of the sort Kanter discusses has been achieved. That is, there have been no legislatures reflecting a 60–40 ratio or better a 50–50 ratio. Therefore, it would be a mistake to take the conclusions here as definitive. Until we see legislatures that are closer to balance and until the effects of that balance are analyzed, the findings here are preliminary. What can be said at this time is that there are circumstances under which women are not immobilized by conformity pressures. When legislatures begin to move from skewed to tilted circumstances, women are accorded and use the leeway that greater representativeness provides.

The Words of Women

To supplement the general picture of women's activity in legislatures, let us listen to what individual women say about how increasing their numbers can result in behavioral effects. The first comment speaks to the ways in which women's voices can be silenced in the absence of support.

> Women's priorities are different from men's. Although women try to minimize their own interests, sometimes women are more oriented toward social issues because of their background and training. But, they are fearful of being labelled outside the mainstream if they pursue these.   (*A northeastern legislator*)

The next category of comments concerns perceptions about how levels of female representation affect policy outcomes. From a western legislator:

> Fewer women would mean no comparable worth, no abortion initiatives and no state ERA. Compare our state to states with few women legislators. There are altogether different attitudes and legislation.

> With 21 women we can't make a difference. We need much more to have a real impact. (*A southern legislator*)

> Absolutely, our issues get attention and supporters out there and the supporters are more outspoken about their position if women [legislators] are in the lead. [Further,] numbers also mean power or a potent voting block. Numbers are one of the reasons we are as effective as we have been. (*A western legislator*)

> Women protect women—with more women, things would be better. The numbers here are too small to make a big difference. (*A southern legislator*)

When asked to comment about whether increasing the proportion of women in their own legislature would result in a different selection of priorities, women offered the following:

> If there were 2 percent women in the legislature, you might not see some issues get raised. If there were 50 percent women, there would be an emphasis on issues that women are likely to champion. [This midwestern legislator was referring to what she called "quality of life" issues such as the environment and water—issues that were more "long term"—and "children's issues."]

On the issue of the impact of a formal women's caucus and its potential to overcome imbalance, there was little question but that it was helpful. A western legislator reported:

> The caucus can be a power block; it can make an impact. [Also,] women would vote together 3/4 of the time if you got rid of party. They think first about the issue, not the politics.

The *California Journal* reported that Assemblywoman Gwen Moore gave a large measure of credit to the women's caucus in passing her bill dealing with the tax status of private clubs:

> [T]he caucus was an important help in her nine-year push to crack down on private clubs that refuse to allow women members. This year [1988], she finally succeeded in winning passage of a bill that will prohibit individuals from deducting dues paid to these clubs on their income taxes.[28]

Women in statehouses also had rather definite opinions about how high proportions of women or the existence of a formal women's legislative caucus affects the behavior of men:

> Men are more sensitive to women's issues because of the presence of women—we've had years of educating these guys. They don't naturally make the connections. Women have taught them how to do that. (*Legislative aide to a western legislator*)

> Numbers make a difference in sensitizing men. Men have grown enormously—they are getting used to women and are learning to trust women. (*A southern legislator*)

> More women in legislatures will make a difference because on the women's issues I have dealt with, I had a core of support from women. Almost all the women sign on and drag some men along. So, not only will there be more support for bills from women, there will be more male awareness. (*A western legislator*)

The magazine *Governing* reported similar feelings on this topic by Assemblywoman (now member of the U.S. House of Representatives) Maxine Waters:

> As women grew stronger politically, "men would come to me to ask me to help them fill out the women's questionnaires" that various groups sent to guide them in making endorsements. Waters knew she had a captive audience, and she used their requests to mention their names in their home districts and the help she gave them as time to educate them. She didn't so much extract a quid pro quo for the favor, she says, as treat it all as an "educational experience" for her colleagues. Some of the men who origi-

nally "had no positions whatsoever on some of these issues are very supportive now."[29]

The words of women in statehouses present a portrait entirely consistent
with the analysis of their survey responses. It can be no surprise in the
world of politics that power and support matter. Women have achieved
some measure of both in terms of greater numbers or collective efforts.
This, in turn, allows their distinctive voices to be heard.

Conclusion

Women and men in statehouses have developed distinctive policy priorities. This was not always the case; in fact, the development of differences
appears to be a relatively recent phenomenon. Throughout this book, I have
argued that society's views of women's proper place within the public
sphere serve to enhance or constrain their behavior. In Chapters 2 and 3, the
changing behavior of women legislators over time was analyzed in light of
societal tolerance for women politicians. Here, the theory was tested in a
cross-sectional fashion. Extent of support was measured by the percentage
of women in legislatures. The findings confirm that reduced conformity
pressures and increased support for distinctive behavior were advanced in
places where the proportions of women were highest; the reverse was true
for places where women were very nearly absent. Put in the terminology of
social science, conformity pressures are reduced as women in legislatures
move from token situations to those closer to parity.

Specifically, the analysis of the 1988 survey indicates that women representatives in states with higher proportions of female membership tended to
introduce more priority legislation dealing with women, and children and
families than the men in their states and were more successful in passage of
these bills. In fact, the levels of success enjoyed by women with respect to
legislation of this sort suggest a greater level of energy, effort, and attention
to bills dealing with women, and children and families. One southern
legislator who was interviewed as part of this study said it best, "Women
tend to look at more issues of women and children. This is not to say others
aren't addressed, but they [women] carry more legislation more quickly
and put in more energy and effort. Women are lead people on this type of
stuff."

5

The Context of Institutional Change

What have we learned so far about the behavior of women in statehouses? First, the dramatic predictions from the reformist half of the typology of expectations that increasing the presence of women in legislative bodies would result in a radically different legislative process and new types of legislation were only half accurate. Women's distinctive contribution has focused on policy, not procedure. They have broadened existing legislative agendas by increasing the attention given to issues of women, and children and families. The realm of the private sphere has become ever more central to the realm of the public one. In addition, issues long hidden from public view, such as sexual harassment and medical research dealing with problems unique to women, have become legitimate public policy issues. To be sure, women legislators could not have achieved these changes, no matter how much they were desired, without supportive environments in the forms of societal acceptance of their presence in legislatures and psychological and numerical support from female colleagues. They have made the most of what was available to them.

The force and relative speed of these changes direct our attention to the power of a newly emergent, enthusiastic, energetic, and determined group as it achieves in the face of great obstacles. Although women as a group (not unlike any other political group) do not have a single set of priorities or a single lens though which they view politics, it is true that they have distinctive life experiences to bring to their deliberations and decisions. And their successful efforts to infuse current legislative decisions and agenda choices with this perspective almost lull us into believing that with enough desire, motivation, and attention almost any sort of change is possible.

But is it? Are some changes in the legislative arena more likely than others? Why have women's differing life experiences and attitudes led them to work for policy changes but not procedural ones? How much can minorities within an organization who have new ideas about what should be done and how it should be done achieve? Is there something about procedural change that is more daunting or more difficult to accomplish than policy innovation?

Chapter 5 concentrates on these questions by examining whether there is any evidence that women legislators desire procedural change, what kind of changes they may want, and what obstacles lie in their path to achieving such a goal. In this chapter, as in the last one, the primary focus is on the interaction of institutional and sociocultural barriers and the extent to which they condition the strategies and pacing of goal pursuit.

Do Women Want Change?

In Chapter 2, we learned that, despite expressing women's distaste for the legislative game, their daily activities did not indicate any effort to alter the rules by which it was played. They did not always embrace the rules, but individual resistance rather than collective efforts to reform them was women's method of protest. For example, in the early years, women tended to participate in the range of typical legislative activities less than their male colleagues. By the late 1980s, this was no longer the case; women tended to participate in those activities as much as men. That legislative bargaining was one of these activities is indicative of the fact that what had once been most difficult for women and perhaps most repugnant was now something that they accepted as part of the role of a legislator. Moreover, whereas women once confined themselves to aspects of the legislative role most in tune with traditional expectations, such as increased attention to individual constituents, by the late 1980s, such extreme differences in focus were no longer visible.

By all indicators, then, women representatives have adapted to the rhythms and methods of legislative life. But is this the end of the story? Does it mean that, despite the myriad predictions to the contrary, female officeholders did not see procedural change as important? Did those who predicted a new world of mutual cooperation in the legislative arena if only women's presence was increased simply project their desires onto female officeholders? Or is there evidence that women politicians do indeed want to see widespread change?

It may not be surprising that evidence exists suggesting that women feel a need for systemic reform. This evidence comes from a variety of sources including both the mail survey relied upon throughout this book and the interviews that accompanied it.

A two-part question from the mail survey provides an indirect feel for whether women in statehouses desired procedural change and whether further increasing their presence in legislatures will contribute toward that eventuality. Representatives in the twelve-state survey were asked whether they were interested in seeing more women run for office, and then, for those who answered yes, a follow-up question inquired about their primary motivations for this desire. A gender gap among respondents was evident in both parts of this query. Ninety-two percent of the women wished to see more women run for office compared with 39 percent of the men.[1] Hence, women were far more likely than men to want to see additional women brought into the legislative arena.

The second half of the question posed to respondents is more directly relevant to our investigation of whether women officeholders desired procedural change. A frequently chosen answer to why they felt as they did was that, with more women in legislatures, the legislative process itself would change. Women were more than twice as likely as men to have chosen this reason for wanting more women in office. Sixty percent of those who selected this answer were women, whereas only 24 percent of those who did likewise were men.[2] The only other statistically significant answer offered by respondents concerned the belief that women had different goals than men and that it was important that these goals receive political and, specifically, legislative attention. In this case, women were almost twice as likely as men to choose this reason for wanting more women to run. Hence, the very areas in which women legislators have made or potentially could make a distinctive contribution were the ones in which a substantively and statistically significant gender gap appears.

Additional evidence to replicate and expand upon these findings is scarce. Because the third wave of research on female officeholders has concentrated on women's distinctive impact on the political world, and because that impact to date has been concentrated on policy alternatives, very little follow-up has been done on women officeholders' views on procedural change. Researchers have seldom pursued answers to whether female legislators desire an alternate set of procedures and, if so, why they have not attempted reform. In spite of these difficulties, there is one more piece of evidence to support the interpretation that women remain critical of the ways in which legislative business is conducted. Over the years, the Center for the American Woman and Politics at Rutgers University has sponsored conferences bringing together women state legislators from across the country. The goal of the closing session of the 1982 conference was to create a wish list of items the officeholders wanted to see accomplished. A two-part list emerged. The first part, fifteen items long, contained wishes that could be translated into reality in the near future; the second, six items long, contained items that were important to women but were ones they did not see as achievable in the near term. The long-term wish list ended with the desire to change the male-dominated institutions in which they worked.[3] It appears that women legislators remain displeased with the way business is done; unfortunately, however, no follow-up to find out the reasons was undertaken.

There is strong, if not abundant, evidence that while women have learned to be successful within the current rules of the game, they are not necessarily satisfied with them and can envision a different process entirely. What sort of change would women, given the chance, usher in?

What Kind of Change? Power and Process

Instead of engaging in confrontation, women are more apt to negotiate. Instead of dealing in win-lose terms, women are more apt to see the gray area in between. Instead of thinking only of today, women are more apt to think in terms of the needs of generations to come.[4]

Those who predicted that bringing more women into legislatures would translate into more change in the ways business was done often talked in somewhat vague terms about a kinder and gentler process—well before former president George Bush ever used that phrase to describe the values he hoped his administration would embody. They spoke about the fact that women would be more cooperative than competitive and less interested in power over compared with power to. The words of Geraldine Ferraro, quoted above, epitomize the sort of change that women legislators from the local to the federal level have echoed over time and continue to echo today. Sifting through the reports of a variety of research studies in which women officeholders were asked about how women might change the process reveals two types of answers: the first set concerns alternative views of power, and the second concerns the outlines of an alternative process.

Women and Power

When talking about female conceptions of power, it seems that feminist theorists, commentators, prognosticators, and women officeholders themselves all agree that women perceive power and use it very differently than men. This is illustrated well by Iva Ellen Deutchman, who, after reviewing a wide sample of writing about women and power, concludes that feminist theorists generally "envision power as essentially social and cooperative. Rather than argue that one person's gain necessitates another's loss, these feminist critics of power argue that everyone can win."[5]

A gold mine of reactions by women officeholders to the concept of power is found in a recent book entitled *Women in Power: The Secrets of Leadership*. In it, the authors interview twenty-five female officeholders from the local to the national level. Among the topics that arose in the interviews was how women perceive power. Generally, they conclude, women are interested in power to make things happen rather than power as a way to control others to uplift oneself. The comments on this subject elicited from the officeholders are numerous, but the following few are wholly representative of the group:

> Power in itself means nothing. . . . I think power is the opportunity to really have an impact on your community.[6]

> Power is basically that sense of strength and understanding about how to pull together resources to get your agenda done.[7]

> To me power means being able to do something for others. I use the power of my office to help other people . . . the potential of helping somebody else out, that's how I view my office. I feel that what I'm doing is worthwhile and rewarding and has direct benefits for other people.[8]

> I don't think women are as affected by the power that's around them. They're not often as awed by it. I don't think women aspire to powerful positions as eagerly as men do. Maybe it's because we don't aspire to the use of power for our own purposes.[9]

The thrust of these comments is one that resonates through gender politics literature from the earliest consideration of the topic. Janet Flammang, in studies of local women officeholders, found that the question of power was one that concerned women and a topic to which they had given considerable thought. For example, she notes that when the subject was approached:

> Some officials even went so far as to describe a distinctive female understanding of power. County Executive Sally Reed characterized women's

power as less authoritarian and more supportive, collaborative and respectful of intuition. Councilmember Shirley Lewis said, "Male power means force and domination. Women use consensus, validation, cooperation, in a win-win direction."[10]

Her conclusions on this topic are best summed up in this comment: "Women do not want power if what that means is business a usual, 'getting yours at someone's expense,' a zero sum game where one person's gain is another's loss."[11]

Procedural Change

Women's alternative conceptions of power translate into concrete changes in the way they envision getting legislative business done. The evidence from my interviews in six states across the nation suggests that there was little doubt in the minds of women representatives from California, Georgia, Mississippi, Nebraska, Pennsylvania, and Washington that female officeholders were more interested in a process that can only be called cooperative rather than competitive. Women, in the eyes of these respondents, whether because of their life experiences as caretakers and nurturers or because of other reasons, were focused on how political processes could be made less zero-sum, less ad hoc, less a fly-by-the-seat-of-the-pants process, less a game of winners and losers, and more a process by which everyone can participate and as many people as possible can emerge with something to praise. With the inclusion of more women in legislative office, the process would look like this:

> The strategies would be different. Women are more democratic and would create a more progressive environment. We would play the game by our own rules. (*A southern legislator*)

> There would be more consensus politics. Women are better at consensus building. (*A midwestern legislator*)

> The legislature would change. Legislation would be more considered and more refined, more in in-depth. The process would be more organized and there would be better communication. (*A southern legislator*)

> Women are more used to mediating and compromising. (*A midwestern legislator*)

> Women see practical, not just political applications. They are cooperative and non-confrontational. (*A western legislator*)

> Women are less inefficient and more straightforward. Patience is a top virtue in politics and women have more of it. (*A western legislator*)

Women put a lot more emphasis on long-range planning. (*Another western legislator*)

Several legislators attributed the change to the fact that, because of their backgrounds, women know how to be conciliators and know how to consider the views of others as equally important as their own. Many discussed the fact that women look out for what is good for their constituencies and look to that goal rather than just their own self-interest. The single focus of self-interest often attributed to men was seen as less of a problem for women. As one southern legislator put it, "Women look at benefits for society and men look at how it will benefit them politically."

The interviews with women state legislators are not the only source of female officeholders' views about the type of procedural change they believe women will promote. A study of state legislators across the nation conducted by the Center for the American Woman and Politics at Rutgers University found that "women are more likely to opt for government in public view rather than government behind closed doors" so that "all points of view can be aired and a consensus can be reached." In this survey, 57 percent of women, compared with 32 percent of men, said that women's increased presence had made a difference in the extent to which legislative business was conducted in public view. Having more women also brought forth a "concern for different segments of the constituency and of the larger society and a different relationship between elected representatives and the citizens they represent," according to the female representatives.[12] The range of citizen interests that were introduced into legislative dialogue was broadened by the increased inclusion of women in office.

Female officeholders envision that when their numbers in legislatures are increased, a different process can result. What sort of environment do they foresee as women become more common in leadership positions? Unfortunately, the center's questions about leadership did not concern whether women and men who held those positions exercised them in different ways; they simply asked respondents the qualities they thought important for leadership to possess. Still, the answers provide some insight into gender-based preferences. On the bulk of the questions, women and men responded in much the same way: those things that were important were a sense of mission, concern with providing leadership opportunities for others, persuasive ability, an ability to encourage everyone involved to express their views, an ability to share credit, and a concern with how those affected by the decision feel about it. There were differences between men and women, however, in how important they felt each of these things to be.

For example, 65 percent of the women, compared with 53 percent of the men, felt that persuasive ability was very important—the ability to convince others to do something they initially might not want to do.[13]

Gender differences among those respondents who held leadership positions were also evident. Women were more likely than men to think that a sense of mission and a concern with how those affected by the decision viewed the decision were very important. Said one woman legislator:

> More than anything else we know we have to create an atmosphere of team effort, share the glory. One of the first things I ever did as committee chair was [to let it be known] that if you did the work on my committee, you [get] to sign the little stupid blurb that goes into the calendar. There is your name signed to that because you did the work. A simple little thing like sharing instead of acting like, "I'm the chairman, I'm going to sign everything. I'm the big-shot."[14]

Evidence suggests that women legislators supported procedural reform and retained a vision of what an alternative process would look like. In its ideal form, it would be a legislative world in which empowerment rather than power over others is the goal as well as the inclusion of long-term perspectives, cooperation instead of confrontation, mediation rather than logrolling, and an eye toward diffused benefits for the community rather than narrow, political victories.

If women legislators desired procedural reform and had in mind specific sorts of changes, then why did they characterize change as a dream for the future rather than a more immediate goal? These are the questions to which we now turn.

Obstacles to Change

> We would like to change the rules of the game, and sometimes hold ourselves back because we don't approve of the way it is played. But then we find if we don't play by their rules, we don't play at all. We would like to be the advocates of political perestroika—a less adversarial and more consensus-built system—that is what we are more comfortable with. But the bottom line in politics is crude and demanding. It's win or lose. Nothing in between. We can't expect the few women in political life to change the values and the rules of the game alone, although that is sometimes precisely the expectation. If you haven't changed the world, what's the point of your being there? Politics is, at best, a reflection of the values of society as a whole. And while political leaders can move the public forward, they can't wrench it around to where it does not want to be.[15]

Madeleine Kunin, former governor of Vermont, captured precisely the feeling that women officeholders had of the legislative process and why their desires to change it were on the wish list for the future rather than the "to do" list for the present: they can't "wrench" the system "around to where it does not want to be." That women were then and are today small proportions of legislatures across the country, that they are relative newcomers to the political elite and must attain collective experience and credibility in the process before they can reform it, and that procedural or structural change, even in the most conducive of circumstances, is extraordinarily difficult together account for why women legislators have not revamped legislative procedures at the same time they brought new policy issues from the margin to the mainstream. The presence of each of these obstacles has influenced a calculated political decision that the time has not been right to attempt all-out procedural reform.[16]

The Dual Nature of Reform

One reason why women representatives have not attempted widespread reform of legislative procedures when they have sought to alter political agendas (and have succeeded in doing so) concerns the nature of the two types of efforts. Reformulating legislative agendas requires a great deal of individual initiative and personal risk-taking on the part of the person or persons involved in pursuing issues outside the mainstream. Anyone promoting a new set of public issues risks getting a reputation for lacking political savvy and being a lightweight. It also necessitates large quantities of time and persuasive skill to convince one's colleagues that passage of a new bill or a set of bills is both beneficial to constituents and without a substantial downside for those who cast a "yea" vote. But augmenting governmental agendas does not require collective perceptions that existing topics of concern are unworthy or deserving of abandonment. In other words, bringing new issues to the agenda does not directly threaten the pet causes of colleagues. Equally important, doing so does not require institutional reform—no rule changes or shake-ups of existing power structures that might threaten carefully protected fiefdoms must be undertaken. In short, adding to the agenda, at least if one is not flooding it, does not threaten the other business of the legislature or the way in which it is being done.

On the other hand, creating a world in which legislatures operate differently than they do today means attacking the system at its core, not just tinkering at the margins. Changes of this sort are infinitely more difficult than passage of an individual bill or set of bills because the rules and structures by which institutions are governed reward some members at the expense of others. Rules are never neutral, and the values that undergird them are geared toward the sensibilities of the dominant group, the people in power. Even rule changes that conform to existing value systems are close to impossible to get agreement on (as illuminated in the next section). Reforms that strike as deeply as the vision held by women politicians are the most difficult of all and can be effectuated only through positions of strength. The minimal elements of a strong position for women are being at or above parity in legislatures and accumulating extensive experience in legislative operations. In that case, women will not only have power through numbers and collective experience and credibility, they will hold positions of influence from which they can structure incentives so that, to meet their own needs, large numbers of legislators must consider the possibility of reform.

Conditions for Institutional Reform

I have asserted that fundamental reform of the type that women politicians envision requires, at the minimum, intense efforts over the long term by participants with a great deal of influence, experience, credibility, and power. Evidence of these propositions is abundant in the literature of political science. Those who study legislative behavior and its determinants offer numerous tales of attempted reform and the circumstances under which successful efforts have been achieved. Exploring instances of substantive legislative reform, reforms that have been extensive but still within existing values and standards of the legislative arena, places the dreams of women officeholders in context. The following three case studies, then, gleaned from the United States Congress, illuminate precisely the institutional obstacles to reform.

The Legislative Reorganization Act of 1946

Deliberate, concentrated (as opposed to evolutionary) procedural and structural reform of the U.S. Congress has taken place twice in recent history. The first of these major reforms was the Legislative Reorganization Act of 1946, and the second was the Legislative Reorganization Act of 1970 and the reforms in its aftermath. The stories of each are illustrative of the difficulties in obtaining agreement for reform and, after formal agreement, making those reforms stick.

In 1946, the situation facing the United States Congress was one in which procedures and the structures that undergirded it had rapidly become outmoded in the new political era. With the increasing responsibilities of the national government resulting from New Deal programs, the work load of Congress had expanded dramatically, and little had been done to accommodate to it. Members were experiencing great difficulty processing the vast amounts of legislation facing them, and agreement that change was needed to help them cope was pervasive.

Congressional scholar Roger Davidson suggests that reform happens in Congress (and, presumably, other legislative bodies) for one of two reasons. External forces, such as social, economic, and political occurrences including war, depressions, scandals, a variety of crises, and technological progress, as well as realignments and shifts in the balance of power among the three branches all compel change. Another incentive to reform is an internal impetus. When member goals are not being met, whether these are goals of reelection, increased status within the chamber, or public policy changes,[17] members become motivated to alter procedures or structures to meet their needs. The Reorganization Act of 1946 was motivated primarily by external forces—the structure within which Congress was working had not changed even though its work load and the demands on members' time had changed dramatically.[18]

The recognition that procedural reform was badly needed and that without it business was more difficult to enact did not mean that Congress could act quickly in devising and carrying out a set of reforms. An agreement that change was needed did not mean that there was agreement on precisely how it was to be carried out. To begin the slow process of creating consensus, congressional leaders decided they needed some rather more objective minds to study the problem. Not unlike today's naming of blue-ribbon commissions to study problems and make recommendations to Congress, members turned to the American Political Science Association (APSA) to form a committee to develop solutions to their organizational problems. The APSA committee came up with ten separate reform suggestions including the creation of independent professional staffs, a Legislative Reference Service and a Legislative Counsel, streamlining and reorganization of the committee system, and consolidation of oversight of the executive branch and bureaucracy by giving responsibility to House Appropriations subcommittees.[19]

Not to be outdone by the breadth or volume of the academic suggestions, a joint committee of Congress held hearings on the suggestions to decide which of them would best meet the needs of members and to which mem-

bers could agree. They came up with thirty–seven recommendations. Legislation was drafted, and as the bill passed through the two chambers, what
was left in the end addressed the leading goal that spurred the effort in the
first place, work load management. Months—indeed, years—of effort resulted in a bill that modernized and streamlined the committee system,
created a greatly expanded professional staff system, and reorganized fiscal
policy-making.[20]

The story so far seems like a very methodical, rational, and successful
effort on the part of Congress to meets its changing needs as an institution
as well as the changing needs of the members within it. But the story does
not end after passage of the reform legislation. Indeed, for our purposes, it
is just beginning. Even in the face of serious need for reform, widespread
agreement that it was necessary, and painstaking and lengthy work to craft
and pass a bill to institute an alternative set of procedures, implementation
was, in stark terms, sabotaged.

The goals of the Reorganization Act were effectively thwarted by the
desires of Congress's more powerful members to protect their prerogatives
and by the desires of many junior members to ascend the leadership ladder
so they could have a say in what was going on. In short order, subcommittees proliferated and more standing committees were created. Further, the
streamlining and fixing of jurisdictions under the new committee structure
was undermined by senior members who preferred the old jurisdictional
relationships that gave them more power. Likewise, senior members' adamant opposition to restructuring fiscal policy-making "doomed the new
procedure." In fact, beyond the increase in professional staff attending
members of Congress, the act had "little immediate impact on day-to-day
operations of Congress."[21]

Despite being "the most ambitious, comprehensive and publicized reorganization effort in the history of Congress"[22] the Legislative Reorganization Act of 1946 was, if not a failure, nothing close to an unqualified
success. One lesson to be learned from this story is that even in what is
arguably the best of circumstances to effectuate change—obvious need,
hindering of progress under the old rules and procedures, widespread (although not unanimous) agreement on need, and absence of attempts to
undermine basic working premises of the process—it is exceedingly difficult to accomplish. The difficulty lies not just in gaining consensus for a
reform plan but in preventing backsliding after the plan has been agreed to.
Roger Davidson calls attention especially to the difficulties of overcoming
the defenses of those in power and how the powerful can thwart any efforts
that may reduce their control.

[T]he act's designers gave insufficient attention to the potential opposition of the power structure within the two chambers. In short, we would conclude that the 1946 act responded to external challenges to Congress, but neglected the institution's internal dynamics. Most importantly, it underestimated the tenacity of the senior "barons" (especially in the House) who controlled most of the key committees and the power of the conservative coalition of southern Democrats and Republicans that buttressed their power.[23] [Further,] it illustrates the futility of such adaptive reform in the face of an internal power structure that sees itself threatened by the innovations. This structure, primarily the senior committee leadership, frustrated or delayed the effects of the reforms.[24]

Applying the lesson of this attempt at reform to the situation of women legislators provides insight into the sort of challenge women face if they are to pursue procedural reform. Female representatives, previously or currently, do not even possess the first necessary ingredient for successful pursuit of reform, large enough proportions of the chambers they wish to alter. Beyond that, the sort of reform women would presumably seek is far more extensive than jurisdictional changes for committees or reformed guidelines for making budget decisions. If legislative barons could thwart reform because they feared losing power over certain types of legislation, how much support for softening the hard edges of political infighting or reconstituting the use of power would there be? The difficulties highlighted in this story of congressional reform place women legislators' acceptance of the existing system in a far more complete context. What was possible to accomplish in the late 1980s at this time and what is beyond reach of the few women who inhabit legislatures is nowhere more clear.

The Legislative Reorganization Act of 1970

The fact that procedural and structural reform of legislatures is a long-term prospect is extraordinarily well illustrated in the story of the Legislative Reorganization Act of 1970 and its aftermath. The 1970 act was largely the result of the failures connected to its predecessor. The problems that were not resolved at that time continued to place obstacles in the path of legislative efficiency and efficacy. In addition to the long-term concerns connected to the growth in governmental responsibilities were problems resulting from the imbalance of ideological and geographical interests between powerful, senior legislators and the rank-and-file members.

A Joint Committee on the Organization of Congress was again created by the leadership to begin the long process of hammering out compromise on

the components of reform. The major problems it addressed were an overa-
bundance of subcommittees in both chambers; in the Senate, an increase in
their power relative to committees; and, in the House, massive power of
committee chairs, lack of disclosure of details of committee and floor
decision making, control of staff by majority party leaders, and inadequate
oversight.[25]

After recommendations were made and legislation offered, the compromise that finally passed the House and Senate addressed these issues by
decentralizing the power of committee chairs (written rules of procedures
were required, some types of proxy votes were prohibited, and the committee majority could call for special meetings to consider legislation); the
autonomy of subcommittees in the Senate was curbed so that it would not
parallel the power of full committees; the minority parties were given staff
and control over them; and to improve the oversight function of Congress,
the General Accounting Office was given new statutory authority to review
and analyze the results of federal programs and to produce cost-benefit
analyses.[26]

The goals of the 1970 act were much more modest than most of its cousin
of 1946, and one result was that a greater portion of its mandate was
successfully implemented. There was less for members, especially powerful members, to be threatened by than was the case with its predecessor
legislation. However, that does not mean that disgruntled members did not
thwart portions of it. Some of its provisions were actively resisted; the most
egregious example was a provision dealing with assignment of a portion of
committee staff to the minority members of committees. These mandates
were virtually ignored.[27]

The Reorganization Act of 1970 is an interesting example of reform
because it suggests that limited attempts to alter the process by which
legislative work is accomplished are likely to be more successfully accepted and implemented than broader attempts at reform. This act is interesting for another reason, however. It is illustrative of the circumstances
under which pervasive dissatisfaction can be channeled into serious reform.
The dictates of the Reorganization Act of 1970 addressed only a small
portion of the discontent felt by a fairly substantial portion of the U.S.
House of Representatives. Among the most common complaints of the
unhappy members was that the power of committee chairs had not been
sufficiently curbed. The charge was that a whole range of legislation was
being stymied by dictatorial, ideologically unrepresentative chairs. Most of
the committee chairs were southern Democrats, and the majority of newer
members were northern liberal Democrats. The chairs used that power to

choke off legislation they did not support, which was most of the agenda of the northern liberals, including civil rights reform.[28] These particular frustrations of the junior, more liberal members of House of Representatives had been brewing since the late 1950s, when the first calls for relaxing the grip of committee chairs were issued.

The accumulation of this long-developing impasse came to a climax in 1971. The Democratic Party Caucus adopted rules abandoning seniority as the only basis for selecting chairs and ranking members of committees. Up until that point, the seniority norm, as it was called, created automatic accession to the chair's slot, a position that was then held until retirement, defeat, or death. To put teeth into this reform, in 1973, both caucuses of the House allowed secret ballots and separate votes on each committee chair appointment. Senate Democrats caught up to the House in this type of reform, and by 1975 they created a parallel system of selecting committee chairs.[29]

The formal abandonment of the seniority rule, which was a bold, serious attack on entrenched power in the House of Representatives, was not the only dramatic move attempted by the liberal and junior members of the House majority party. Another way to curb the power of committee chairs was to put more power in the hands of the chairs of subcommittees. This was done in the House in a series of moves from 1971 to 1976. Over that time, committee chairs were denied control over the creation of subcommittees, their jurisdictions, the appointment of subcommittee chairs, and members and the determination of budgets and staffing.[30]

The lessons of the reforms of the 1970s appear to be that bold and dramatic procedural and structural change in how legislatures do their business can be accomplished. Change, even extensive change, is possible when conditions are right, such as a decades-long dissatisfaction among some members that grew in intensity as an increasing number of liberal Democrats moved into the system, years of lobbying behind the scenes, and social and political upheavals in the form of the Vietnam War, the demands of the civil rights movement and the New Left, and Watergate. Most important, perhaps, no aspect of this reform challenged the basic premises and values by which the legislature did its business. Yes, power was decentralized, but it was not redefined or refocused. Nothing approaching the sort of reform envisioned by women was contemplated. Even with all these favorable conditions, the reach of the reforms was not as great as might initially be assumed. As it turned out, the attack on the seniority system, while successful, was not wholesale. After an initial rejection of three powerful southern committee chairs, the norm of seniority has continued despite the rule of seniority being abandoned. The practice today is that seniority still affords one the opportunity to be committee chair in all but the most unusual circumstances.[31]

So far, the case studies examined here have had to do with formal alterations in legislative procedures. The sort of change that women legislators envisioned does not just entail reforming rules and committee jurisdictions; alterations in the values that influence legislative decisions and in the norms of professional behavior that underlie formal rules, procedures, and structures are central to their task. There is no reason to believe that rapid, wholesale changes in the norms and values operative in legislative environments are more easily accomplished than procedural reform. Indeed, studies of the United States Senate offer insight into the pace and extent of such change.[32]

The Transformation of the U.S. Senate

In an award-winning book, Barbara Sinclair describes what she calls the transformation of the U.S. Senate. She analyzes the reasons why the norms and folkways that guided individual actions of senators and the daily life of the Senate have changed so dramatically over the previous thirty years. From the 1950s to the 1980s, the Senate went from a conservative men's club with the norms of apprenticeship, seniority, specialization, workhorse behavior (keeping one's nose to the grindstone and avoiding showboating—especially for the media), reciprocity, courtesy, and institutional patriotism to an atomized, individualistic chamber. The norms, which were fairly elaborate and strict, allowed senior members to control the flow and direction of legislation and kept rank-and-file senators focused on the work of the chamber rather than outside lures. Even though these folkways constrained behavior, they were not challenged because the needs of members, whether they concerned reelection, prestige within the chamber, or good public policy, were being met under the guidelines.[33]

By the 1980s, however, the picture had changed. Similar to the dissatisfactions that spurred the Legislative Reorganization Acts of 1946 and 1970 as well as the subsequent 1970s reforms, it was the interaction between the wider political climate and the needs of the members that resulted in a severe diminution of the norms of conduct that had long guided the Senate. The influx of liberal northern Democrats, the expansion of the role of govenment, the decline in influence and effectiveness of political parties, the increasing coverage of the Senate by the national media, and the major changes in issues facing Washington all contributed to the changing needs of members.[34]

Sinclair argues that as soon as the norms failed to serve the needs of the majority of members of the Senate, their decline was inevitable. For example, as parties were no longer guarantors of a seat or the voting allegiance of members of Congress, senators found it increasingly important to make an individual impression rather than an institutional or party one. An outgrowth of this need was a mad scramble by almost every senator to get his or her face before national and local media outlets. Success could no longer be had by playing by the old rules; in order to enact public policy and get reelected, one had to attain national prominence. The norms of apprenticeship or workhorse behavior went out the window with nary a second thought by members.[35]

The message here: long-term change of norms and folkways that guide legislative behavior is gradual but not impossible.[36] Here again, though, the norms and standards so prevalent in the 1950s are not all dead. Some have perished, but a good many still live on—diminished, but detectable all the same. Just as formal legislative reform is not successful in its entirety, the changing standards of conduct and behavior within an organization do so slowly and unevenly. Traditions are hard to break, and established patterns of operation do not end dramatically and conclusively.[37]

What women legislators can learn from changing Senate norms is that they will increase the likelihood of success in altering the ways in which legislatures do their business if rewards (reelection, passing of legislation, or attaining leadership positions) are made contingent upon abandoning old norms and conforming to new ones. While that is no easy task, it is one way to guide evolution from current circumstances.

Taken together, these examples of deliberate change of rules and procedures and evolutionary change of underlying norms that guide behavior illustrate why women officeholders, despite disliking the procedures by which legislatures go about their business, have not worked for all-out alterations. They have only, in the last twenty years, begun building up their numbers in legislatures, begun to gain individual and collective experience, and developed a distinctive set of policy priorities. Moreover, the sort of change they envision is more complicated and far-reaching than any of the examples presented here. If we are to see procedural change of the sort some observers predicted and many others wished for, we are going to have to wait a good deal longer. The message for women officeholders who desire procedural change is to continue to work for increased representation and only then to pursue extensive reform agendas. Success can only be accomplished in the future if the groundwork is laid well in advance.

Women as Rational Political Actors

> I don't like the process, but in order to make a change, you have to get power, and in order to get power you have to play the system.[38]

As this quote by Jean Marie Brough, former Republican floor leader in the Washington House of Representatives, suggests, women officeholders, while disapproving of the process, concentrated on that which was politically possible. They chose to focus efforts where they could make a difference and perhaps, as Representative Brough noted, to aquire the power necessary for changes down the line. If the definition of politics is the art of the possible, then women have been supremely political—in other words, they pursued the course of political rationality.

Given the political realities they were faced with, women had two choices regarding their desires for procedural change: they could master the ways of the legislative world in order to gain the experience, skill, and credibility necessary to set the groundwork for change, or they could expend all their political capital on an all-out assault on the process.

What are the costs and benefits of each of these choices? An unsuccessful attempt at procedural overhaul would, most likely, consign those involved either to isolation and ineffectiveness or, ultimately, to loss of position. An attempt at widespread change without sufficient groundwork and support means that one must be willing to give up any benefits of a potentially long and successful legislative career. Although any officeholders involved in advocating reform of this sort may gain personal benefits of holding fast to their principles and acting on strongly held beliefs, they would lose the opportunity to garner benefits for women at large and for the districts to whom they are accountable.

On the other hand, if female legislators follow the model of Representative Brough and use whatever leeway for reform they have to do what is possible, several benefits, personal, political, and societywide, might be anticipated. The personal benefit gained is expanding the likelihood of a long and successful political career. Benefits for women as a group are also attainable. By staying in the legislative arena, female officeholders can introduce and enact legislation to benefit women. Moreover, the longer individual women are in the legislature, the more experience, credibility, and seniority they accumulate that can be channeled toward both improved policy decisions for women and the long-term potential of a reformed process. Finally, if female officeholders decide to play by current rules in order to secure long-term gains, they also make an important contribution to the way in which society views the proper public sphere role of women. It will undoubtedly be easier for the women who follow to take their place as full and equal partners in political life. Moreover, more girls and women will see elective officeholding as a viable choice for their professional lives.

This choice is not without costs, however. Part of the cost is personal dissatisfaction. Operating each day in an environment that is, at best, uncomfortable in that it is at odds with one's usual standards and, at worst, antithetical to one's closely held beliefs is a strain. Equally important, deferring an aspect of one's political goals, even if only temporarily, is frustrating. For those who are politically motivated—and who could be more motivated to make a political impact than elective officeholders?—not to take aggressive action to further a vision of the political future diminishes, in some fashion, the motivation to be politically involved.

The reason, then, that women officeholders chose to switch rather than fight aggressively is that the cost-to-benefit ratio is weighted toward the former option. To have chosen to make what progress they could toward the eventual goal, even if it was limited, does not mean that women have given up on its long-term viability. The choice might be characterized as one between the potential for success in the long term and the short-term impact of a dramatic, bold, but losing gesture. Some might characterize it as a choice between political rationality and political suicide.

Comments from a recent study of interest group representatives in Washington, D.C., make this point as well as it can be made:

> The strategy of acting like the boys while joining forces with women is not unique to Washington pressure politics. Women legislators seem to adopt a similar strategy—as do women who are attempting to make their way in academic departments, law firms, and many other institutions long dominated by men. A question much discussed both among feminists and in the media is whether, as more and more opportunities become available to women in what were once exclusively male preserves, women must simply act like men or whether they can enjoy the fruits of these opportunities without sacrificing a distinctive style. The experience of advocates for women in Washington pressure politics suggests that wherever they are a

small minority lacking critical resources (money, tenure, partnership, seniority, whatever matters for the institution in question) and operating in an arena with a long history and deeply established folkways, *women are in no position to write, or rewrite the rules.* [Emphasis mine.] If they wish to participate in the pressure politics—and not to participate would have undeniable consequences for the way in which the federal government treats women—those who represent women in Washington have little choice but to follow rules they did not set. In fact, the way policymakers treat women in government affairs may dictate that these women have less autonomy than their male counterparts in defining a distinctive style. As mentioned earlier, a number of the respondents in the survey indicated that they felt constrained by their gender to work harder in order to be taken seriously. Under the circumstances, to follow rules constructed by men while supporting other women on behalf of issues affecting women may be the most instrumental response.[39]

Women representatives are not the only ones for whom the constraints of the procedural status quo are stronger than those regarding issues pursuit. Research on the behavior of African American politicians shows similar patterns: while local-level African American representatives learn to work with existing sets of political rules and procedures, they also use these tactics to advance unique goals. The fact that both women and African American politicians display the same pattern with respect to the eschewing and embracing of the status quo suggests that political rationality dictates achieving change where it is possible and leaving that which is currently impossible for another day.[40]

A Viable Political Option?

A circumstance in which women currently holding office would be inspired to initiate the groundwork for procedural reform is if they thought that they would soon be joined by a tremendous influx of female colleagues. At this point, women hold only 20 percent of statehouse seats, so incremental increases of the sort that have transpired over the last fifteen or twenty years would be insufficient for purposes of achieving anything close to parity, not to mention the sort of proportions that would be required for success in such endeavors. Current levels of increases, projected into the future, would lead to parity in state legislatures well after the year 2000. Since incumbency is the single greatest obstacle to increasing the number of women in legislatures,[41] the only way that women would have adequate influence on procedural reform in the near future is if women were to gain seats quickly—a scenario that looks unlikely.[42]

Will Women Be Co-opted?

Readers may wonder if the analysis advanced thus far does not consign women to forever living with business as usual in legislatures. That is, if women legislators must wait for change until they have individual and collective experience and power, will the time spent in the status quo co-opt them? Will socialization influences impel them to see the system that they once criticized as acceptable? Will exposure to and success in the system result in living with it as is? It can be argued, for example, that discussion on conformity from Chapter 4, which points out that the longer one is part of an institution or organization, the more likely one is to accept its dominant viewpoint, has validity in this situation as well.

On the other hand, a fundamental message of Chapter 4 is that comformity pressures do not operate uniformly on everyone within organizations; much depends on whether one belongs to a group lacking social and political power inside and outside the specific organization in question and whether or not one is part of a numerical minority. Members of nondominant groups generally possess distinctive perceptions and sets of values through which they perceive political life. Further, they often have distinctive goals. Because of these identifiable differences from the mainstream, members of minority groups experience conformity pressures more when their numbers are very small than when representation increases. That is, the smaller the size of the minority group in relation to the majority, the more likely that minority members will feel conformity pressures exceedingly strongly. It is also more likely that they will chafe under those restrictions and look for opportunities to escape them. When the size of the minority group in relation to the majority approaches parity, the tug of conformity pressure is loosened and members of the minority take the opportunity to substitute their own standards for those of the dominant group. Easing of restrictions does not coincide with abandonment of unique perspectives or the actions that result from it. There is, therefore, little reason to believe that the women legislators who displayed courage enough to bring their distinctive priorities to legislative agenda would become so distant from those priorities and the life experiences that guided them that all desire for procedural reform is abandoned. It is also unlikely that at the point at which women constitute a sufficient proportion of legislatures to make reform a possibility, all thought of reform would die. As Mary Katzenstein notes, it is well to remember:

> [T]here needs to be recognition that institutions shape women's experiences in distinctive ways. Individual consciousness of the meanings and implica-

tions of gender is conditioned no less by the person's institutional affiliations and connections than by her race and class background.[43]

Some evidence that women do not get co-opted the longer they are in office or once they hold leadership positions in legislatures shores up to this argument. An indirect indicator that as women gain seniority in the system, they do not lose their distinctive perspective is available in the work of Lyn Kathlene. Her research concentrates on whether women officeholders hold different attitudinal orientations that lead them to look at policy formation differently than men. The focus here is not whether women representatives have different priorities than men but whether they approach legislation of all sorts from an alternative standpoint. In tests of her hypothesis that women in the Colorado legislature are more contextual than men (perceive life as a web of interrelations rather than a hierarchical ordering), she finds not only that her expectations are correct but that women are still more contextual than men no matter how long they are in the legislature.[44]

The recent work of Sue Tolleson Rinehart concerning mayoral pairs in five large cities (cities in which women were succeeded or followed by a male leader) also suggests that women in leadership positions do not lose their unique perspective in order to gain or retain power. Tolleson Rinehart finds that meaningful gender differences appear among the female and male mayors she interviewed and concludes that they exercised different leadership styles: women had more hands-on style and emphasized collegiality and teamwork more than men.[45]

The Center for the American Women and Politics study, mentioned earlier, provides additional indirect insight into whether women legislators lose their distinctive perspective when they achieve legislative leadership. Since the aspect of women's contribution that is unique is their policy priorities, the researchers at the center explored whether women leaders had to become copies of male power brokers to achieve or retain those positions, whether they had to choose between "making a difference and being an insider." What they found was that, "regardless of self-labeled party insider status, women were usually more likely than male colleagues of the same party to support liberal and feminist policy positions"; women insiders were equally as likely as other women legislators to have worked on women's bills; and women in legislative leadership were more likely than men in leadership to have had a women's bill as a policy priority.[46]

The center's researchers conclude that women hold to their principles even after assuming positions of leadership and that the real challenge for women is attaining those kinds of positions in the first place, not losing their singular perspectives once they get there.[47]

> For those concerned that a woman officeholder might become "one of the boys" and, in the process, abandon the policy needs of women, our results suggest that such fears are unfounded. The increased presence of women in public office and their increased influence within these institutions should give women greater power to shape policy agendas. These changes do not seem likely to deter them from pursuing policies that improve the welfare of women.[48]

If this story about Geraldine Ferraro is representative of other women who have or will achieve leadership, then the conclusion by the center's researchers are accurate:

> But she split for a time with the House Speaker last September when she opposed a resolution allowing Reagan to keep U.S. Marines in Lebanon until early 1985. Her own son, John, was nineteen at the time and she'd been to Beirut and talked with the young Marines. "I am a mother and I saw those kids over there," Ferraro said. "When we had the debate, Tip came up to me and said, 'Gerry, you're with me, aren't you?' And I said, 'No, Mr. Speaker.' And he said, 'Gerry, you're part of the House leadership.' And I said, 'Mr. Speaker, I just can't.'"[49]

Conclusion

Empirical indicators that female legislators acclimated to existing legislative activities might, at first glance, suggest that they were satisfied with the procedural status quo. Deeper analysis, however, reveals that they were no more accepting of the ways in which legislators go about their business than were their sisters in the 1970s. Indeed, they envisioned an alternative standard in which power and procedure are geared toward ends more responsive to their colleagues in the legislature and the constituents to whom they are accountable. Why, then, didn't women officeholders work to systematically and comprehensively revolutionize the legislative world? The answer concerns the nature of institutional reform—institutions and those who inhabit them are notoriously resistant to anything that might attenuate their hold on power—and the position of weakness that still characterizes the circumstances of political women. That female legislators made pragmatic political calculations not to court extensive procedural change does not suggest, however, that they are not preparing to do so in the future.

6

The Impact of Women

Have women in legislative office had an impact on political processes and products? And if so, is that impact similar to or different from the impact of men? Whatever the impact, how best ought it to be judged or evaluated? What information about the political, social, and cultural environment is important to understand why and how women participate as they do?

These are the questions that spurred my interest in studying women officeholders and the ones with which I began this book. Previous chapters focused on measuring the impact of female representatives on policy and procedure and exploring the context that shaped their choices and actions. The task of this chapter is to offer judgments on women legislators' contributions to and impact on the political arena and to weigh their significance.

Arriving at judgments of impact and significance requires delineations of the standards to be used in assessing them. As commonsensical and uncontroversial as this recommendation sounds, creating a set of standards and systematically evaluating accomplishments based on each of its elements is something routinely overlooked in the gender politics literature. What is more usual is the offering of conclusions largely unattached to an articulated or comprehensive framework. Without an adequate baseline for measurement, we cannot fairly or accurately judge where women representatives are now compared with where they were fifteen or twenty years ago, what they have sought to accomplish with what has been achieved, and what the possibilities are for the future. Equally important, without a framework, the standards of judgment will constantly be shifting with the passage of time or the individual perspective of the evaluator.

Previous Standards

By what standards should women politicians be judged? A first clue is to examine those currently or previously in use. In fact, the journalistic and scholarly literature about women in political office is replete with judgments about their contributions, achievements, and impact. Not surprisingly, however, they are conflicting ones. This may be because, as a group, they tend to be scattered, unsystematic, and lacking comprehensiveness. Moreover, the majority of conclusions about what women have achieved suffer from narrowness of scope, which, somewhat like the typology of expectations introduced in Chapter 1, has fallen along two dimensions—what I call the political integrationists and the political reformists.

Integrationists have tended to judge women officeholders on whether they have assimilated into the current system, learned the ropes, and used available opportunities to further their careers in traditional ways: developing expertise in and obtaining passage of high-visibility and high-profile issues, spearheading issue area reform efforts, and using exposure from such efforts to ascend leadership ladders. Significance of impact is then determined based on traditional definitions of individual success rather than on whether women, as a group, have made a meaningful contribution or had a distinctive impact.

The ideological predisposition underlying this set of evaluative standards, naturally, concerns the assumption that women will not or should not seek to alter the system in any meaningful ways. It is possible that some minimal, incremental alterations to policy or process may result from an influx of women, but, according to this perspective, neither the topics under consideration nor the way business is done (including, especially, the values at its base) should or will be challenged. These assumptions are based both upon bias against anything but gradual, hierarchical, and structured change and upon the belief that only the foolhardy would risk individual success and impact by promoting all-or-nothing attempts at overhaul rather than working through the system. Once again, the bottom-line criterion for assessing impact is individualistic rather than group or society based.

On the basis of these criteria, women officeholders have been given mixed reviews. On the one hand, women have not reached a level of impact equal to that of men. Few female representatives have achieved significant leadership positions, and it is the rare case that a woman officeholder is visibly in the lead on an issue that confers high-level power. Typically, the powerful committees and powerful people are those closely involved with matters of money. Those are the players who have a greater-than-average chance of ascending through the ranks, achieving power and influence in the eyes of their colleagues and the eyes of the general political establishment. Seldom do we see female legislators as leaders and spokespersons for issues of taxes, budgets, or commerce, for example.

On the other hand, women have made progress over the years. As indicated early on in this book, and as acknowledged by integrationists, female officeholders are represented on the full range of committees and have policy priorities in all legislative areas. Moreover, women now hold committee chair positions, and in the occasional state, a few women have ascended the ranks to hold leadership positions at or near the top of the hierarchy. Similarly, women legislators are occasionally in the lead on high-profile issues and strategies and are occasionally those relied upon to foster progress when legislative impasse has been reached.

Whether women will be judged as being fully successful in the future depends, in part, on whether they become as powerful within the system as men have been. If women embrace the values of individual success, it may be merely a matter of time until women officeholders are considered to have had a significant impact on the political arena.

Contrary to integrationists, reformists judge the accomplishments of women officeholders on a far different set of standards. These center not on whether women politicians have been integrated into the legislative world as it exists or are powerful within it but on whether they have used their distinctive life experiences and values to foment widespread change of the status quo. This perspective is well articulated in this comment by Barbara Ehrenreich:

> But, I'm sorry, sisters, this is not the revolution. What's striking, from an old-fashioned (ca. 1970) feminist perspective, is just how little has changed. The fact that law is no longer classified as a ''nontraditional'' occupation for women has not made our culture any less graspingly litigious or any more concerned with rights of the underdog. Women doctors haven't made a dent in the high-tech, bottom-line fixation of the medical profession and no one would claim that the influx of executive women has ushered in a new era of high-toned business ethics. It's not that we were wrong back in the salad days of feminism about the existence of nurturant ''feminine values.'' If anything, women have more distinctive views as a sex than they did 20 years ago. The gender gap first appeared in the presidential election of 1980, with women voting on the more liberal side. Recent polls show that women are more

likely to favor social spending for the poor and to believe it's "very important" to work "for the betterment of American society."[1]

The ideological bias inherent in the reformist position is, therefore, one toward group and societywide change. Individual and incremental goals, if not meaningless, are of considerably lesser significance. Further, the impact of female officeholders is judged as a package: whether they have successfully brought private sphere issues to legislative agendas and whether they have brought private sphere values to the ways in which legislatures do their business. The two halves of the package appear not to be equally valued, however; the latter element is judged as its most important aspect.

On the basis of this standard, women's contributions have come up short. While the import of highlighting and championing new issues, issues that link private and public spheres, is granted, to this way of thinking, obtaining passage of individual bills does little to change the underlying foundations of a system whose goals and methods are wrongheaded. The point of including women in the political elite was to have them transform the system—indeed, transform society—not simply tinker at its margins.

Whether one uses the approach of the political integrationists or the political reformists, the significance of women's impact on the legislative arena is seen as less than awe-inspiring. But does using one or the other of these approaches give us the best standard for evaluation—or is there more to the story? Should complete assimilation or complete transformation be the basis on which we judge the impact of women legislators? Or should we devise standards that take into account another set of criteria?

Impact: Options for an Alternative Standard

Just as the dichotomous nature of the typology of expectations offered alternatives that failed to take into account all that is necessary to understand the actions and reactions of women officeholders (such as change over time or an outcome that might reflect a blending of two sides of the typology), the two perspectives for evaluation presented above are options for assessment that may not provide the best answer to the question "How might we judge the significance of the impact of women officeholders?" Just as using the typology as a heuristic device was useful to structure inquiry, recognizing where the integrationist and reformist approaches fall short is a useful way to develop a more sophisticated, inclusive, and systematic standard.[2]

Three possible alternative foundations for judging the contributions of women officeholders are available. The first is, of course, a standard similar to those promoted or preferred by either the integrationists or the reformists—an ideological one. While this type of framework has dominated debate to this point, standards of this sort are ultimately of limited usefulness because they assume a purity and singularity of influence on the actions and motivations of officeholders that do not reflect multidimensional political reality. In short, the narrowness and one-sidedness of ideological standards render them unsatisfactory.

A second possibile foundation for judging women officeholders' impact is based on what the people who are being represented expect from the representatives they elect. This standard is highly defensible: whose opinions could be more relevant in a democracy than those of citizens? To apply it, we need to take into consideration citizen expectations of women officeholders. No clear-cut answer to what citizens expect of their representative is available, but we have a few clues. First, the general increase in societal tolerance of women in the public sphere tells us something about approval of their presence. Does this acceptance of women in public office signal anything specific about the direction of policy or the ways in which it is achieved in addition to a basic support for equality of opportunity? Two pieces of evidence suggest that the answer to this question is yes. The first relates to beliefs that female representatives are more honest and less "political" than male representatives and are better at domestic issues such as education, health, and welfare.[3] To the extent that women are elected to office, one might conclude that citizens expect women to champion certain issues and to lessen the extent to which the "political" is valued over the good, the fair, or the just. If all else is equal, this assumption is probably a pretty safe one—at least if referring to women officeholders collectively. It must be noted, however, that all else is rarely equal, and in any individual case, there are many other possible explanations as to why a woman candidate won a particular race over a male candidate.

Another hint about what the citizenry expects from women officeholders concerns the outrage of many women at the way in which Anita Hill's sexual harassment charges against Clarence Thomas were handled by the Senate Judiciary Committee of the United States Congress. The subsequent successful candidacies of female Senate candidates who highlighted this issue, such as Carol Moseley-Braun in Illinois and Patty Murray of Washington, may also suggest that some sections of the female voting population expect that increasing women's presence in legislatures will increase the sensitivity accorded to issues of particular importance to all women. Even if this is true, however, it is not yet clear how much of the constituency is sending this message and what the remainder of the voters expect from women in office.[4]

Looking toward the constituency however narrowly or broadly defined is both a reasonable standard by which to judge the impact of women officeholders and a difficult one to implement. Beyond the appeal of its responsiveness to issues of democracy, there is the problem of accurate and adequate knowledge about the preferences of the electorate upon which to base a framework. The usefulness of this approach is therefore limited.

Another possibility for judging women's impact is to measure it relative to the goals that women officeholders hold for themselves.[5] Doing so has several benefits. First, the survey and interview research conducted by scholars over the last twenty years is rich with information about what goals female legislators have held and currently hold. Unlike information on citizen preferences, this is available and easily interpretable.

Second, focusing on the goals of women officeholders circumvents the problems related to the one-sided nature and narrowness of ideological standards, not to mention their only passing respect for the multiple and overlapping motivations of and influences on representatives. It also allows evaluators to factor in the political realities any legislator confronts as well as the specific ones faced by female representatives. Using the goals of women legislators as a baseline to judge their impact rather than ideological tests is, for example, conducive to considering the obstacles women have faced and the opportunities available to them that relate to success or failure of goal fulfillment.

Finally, standards of judgment that are based on women's goals are inclusive of the wishes of citizens they represent. Legislators do not set objectives, especially policy objectives, in a vacuum; one of the most important influences on determination of goals is the needs and wishes of constituents. Thus, using this standard means that we do not have to make assumptions about what the citizenry prefers; those wishes are indirectly taken into account. Given this, it does not seem surprising that what the public appears to want from women officeholders—avoidance of what is seen as corrupt politics and championing or at least exhibiting a sensitivity to issues concerning education, health, and welfare (all interests that are, by the way, correlated with women's, and children's and family issues)—is also at the center of women legislators' agendas.

Of the three possible ways to judge whether women legislators have had an impact, distinctive or otherwise, on the political arena, the last, using the goals of the women themselves, is the one that, for reasons of information accessibility and comprehensiveness, has the greatest possibility for providing a useful assessment. Women officeholders' goals are therefore the first element of the new standard of evaluation I propose.

Goals and Possibilities:
Toward an Enhanced Framework

If objectives of women politicians are the central element in constructing a new standard of evaluation, we must start by illumination of each of their goals. The dual focus of this book, which concerns matters of both procedure and policy, directs our attention to the goals of women officeholders related to these two areas. The structure of analysis makes women officeholders' individual and group-based goals less immediately apparent, however. Exploration of each of these four areas is nevertheless essential if thorough assessment of women's impact on the legislative arena is to be accomplished.

Certainly, the policy goals of women have been evident throughout the period under study. Even when female officeholders did not display distinctive priorities, they did exhibit distinctive ideological viewpoints, voting records, and issue attitudes. In each of these cases, women officeholders were more supportive than their male colleagues of issues concerning women, and children and families. Women were not only more supportive of these issues, they championed them by sponsoring them, making them top priorities, and seeing that they became public policy. Hence, altering the agendas of the legislatures they inhabit to include a wider array of subjects, subjects of direct relevance to the changing roles of women in society and the effects of these changes on familial relationships, has been a long-standing and central goal for female politicians.

Policy goals of women legislators also went beyond their distinctive contribution to the success of women's, and children's and family issues. Female representatives sought the fulfillment of another related and more distant goal: having the priorities of male colleagues include bills of this sort. In other words, they wanted more than men's votes on the occasional bill; they wanted men to participate to the same extent as women in sponsoring such legislation. Whether engaging in quiet educational efforts for individual colleagues or public forums on women's issues, female representatives have sought to integrate issues of special concern to them into the general political environment.

Available evidence indicates that women officeholders also envisioned a different procedural framework in which to conduct legislative business as well as a different set of values upon which to base those procedures. Whether it concerned alternative definitions and uses of power or more systematic and comprehensive decision making, female representatives articulated a long-term goal of revamping the standards that govern political decision making. As Chapter 5 suggests, the fact that women fully participated in the rules of the game does not translate into approval of them; instead, these actions are better viewed as necessary for effectiveness in the short term and a preliminary step toward gathering requisite credibility and power to guide the procedural future.

Analysis related to the central focus of this book, whether women representatives altered or embraced the policies and procedures guiding legislatures across the nation, yields a dividend related to uncovering additional goals. All the empirical indicators preceding direct measures of how women dealt with matters of policy or procedure offer a wealth of insight into individual and group-based goals. The individual goals of female representatives have, over time, included effectiveness in meeting constituent needs both through service and legislative action, contributing effectively and substantially toward policy debates, mastery of the legislative process, credibility and respect from colleagues, achieving leadership positions, and making a mark sufficient to fuel any higher ambitions each might harbor. Women's efforts to achieve each of these objectives ranged from increasing their participation in all aspects of legislative life to conducting the requisite preparation and entering competitions for leadership positions and higher offices.

Finally, a last set of goals women legislators developed in relation to their presence in legislatures concerns group-based ambitions. That is, women did not just want to see individual achievement and progress for themselves, they expressed a strong aspiration to see women in general succeed in political life. The desire to see more women in legislative office and to reduce discrimination against women in the political arena (as elsewhere) is reflective of this group-based goal. Female representatives engaged in multiple strategies to further this set of goals from forming women's legislative caucuses to raising money for and recruiting women candidates for elective office. On this aim as all the others, efforts to achieve success and progress on one assisted in progress toward each of the other three. As is true in all facets of life, political or otherwise, actions have multiple motivations and applications and contribute toward multiple objectives.

Taken together, these goals reflected a desire on the part of female officeholders to progress in the system as well as to work toward transforming it. Their ambitions spanned the ideological spectrum illustrated by the reformists and the integrationists: women wanted both to integrate and to progress in traditional political fashion, but they did not want to stop there; they were not content to create an exact replica of the traditional political role as defined by men. The integrationists and the reformists both overlooked that which is crucial in understanding how to judge the impact of women in legislatures—that those people, women and men alike, who become involved in politics do so because, on some level, they value our political institutions and traditions. The women who pursue elected office do so first because they want to take their rightful place beside men in our political life. And while they, as a group, do not want to mimic completely the role played by men, neither are political women anarchists. Instead, they are visionaries of sorts who want to enhance and perfect our institutions and traditions.

The Context of Possibilities

If the goals of women officeholders are the first element of a new and comprehensive standard by which to judge their impact, what are its other elements? In a phrase, the answer is consideration of context—the context in which the goals are being attempted, or, put another way, the opportunities and obstacles met on the path to success. These can be thought of in the language of possibilities.

The realm of the possible relates to the goals of political women in two ways. One concerns societywide perceptions about the role of women in the public rather than the private sphere. When it was unusual for women to inhabit legislatures, individual women tended to circumscribe their behavior so that they did not stand out; they wished to highlight the ways in which they were similar to the norm, not different from it. Closely held beliefs about women as somehow more pure, more honest, less guileful, and less shrewd than men so dominated our collective psyche that political women were discouraged from stepping into the legislative arena in any forceful way. When female legislators were no longer as unusual as they once were, political women began to be accepted on similar terms as political men. Hence, restrictions they previously placed on their behavior began to be relaxed as it became clearer that they would not be as heavily sanctioned for failing to conform to stereotypes. The first set of possibilities, then, relates to notions of appropriate behavior for women who work in the public sphere: the obstacles were narrow beliefs that limited women's options; the opportunities related to expanded belief systems.

The realm of the possible also encompasses the institutional environments in which women work. Whether it be their level of power relative to other groups within the legislative world or the relative flexibility or inflexibility of rules and procedures governing legislatures, the particularities of institutional life have also influenced the extent to which women have been free to deviate from existing norms or forge new pathways for action. In the case of the creation of distinctive policy priorities, for example, it was when women developed a position of power—in the form of greater numbers—that an emphasis on the introduction and passage of bills dealing with women, children, and families emerged. Despite a demonstrated interest in these issues, female representatives of an earlier era did not display such priorities. As opportunities expanded, so did female representatives' willingness to act in a distinctive fashion.

The Time Factor

If we are to develop a set of standards by which to judge the impact of women legislators, another element related to opportunities and obstacles must be factored into the equation—time—the time it takes to transform goals into realities. This variable is relevant when judging the impact of any individual or any group on the political arena, but it is a particularly critical one for women. Because women have been systematically excluded from the ranks of the political elite (as have other groups), they are in the situation of being newcomers. Equally important, women remain in the minority in legislatures and are still seen as creatures of the private sphere more than inhabitants of the public one. All this means that in order to meet their goals, they need time for more than a simple adjustment to a new job: time must be allowed for other political actors to adjust to their presence. Female officeholders must both carve out their role within legislatures and win acceptance from the majority for their choices.

The Lessons of History

One way to illustrate the necessity for making time a component in a new evaluative standard for judging women's impact is to look back on the pursuit of other political goals of women and their progress. In Chapter 1, I

offered a brief but comprehensive overview of the political and legal history of women in the United States so that we would be equipped to place
the circumstances of political women in historical perspective. This history
is also useful for judging the impact of modern elective officeholders.

One of the best examples of what it takes for a previously excluded group
to further its political objectives is the women's suffrage campaign. Suffrage was formally put on the political agenda in 1848 in the Declaration of
Principles of the Seneca Falls Convention, the first meeting convened in the
United States on the subject of women's rights. The central focus of Seneca
Falls was organizing to promote legislation providing full legal status to
women independently of their relationship to husbands, fathers, and
brothers. In fact, suffrage was a marginal issue at the time and one considered tremendously radical. Yet, by a narrow voting margin among the
delegates, the call for a franchise was included in the declaration that
emerged from Seneca Falls. Through the work of women such as Elizabeth
Cady Stanton, Susan B. Anthony, and many, many others, the notion that
women deserved the vote was nurtured along at a slow but sure pace.[6]

The first real hope that these political reformers had of turning their
efforts into success was just after the Civil War. In 1865, when Negroes
were to be given the vote, women's rights activists believed that in addition
to Negro men, all women would be enfranchised. Surely, they thought, the
contributions women had made to the nation during the war combined with
their unceasing work for abolition earned them the right to broaden their
participation in politics. Yet, when the Fifteenth Amendment to the United
States Constitution was drafted and passed, nowhere was it written that
women would get the right to vote. Feminists emerged from this loss bitter
and even divided among themselves as to how to proceed in their renewed
quest.[7]

After the Civil War, women's suffrage took center stage for the activists,
and despite relentless effort on both the state and federal level, it was not
until the 1880s that Congress took the issue seriously (select committees on
women's suffrage were established in both chambers in 1882), not until
1914 that a favorable vote emerged from even one chamber, and not until
1918 that bills passed both chambers of Congress. Finally, in August 1920,
the required three-fourths of states ratified the Nineteenth Amendment and
the battle was won.[8] The journey from Seneca Falls to final ratification
of the Nineteenth Amendment took seventy-two years. When one compares
the efforts of women to obtain the franchise in federal elections (something
they had been doing in some local and state elections well before this time)
with the approximately fifteen years that women have participated more

routinely in legislative office, one gets a better sense of how long it takes for those outside the political mainstream to achieve their objectives.

Contribution and Impact

I have offered a standard for evaluation of the impact of women on the world of legislatures that includes the four sets of goals of political women and the context in which they have sought to achieve them. What remains is to apply these standards. The question is how completely have women fulfilled their goals, and what variables have influenced their achievements or failures?

Women's Impact: The Individual and Group Goals

The progress of women legislators in meeting the goals that might best be categorized as integrationist has been substantial. Female legislators have mastered legislative technique (as evidenced by their success in bill introduction and passage), proved their credibility by winning seats on the range of legislative committees and winning some leadership positions, demonstrated effectiveness in their role (as evidenced by their comparable reelection rate compared with men), increased their numbers, and succeeded in overcoming a great deal of the overt discrimination against them. This progress does not mean, however, that each of their individual and group goals have been fully met.

Despite continued, incremental success in bringing more women to public office, their numbers are still very small in the vast majority of states and even worse in the U.S. Congress. While there are some places where women compose 30 percent or more of the legislatures (such as in Arizona, Washington, Vermont, Maine, New Hampshire, and Colorado), there are also states in which women still make up less than 10 percent of the total (such as Alabama, Arkansas, Kentucky, and Pennsylvania). Despite the much publicized gains of 1992, women still constitute only 10 percent of the U.S. Congress. Further, women are still woefully underrepresented in leadership positions relative to their proportion in legislatures and their seniority. This is especially true when the highest levels of leadership are considered.

Similarly, while women have worked hard to overcome discrimination against them in the political arena and have even managed to succeed in spite of its continued although more muted existence, the success has been only partial. Overt discrimination has been reduced dramatically in most places, but the more subtle covert variety is a repeated complaint voiced by women officeholders across the nation. The lament is loudest when it comes to women's bids to attain leadership positions. While women have, in some places, won some of these positions, almost no woman who has done so says it was anything but an uphill struggle. Assertions that they have had to work harder than men to prove their credibility and had to quell fears that they would create chaos where rationality once reigned are legion. In the words of Edith Green, a former member of Congress:

> You know the saying: "Negroes are fine so long as they know their place." The same goes for women in Congress. A woman is fine as long as she knows her place. If a woman were to announce she was running for a party position, she would be considered an "uppity female."[9]

The goals not fully achieved have not been so for want of trying. In the case of obtaining greater presence in legislatures, the literature indicates that when women run, they do win. There is no evidence that, all else being equal, women candidates lose more than their male counterparts. However, the impediments to increased access have been greater than the opportunities. Perceptions of women's public sphere roles, institutional environments, and time factors are all relevant. For example, women's presence in legislatures is not closer to parity, in part, as a result of one form of institutional resistance to change: the difficulty in unseating incumbents. This is true whether the challenger is a woman or a man, but since men are generally the incumbents, the only way to greatly enhance the numbers of women in legislatures is to unseat men . . . or to wait until they retire.[10] Either way the process is time-consuming.

Narrow perceptions of women's public sphere role serve to limit the numbers of women in what Darcy, Welch, and Clark refer to as the social eligibility pool. This pool is merely the set of qualifications that we generally associate with viable and strong candidates for elective office including a college education, a legal or business occupation, military service, community service, and the like. Because women have only recently been in positions of meeting these qualifications, they have had less access to office. Another way to think about this concept is voiced by Susan Carroll in her discussion of barriers of socialization. She notes that women in the general public have tended not to see public office as a viable option for their own lives. To the extent that that view is changing, women have run for and won elective office in ever-greater numbers.[11]

Women's Impact: Process and Procedural Goals

Women have made substantial progress on goals that might be categorized as reformist. Certainly, this is true when it comes to the policy goals that have been the focus of many women in legislatures across the land—to bring issues of the private sphere to public agendas. This contribution is a unique one, and without women's presence in legislative bodies, it is unlikely that the same result would have obtained. Perhaps this female state representative from Massachusetts said it best:

> You bet we're unique. We bring to this legislature many issues that would not even be considered by the male reps. Gender-neutral insurance, Healthy Start for Kids, changes in the code on domestic violence. I could go on . . . But let's face it—without the women, people like [names omitted] and the Caucus these issues would be non-issues. Today these things are law.[12]

Women's impact on policy also goes beyond the introduction of new issues to legislative agendas. If one deals with policy goals more broadly, an important question is whether women legislators have brought a unique perspective to all issues, not just those directly related to women's, and children's and family concerns. Put more simply, have female officeholders infused those concerns into all legislation? Have they, for example, considered transportation policy from the perspective of its impact on family life? Is there any evidence that women legislators have made such a broad-based worldview a part of their objectives in office?

The limited evidence available suggests that female officeholders do apply their singular point of view to the range of issues. The Colorado research introduced in Chapter 5 indicates that women tend to respond to issues on a contextual basis (evaluating the impact of legislation in terms of interrelationships), whereas men tend to respond in an instrumental fashion (hierarchical ordering).[13] Additional research from the same data set analyzes one area of public policy, crime and prison issues, to discover whether women and men approach it differently. The author finds that women see "the causes and effects of crime to society at large" and focus on preventative solutions, while men talk more about "criminals as individuals responsible for their choices" and focus on the immediate goal of punishing them for their illegal actions.[14] Although limitations exist on our knowledge of how extensively this perspective is applied by women or what obstacles they encounter in using it as fully as possible, it would be fair to conclude that female legislators' impact on policy has been multilayered.

The final policy goal of women officeholders concerns their diffusion through the legislature. Female officeholders have sought to introduce and successfully pass the type of legislation of particular concern to them, but they have not been content with taking sole responsibility for its introduction and nurturing; they have wanted to see male legislators embrace these bills as important.

Achievement of this goal has been less than total. As the analysis in Chapter 4 indicates, even in states in which women were most numerous, there was no strong overall commitment to the introduction of legislation dealing with women, and children and families. In other words, while there was variance among the states, overall introductions were still at low levels everywhere, and in no state were men equally likely as women to prioritize these bills. The picture was brighter when it came to passage of bills dealing with women, and children and families. Where women were most numerous or where they had a formal women's legislative caucus, we saw the highest passage rates of these bills. Although men were generally not committed to the work of introducing bills on subjects most dear to women, they have contributed to their passage and did so to the greatest degree in places where women were at their most powerful.

Having analyzed achievement of policy goals, I turn now to procedural ones. Since it is clear that women legislators' vision of an altered procedural environment was one applicable to the future, the most relevant question is, "What progress have women made to lay the groundwork for eventual alteration of legislative procedure?" Three contributions are relevant. First, as explicated fully in Chapter 5, female representatives have sought to overcome their hesitancy and distaste with aspects of everyday legislative activity in order to both meet their other goals and to gain the skills, credibility, and power necessary to leave an imprint on the process down the line. While still admitting to disliking some of what is necessary to participate fully in legislative life, women officeholders have done so as a means to a different end.

A second way in which women kept alive the long-term goal of procedural reform was by continuing their practice of performing legislative tasks according to a different standard than they perceived was the case with men. Female officeholders reported that they dealt with legislative tasks differently than men—for example, they were more thorough and detail oriented in preparing, advocating, and opposing legislation and more attentive to various consequences of policy actions. By continuing these practices at the same time they engaged fully in routine legislative activity, women modeled an alternative to the traditional ways in which decisions were made. Although approaching decisions in a new fashion does not have an effect on formal rules and procedures, it does have an effect on the values that underlie them. One might interpret this as laying the groundwork for future change.

Another way in which women prepared a path for the future concerns a by-product of their dissatisfaction with the status quo—it is now subject to broad-based reevaluation and reassessment. The nature of reform debates has been broadened to include not just narrow options that accept traditional frameworks; the debates have been expanded to include options that could dramatically alter the values and practices of legislative life. To the extent that reforms, either formal or informal, of the ways in which legislatures do their business are considered, women legislators have to be given a large share of the credit.

In the realm of policy and process goals, women, then, have been, while not completely successful, quite so. In cases in which full success was not achieved (such as parity in representation—either in the legislature or in leadership positions), the possibilities for doing so were limited by daunting obstacles.

Significance: Marginal or Robust?

Women legislators have met with a great deal of success in achieving their goals. Their impact has been both wide-ranging and distinctive. One last question remains—is this impact a significant one? That is, has it been great or marginal?

My answer to this question is straightforward and positive. That the significance of the contribution made by female officeholders is high is related to several factors, the first of which is that the goals have been aimed high, not low. The correspondence between goals and their achievement tells a great deal about the type and direction of impact women have had in the legislative arena. The ambitiousness of the goals speaks volumes about the significance of the impact—assuming, of course, that the goals have been met—and in this case, that is generally true. Whether one is considering their scope (which ranges from individual success and effectiveness to alterations in legislative agendas) or the fact that women have sought major changes in the legislative world (especially with respect to the sorts of public policy enacted), it is clear that women did not restrict themselves to low-level, easily met goals. Most impressively, they chose goals that were multidimensional, goals that went beyond proving that women could operate in the legislative world as effectively as men. Female officeholders chose to strive toward distinctive goals, and, in most cases, they achieved them.

Just as significance can be assessed based on whether goals have been ambitious or minimal, whether opportunities have been great or limited also bears on that judgment. Little in the circumstances faced by women legislators could be construed as conducive to success. Rather, they have had to break through a variety of barriers in order to gain their jobs, keep their jobs, and perform effectively within them. These include their paucity of numbers, their newcomer status, their relative disadvantage compared with men in terms of collective legislative experience, discriminatory attitudes of colleagues, the lack of latitude on the part of society for their full participation in the public sphere, and institutional obstacles to change. While all barriers are not created equal, with the exception of lower collective levels of legislative experience (which is, of course, remedied as time passes), each of the barriers faced by women can be classified as ranging from difficult, but surmountable, to almost completely impossible to overcome.

What is particularly impressive is that women have found ways to make progress regardless of the difficulty of the barriers. Where they were least confining, female representatives took advantage of the opening and moved rapidly and in a sweeping fashion. Where the obstacles were the stiffest, women set and were successful at taking small, incremental, but consistent steps toward the goal.

For example, recognizing that obstacles to policy change have been weaker and less resistant than those related to procedure spurred women to devote considerable effort to the former area. Women overcame sentiment against concentration on issues of women, and children and families by using any condition that could be construed as favorable to introduce and reintroduce such legislation. Most often, the favorable condition was support from other women in the legislature. Remarkably, even in places without this type of support, where women legislators' pursuit of those issues posed considerable personal risk of being branded a lightweight and losing credibility, some courageously continued to push them.

When women confronted a barrier so considerable that direct and immediate progress toward a goal was impossible, they refused to abandon it; instead, they simply operationalized a longer time frame and pursued intermediate objectives. For instance, to effectuate even minor procedural changes is a daunting and time-consuming task; to effectuate the sorts of procedural changes that women politicians envision requires, at the very minimum, parity or above parity in numbers in legislatures, a consensus among colleagues that the system as is cannot meet their individual and collective needs, and an incentive structure that will guide changes in the anticipated direction. None of these baseline requirements were ones that modern women legislators were even close to obtaining. But women legislators did not abandon their desire to see procedural change; they merely created another path to achieve it.

To put the discussion of the significance of women legislators' achievements in the face of serious barriers into a slightly different and perhaps more amusing perspective, consider the following: during in-person interviews of women legislators in California, Georgia, Mississippi, Nebraska, Pennsylvania, and Washington, I routinely asked women what kinds of obstacles they face that men do not. In addition to answers focusing on discrimination, minority status, newcomer status, and all the substantial obstacles highlighted throughout this book, women in almost every state raised an issue of another sort entirely: bathrooms in state capitol buildings. Female representatives told me that they had, in some cases, spent years trying to convince the leadership to convert one of the rooms off the floor into a women's restroom. Since legislatures were not designed with the notion that women would inhabit them, women's restrooms were not available for use anywhere near chambers. Women had to run to another floor of the capitol or somewhere on the same floor, but very far from chambers, in order to meet basic biological needs. Often, this caused them to miss votes or significant portions of floor debates. In some states, it didn't take too long to get the leadership to relent; in others the battles were multiyear and contentious. It is remarkable that, when some portion of women's time and attention had to be devoted to issues such as this, they had time, energy, and fortitude to face and overcome barriers to meeting their more substantive goals.[15]

Achieving ambitious goals in the face of serious obstacles is directly relevant to judging the significance of impact. The time expended in the effort also must be factored into the equation. That women's achievements have been impressive given their scope and the limited opportunities that were afforded them is of little doubt. That they have achieved them in so short a time period is, ironically, made that much clearer by Barbara Ehrenreich's disappointed comment that what has transpired so far does not resemble the anticipated revolution. Remembering that women legislators have only inhabited legislatures as anything more than occasional exceptions for the last fifteen or twenty years makes clear that the correct question at this point is not "Why haven't women officeholders revolutionized political standards?" The better one is "How have women accomplished all that they have in such a short amount of time?'' With only a limited opportunity to use their unique attitudes about the process, the issues, and their own role within the political arena to influence their colleagues, women legislators have made progress toward their goals and have had a distinctive impact on the system. Put in this light, what has transpired appears extraordinary. As one commentator in the mid–1980s noted:

> In half a decade, women have moved day care, welfare reform, child support payments, and maternal and child care out of the social fringe and into the political mainstream of the state legislatures. The years of effort are paying off in more and more bills ensuring equality for women on every front from insurance to taxes to pay and pensions.[16]

Ambitiousness of goals, opportunities, obstacles, and time—these variables are necessary to judge the significance of impact of any type of political contribution. In the end, though, another criterion matters equally as much: do the contributions make a difference? The answer here is an unequivocal yes. Although many benefits result from the direct efforts and successes of female legislators, arguably the most distinctive, dramatic, and fully developed contribution has been bringing issues that were heretofore considered marginal and of lesser significance squarely into the center of public agendas throughout the nation. These laws have transformed the lives and options of many people, and without women in elective office, it is doubtful that these benefits would be available today.

Significance More Broadly Defined

No discussion of the significance of women's impact on the legislative world is complete without acknowledgment of two broader and less direct benefits of women's presence in elective office: the symbolic benefit that accrues from conditioning society to the presence of women in a wide range of public sphere positions, and the improvement to public decision making as a result of using a greater share of the intellectual and experiential resources available.

First, as women take their place as legitimate players on the political stage, society will likely become ever more tolerant of them in myriad positions of power: no longer will women in high-level, high-visibility positions be seen as exceptional, or as Barbara Ehrenreich puts it, ''nontraditional.'' Not only will this allow adult women to expand their career possibilities, it will allow young girls to grow up with the knowledge that women can perform all of society's roles and that their sex will not be a limitation on their dreams.

Increasing women's presence in the political sphere creates another benefit to public life generally: access to a greater diversity of ideas and experiences that fuel definition of problems and the creation of solutions. Leaving any group out of policy formulation and legitimation necessarily means that the range of ideas is artificially limited. It is hard to imagine a worse way to restrict the visions of a society. Whatever else women have achieved, however quickly, and under whatever sort of constraints, these stand out as important contributions.

Implications

It has been a long journey from formulating the questions that guide this book to arriving at answers to them. But, for the patient, answers have been proffered. What are the implications of this endeavor? Several general implications come immediately to mind. The first takes the form of an admonition to those who study the impact of groups in the larger political process. The analysis in this book makes clear that our knowledge of the effects of minority status on the behavior of minority and majority members of political bodies must be rethought and expanded. Questions still remain about whether conformity pressures, for example, are felt and responded to in the same way by other groups within the political arena. The combination of obstacles and opportunities faced by various minority groups is likely to differ; therefore, each may conform or deviate in different ways or in response to different pressures. Further, each group will likely develop different goals and seek out unique ways to respond to the process.

Until we have explicated and analyzed these types of questions, the general theories of legislative behavior we develop will provide insufficient understanding of legislative and political life. The big picture will be a distorted one, and comprehension of the variation that underlies the generalities will be limited. In short, our knowledge of the legislative arena will remain incomplete and will, in certain instances, be inaccurate.

Social scientists, however, are not interested only in accurate description or explanation. We seek accurate predictions of the future, and as citizens and participants in the political world, we want to contribute to debates about what the future should look like. If attention is not paid to minorities within politically elite majorities, we risk missing the trends that lead to the future. Groups that are now small, but destined to be large portions of political bodies in time, will play a significant role in determining the shape and content of the future. How can we credibly assert a clear-eyed vision if we continue to ignore crucial aspects of the present?

On a separate level, the results of the inquiries pursued in this book speak to the issue of how well we are represented. Unless views of what are proper topics for the governmental sphere continue to be broadened to include diverse concerns rather than just mainstream or majority concerns and unless topics that have heretofore been ignored, never considered, or considered but not deemed important continue to be introduced into the public arena, our society will have achieved only partial representation. This leaves our system vulnerable to charges of illegitimacy and elitism. Similar problems arise when all groups in society are not mirrored in its governing bodies. In other, perhaps more elegant words: "Is democracy workable if a majority of American citizens (women) lack an equal opportunity to participate in the governmental decision-making process? The answer must be no."[17] On the other hand, providing broad-based representativeness preserves the elasticity and legitimacy essential to a stable political system.

Finally, exploring legislative behavior from the perspective of those outside the dominant group allows us to perceive much more clearly the values that underlie our system. As James March and John Olsen point out:

> Political democracy depends not only on economic and social conditions but also on the design of political institutions. Bureaucratic agencies, legislative committees, and appellate courts are arenas for contending social forces, but they are also collections of standard operating procedures and structures that define and defend values, norms, interests, identities, and beliefs.[18]

Not only may we better identify these values, norms, interests, identities, and beliefs, bringing them to the forefront provides an opportunity to reconsider whether they are the ones we most desire.

7

Predictions for the Future

In the summer of 1985, a lower-court judge in western Montana made a bit of political history by swapping her gavel for a seat on a county board of commissioners. With that, Missoula County, as well as can be determined, became the first county in the nation to be run by women. Nearly three years later, a question forms: Is this nothing but an interesting bit of trivia, or is there a fundamental difference in the way three women govern? There is some disagreement on the answer, but the three commissioners, as well as most who have watched their performance closely, say gender has made a difference.[1]

Missoula was the first county board composed solely of women, but it was not to be the last. In 1986, the five-member Multnomah County (Oregon) Board of Supervisors became the second all-female board in the nation. Situations like these two, in which women are not just tokens in a male-dominated political group, are among the few opportunities to see how having women in charge affects the range of goals pursued by women representatives. Although it is risky to draw conclusions from just one or two cases, these experiences cannot be ignored. And the experiences suggest that more than anything else, when they have the opportunity, women do conduct governmental business in new ways. In fact, almost everyone involved in Missoula County government is convinced of this fact.

The commissioners of Missoula report that they work together very well and that they have settled any disagreements and differences in perception by confronting them head-on, rather than avoiding conflict. This is possible, said Commissioner Janet Stevens, because "society has traditionally permitted women to express themselves in a broader range of emotions." Commissioner Ann Mary Dussault added "[T]he women she [Dussault] knows in office tend to be more directed toward the job at hand than toward the next rung up the ladder." Consequently, she noted, "it's easier to trust the motivations of female colleagues."[2] Given the ideological diversity on the Missoula board (one conservative Republican, one liberal Democrat who also describes herself as a feminist, and one moderate Democrat), this feat is even more noteworthy.

The same qualities that allow Missoula's commissioners to bridge their differences and find ways to work together help them bring the concerns and needs of the community to their decision making. A good example concerns action to reduce pollution from wood-burning stoves by linking lower-income people to a human service agency to obtain grants to pay for heat. Because previous boards had not bothered to uncover the source of strong opposition to alternative heating sources by the county's lower-income population, they lost the opportunity to take steps to solve the problem. Says Commissioner Dussault: "I think that women, regardless of whether they are in council positions or legislative positions, do bring that nurturing and, in a lot of cases, a far less aggressive or combative style to the position." Further, "We can attempt to do the old traditional thing, which was to ram this down their throats, or we can take a different tack. What we decided to do is to take the different tack, which was to empower them."[3] The alternative style engaged in by the women leads, as implied in that statement, to approaching problems from a different perspective. Hence, women's contribution to policy went beyond introducing new issues to the agent, to include new ways of formulating policy.

If women do bring a different style to governing and if they do tend to promote different programs to meet constituents' needs, what of the overall quality of the job they do? Does it measure up to the job done by all male predecessors, is it equal to that of previous boards, or does it surpass them? The majority of opinion in Missoula has been that the board has done an excellent job. Said the male president of the Chamber of Commerce: "This is the most well-reasoned, stable, trustworthy body I have dealt with in 10 years of chamber management in three states."[4]

The success and innovations of the women of Missoula County and the positive reception they have been accorded has not, however, erased stereotypical notions of women's capabilities from the minds of all the county's political actors. Says Commissioner Ann Mary Dussault, "In order to be perceived as successful you have to be twice as good and twice as smart, and I think most women in politics know that. . . . In some cases, the sexism was extraordinarily overt. The classic example of someone who thought he could bludgeon his way through was the sheriff. He thought he could put on a uniform, play macho, and walk in and get anything he wanted."[5] Says Commissioner Stevens: "The only time I resented people's reactions was when they treated us like we were a bunch of girls and dimwitted ninnies.''[6]

The successes, obstacles, priorities, and approaches to governing tasks of the women of the Missoula County Board of Supervisors spur a host of questions about future political configurations. For instance, when women reach parity or above in governing bodies across the country, will the trends cataloged throughout this book continue? That is, as women politicians achieve individual and group-based goals of bringing more women in public office, will they permanently alter legislative business and the way it is conducted? The Missoula County board may signal what will happen in the future. But what else is possible, and what is likely? After all, as the following quotation illustrates, our expectations may not always manifest themselves in the expected fashion.

> On a trip to London a few years ago, I was told the following story. A parliamentarian overheard two children playing "grownup." The little boy turned to the little girl and said, "I want to be prime minister." The little girl responded, "You can't, you're a boy."[7]

Portraits of Possibilities

As we draw on the history of women in politics, on the expectations of their political behavior and contributions, and, most important, on empirical evidence of their beliefs and actions, several plausible scenarios envisioning the collective future of female politicians emerge. The first possible scenario is that the future of women politicians will look much like the experiences of the women of Missoula. Governing bodies will become increasingly populated with women, and female representatives will use their ever-increasing clout, experience, and confidence to construct a new political reality—one in which new approaches to the problem solving will predominate. Women will bring their distinctive life experiences and perspectives to bear on the challenge confronting government and reach out for new, more inclusive solutions. They will explore problems from the ground up, not the top down (as in the pollution example in Missoula). In short, the changes women representatives have already brought to public policy in legislatures across the states—a broadening of the governmental agenda will be accompanied by a new way of tackling a wide range of issues.

A variant of this scenario would be a political world in which women's more inclusive governmental agenda and new ways of doing business restructure general norms of political action. As women and men equally embrace the values, structures, and procedures of which women politicians now simply dream, female representatives will no longer be the prime movers of legislation dealing with women, and children and the family. Female representatives will not be the only ones looking at legislation in the contextualist sense;[8] men will too. Additionally, men and women alike will respond to the process in a less competitive, zero-sum fashion: the incentive structure of legislatures will lure both sexes into new procedural patterns. In other words, the feminist transformation that many have long desired and continue to support will best describe the future.

This scenario is not intended to reflect an idyllic or utopian vision of tomorrow. I am by no means asserting that the problems and obstacles that face us would disappear if women legislators brought this sort of change to the political arena. Rather, the "feminist transformation" in politics would mean that women would be fully accepted in all public sphere roles and use their numbers and distinctive perspectives to broaden governmental agendas and bring changes to the way govenment's objectives are pursued. When such overhaul is accomplished, men will have incentives to reformulate their own tactics, stategies, and goals.

What if a feminist transformation doesn't come about? There is little doubt that as time goes on, women will increase their numbers in public sphere occupations, including politics. However, some prognosticators assert that the more involved women get in politics, the more they inhabit all types of positions, and the more they become insiders in the system rather than newcomers to it, the more they will recognize that the rules are the rules because little else is possible. Politics still is, as former governor of Vermont Madeleine Kunin argues, a zero-sum game. No amount of desire to be more consensus-oriented or inclusive will change that fact. Women politicians can theorize and dream about a different way of working in the political arena, but when it comes right down to it, power is power, and those that have it exercise it to get what they want. Women will be no different, or they will not long share its reins with men.

Further, women politicians will ultimately have an answer to the same constituencies men do if they want to stay in power. An outcome between these two extremes is also possible. The near future may look almost precisely like the most up-to-date evidence we have. In the next ten years (or twenty or thirty) women politicians, while increasing their numbers in most places, may still hold relatively little power and have relatively little ability to convince their male colleagues that the change is viable and appropriate. The role of women in the public sphere is still in transition, and that transition may take a good deal longer than many desire. If this turns out to be the case, something like the recent pattern will continue. Women legislators will continue to expand governmental agendas and make sure that matters of the private sphere that were once left out are now included, but while the topics of legislative attention will be altered to some degree, the process itself will remain relatively static.

The Most Likely Scenario

Throughout this book, I have expressed distaste for discrete, reductionist categories in the analysis of political behavior. Consistent with that proclivity, my predictions for the future reflect elements of several of these scenarios. To begin, the actions that women are likely to take are primarily related to their proportions in governing bodies. If the past is any guide, the proportions of women in legislatures will increase steadily but incrementally. It is also quite likely that the increments will be greater than they have been before. After fifteen to twenty years of getting acclimated to women running for office, winning office, and performing effectively once in office, society will become increasingly comfortable with expanding their numbers.

It is also probable that at certain times, the proportions of women in legislatures will increase in substantial spurts. As noted above, the 1992 elections proved to be an example of such sudden growth on the federal level. Dubbed by many the "Year of the Woman," in 1992 large numbers of female candidates ran in and won races for the U.S. House of Representatives and the U.S. Senate. This spurt can be attributed to many factors, including decennial and minority redistricting, a record number of retirements from the House of Representatives, the House bank and post office scandals, and a strong desire on the part of the electorate for a change in personnel and politics as usual. Women were able to capitalize on this situation because their twenty-year history of incremental ascent up the ladders of local and state politics positioned them for effective federal candidacies. Additionally, as relative newcomers to politics and as a group with a strong reputation for honesty and integrity on the one hand, and expertise on many domestic issues on the other, women were looked upon to initiate reform. Whether or not circumstances conspire in the near future to create growth spurts on each level of government, steady future increases in the proportions of women in legislative bodies are inevitable.

With the number of women in governing bodies rising, the changes they desire will have an ever-greater chance of becoming reality. However, the threshold for change will be different depending on whether we are examining policy goals or procedural ones, group-based or individual goals. With respect to policy, women legislators have already achieved a great deal of success in bringing their distinctive concerns to legislative agendas and making sure these concerns have been ushered through successfully. There is no question that the blueprints for action have been altered rather dramatically since women arrived in legislatures in greater numbers. Yet, in very few places (only those with formal legislative caucuses or very high numbers of women) have those concerns begun to permeate general legislative environments. This will change, I predict, when women regularly represent at least 35 to 40 percent of any given legislature. Since male representatives already supply votes for the passage of bills dealing with women, and children and families, it stands to reason that when women legislators come close to parity in representation, their efforts to educate, support, and influence male colleagues will find a far more receptive audience.[9]

One preliminary indicator that this hypothesis is reasonable is a study Susan Carroll and Ella Taylor of women in U.S. statehouses. These authors explored the extent to which female representatives champion legislation to help women. Consistent with my findings, they discovered that women were much more likely than men to make a priority of legislation of this sort. They also discovered that in statehouses in which women constituted at least 25 percent of legislators, about 65 percent of the women representatives worked on legislation to help women. However, in statehouses in which women represented 25 percent or more of the representatives, only about 40 percent of the women worked on such legislation. The authors go on to say, "These findings suggest the possibility that there may be a critical point somewhere near the 25% mark where women become such a sizable minority that individual women legislators no longer feel as strong a personal responsibility to represent women as they do when women are a smaller minority."[10] This is likely true, in part, because more men have embraced these types of issues.

Whether the critical point for making a priority of legislation to help women is indeed about 25 percent or whether that percentage varies over time and location, the concept that greater percentages of women legislators will lead to a diffusion of their perspectives throughout the governing bodies is sound. And the issues of special concern to female representatives, those dealing with women, and children and families, will permeate legislative bodies as women's representation is closer to parity.

Procedural transformations will not follow the same path or be as likely to occur at near-parity levels as will policy alteration. Achieving 35 to 40 percent representation in legislatures will not change the situation much from what women face today. This is especially true if women are not routinely members of leadership teams and thus holding positions of power and respect. Unless and until women at least reach parity with men in governing bodies, numerically and in terms of leadership positions, there will be only small movements toward a new vision of procedural conduct. The immediate future will then look very much like the present, with women desiring change and taking small steps toward it but holding back from full-scale attempts to transform the environment. A lack of conducive circumstances or necessary opportunities will be the primary reason for this stasis.

As the proportion of women in governing bodies increases, the progress women have already made toward individual and group goals will be nearly complete. Female representatives effectively meet the needs of their constituents through service and legislative action, contribute significantly and meaningfully to policy debates, earn respect from their colleagues, and master the legislative process. As their numbers increase further, individual goals related to higher ambition will accelerate and legislative leadership will, more often, become the realm of women.

Group-based goals of bringing more women to office will, by definition, be furthered. Reducing overt and covert discrimination toward women will, however, be a slower, rockier path on which to tread—one that might, in certain ways, get worse before it gets better. The reason for probable slower progress on reduction of discrimination is that as women's numbers increase and as they begin to win more leadership positions, the men who have held central positions and power and who believed they would do so despite the influx of some women will likely react strongly to the challenge to their ascendancy. It would be naive to believe that no backlash, no struggle to maintain power will ensue. That this will occur is certain; what is also certain is that with time, women will overcome resistance and take their rightful place beside men in the public arena.

In sum, the path I envision is a gradual but steady progression toward the very things on which women are already working. I predict neither total transformation nor total submission to the status quo. In a sense, my forecast will disappoint both extremes of the ideological spectrum. I will first address those who believe that women will simply end up reflecting the status quo—that power is power no matter who holds it and that women will, in their time, discover this. Clearly women's action in legislatures already contradict this view. Steps taken by female politicians have ineluctably altered the status quo. Although the changes that have occurred are subject to further alteration, and, no doubt, the future will not be simply a linear progression of the present, one element of an equation cannot be altered without affecting its results. Ultimately, it makes little sense to suppose that bringing any new group to an existing institution or existing human endeavor will not substantially alter its gestalt.

I have also rejected the feminist view of complete transformation. No subgroup of political elites has a vision so strong and an influence so powerful that its will can be imposed on people and institutions unaltered. The status quo assumption is that the existing system is so resistant to change that bringing new groups to its door will not substantially alter its basic foundations. The transformation assumption is that institutions and groups are sufficiently malleable that they will swallow a vision wholesale without modification. Each of these suppositions are narrow and neglect the multivariate realities of human nature, social interaction, and the nature of institutions that support both. What will occur in the future will reflect an interaction between the various visions of preferred reality and will almost certainly reflect a hybrid of them. This is precisely why I have suggested that the elements that constitute the political future are separated and examined independently of each other. This is also why I have steered a course of moderation between the two extremes. Anne Phillips's comments about the power of feminist theory to transform democracy express a parallel sentiment.

> [W]e cannot presume in advance that these [the implications of feminism on democracy] will transform the very foundations of debate. The scale and ambition of contemporary feminist argument recall similar arguments made on behalf of the proletariat, whose emergence in the course of the nineteenth century likewise provided the grounds for escalating claims. . . . The history of Marxism warns against over-vaulting ambition and conveys an uncomfortable message to those who make too grandiose a claim. So while I believe that feminism, for its part, does revolutionize previous thinking, I think the success of that revolution can be hindered by arguments that go over the top.[11]

A Cautionary Word about Tactics

Whatever scenario of the future is correct, and whether or not the one I think is most likely does indeed transpire, it is important for women politicians, as they move toward achievement of each of their goals, to keep in mind the potential obstacles in their paths. Because women continue to be seen as outside the "normal" political configuration, their distinctive skills and interests are seen as precluding other important political necessities, most notably those that have dominated legislative politics to this point.[12]

Sometimes that perceived lack may not hinder women; indeed, it can occasionally be a bonus—witness the federal elections of 1992. Because voters have been extremely disillusioned with politics as usual, they looked to outsiders to fix a broken system. Among those considered to be attractive outsiders have been women—whether or not they held political office in the past. Perhaps because it is clear to everyone that women do not hold the reins of power, they are seen as not responsible for the mess and able to reverse its downward progression. There was extra emphasis on the attractiveness of female candidates this past election year because of our historical situation in the post–Cold War world. Now that threats from the former Soviet Union are, if not nonexistent, greatly diminished, the country sought to turn inward to improve the lives of those battered by the economic decline, to right our wrongs, to heal our national soul. As a group focused on domestic issues like education, health, welfare, and family life, and as people perceived as nurturers, women candidates were looked to as those having the most ability and greatest likelihood of improving the lives of average Americans.

The downside of gaining office based only on distinctive issue expertise or as outsiders is that when conditions change, women may once again be consigned to a lesser role. For example, once a dramatic and controversial foreign policy issue moves to the front burner, women may be assumed less able to cope than men. This not only limits women's credibility to certain areas at the expense of others, it also limits the sorts of political jobs for which they will be considered serious contenders. One of the first things 1984 vice presidential candidate Geraldine Ferraro had to face when she accepted the invitation to join Walter Mondale's ticket was the never-ending set of questions concerning her fitness to handle foreign policy problems. Even though women benefited in this most recent election cycle, the long-term ramifications of a pigeonholing strategy are clear.

The reasons women have either packaged their candidacies on the same basis as men or sought to emphasize collective distinctiveness in the form of issue priorities or outsider status are understandable. Simply put, women politicians are between a rock and a hard place. If they reject and fight against depictions that women's skills and knowledge are superior to men's on certain issues, they will lose the advantage of support from an electorate that, at least at the moment, wants people in office with those qualities. On the other hand, if female candidates play to those expectations, they risk limiting their current and future political input to those areas.[13]

When the situation is viewed from this either-or perspective, it is difficult to find the ideal long-term strategy to increase the numbers of women in political office. There are bound to be disagreements among those seeking this goal. Not unlike the political battles waged by those fighting for political rights of women throughout our history, some strategists will opt to portray women as no different from men, and others, with a variety of justifications, will highlight their differences from them. Just as the forces of suffragists split over strategy, and just as alliances have shifted as the political winds and women's fortunes have changed, the debate will be long lasting and vigorous. It can only be won, however, by those who learn the lessons of history and search for approaches that transcend the narrow configurations of old battles. It may well be time to acknowledge that the true portrait of women politicians is multilayered. The broadest view shows them to be interested and active in the full range of legislative issues and activities and competent across the board. A closer view shows that women representatives generally focus special attention on underrepresented issues and will likely continue to do so until such issues are accorded attention by all groups of legislators. It is also true that, more often than not, female officeholders share a vision of the future that includes both a procedural transformation and an alternative view of policy formulation. Only when the public is given the opportunity to promote women based on their individual strengths and weaknesses and their evolving collective proclivities will they be true equals in the political world.

Notes

Introduction

1. Sociologist Margaret L. Anderson, in her comments about the work of another feminist scholar, warns of the dangers of excluding knowledge about all facets of a subject, a group, an organization, or a discipline: "Minnich writes about the fundamental conceptual errors brought about by taking a particular few to be 'simultaneously the inclusive term, the norm, and the ideal.' Knowledge that ignores gender—both as a subject of study and as a process influencing the construction of knowledge—is exclusionary, and therefore, leads to distortion and mystification." Margaret L. Anderson, "From the Editor," *Gender and Society* 6 (June 1992): 165. In this introduction to the June 1992 issue of *Gender and Society,* editor Anderson is commenting of the work of Elizabeth Kamarck Minnich, *Transforming Knowledge* (Philadelphia: Temple University Press, 1990).

2. For information on the gender gap, the following may be helpful: Sandra Baxter and Marjorie Lansing, *Women and Politics: The Invisible Majority* (Ann Arbor: University of Michigan Press, 1980); Carol M. Mueller, ed., *The Politics of the Gender Gap: The Social Construction of Political Influence* (Newbury Park, Calif.: Sage, 1988); Pamela Johnston Conover, "Feminism and the Gender Gap," *Journal of Politics* 50, no. 4 (1988): 985–1010; and Elizabeth Adell Cook and Clyde Wilcox, "Feminism and the Gender Gap—A Second Look," *Journal of Politics* 54 (November 1991): 1112–1122. For information on women's political participation and its motivations, see Kristi Andersen, "Working Women and Political Participation, 1952–1972," *American Journal of Political Science* 19 (August 1975): 439–453; Karen Beckwith, *American Women and Political Participation: The Impacts of Work, Generation, and Feminism* (New York: Greenwood Press, 1986); Pamela Johnston Conover, "The Influence of Group Identifications of Political Perceptions and Evaluations," *Journal of Politics* 46 (August 1984): 760–785; Pamela Johnston Conover, "Group Identification and Group Sympathy: Their Political Implications" (Paper presented at the annual meeting of the Midwest Political Science

Association, Chicago, April 10–12, 1986); Patricia Gurin, "Women's Gender Consciousness," *Public Opinion Quarterly* 49 (Summer 1985): 143–163; Ethel Klein, *Gender Politics: From Consciousness to Mass Politics* (Cambridge: Harvard University Press, 1984); Virgina Sapiro, *The Political Integration of Women: Roles, Socialization and Politics* (Urbana: University of Illinois Press, 1983); and Sue Tolleson Rinehart, *Gender Consciousness and Politics* (New York: Routledge, Chapman and Hall, 1992).

3. The literature on women's candidacies is substantial. Readers may wish to consult Susan J. Carroll, *Women as Candidates in American Politics* (Bloomington: Indiana University Press, 1985); R. Darcy, Susan Welch and Janet Clark, *Women, Elections, and Representation* (New York: Longman, 1987); Barbara C. Burrell, "Women's Candidacies and the Role of Gender in Open Seat Primaries for the U.S. House of Representatives, 1968–1990" (Paper presented at the annual meeting of the Midwest Political Science Association, Chicago, April 18–20, 1991); Charles Bullock and Susan MacManus, "Municipal Electoral Structure and the Election of Councilwomen," *Journal of Politics* 53 (February 1991): 75–89; Lois L. Duke, "Paying Their Dues: Women as Candidates In the U.S. House of Representatives" (Paper presented at the annual meeting of the American Political Science Association, Chicago, September 3–6, 1987). Diane L. Fowlkes, "Women in Georgia Electoral Politics: 1970–1978," Fowlkes *Social Science Journal* 21 (January 1984): 43–55; Lois L. Duke, *Women in Politics: Outsiders or Insiders?* (Englewood Cliffs, N.J.: Prentice-Hall, 1993); Gary F. Moncrief and Joel A. Thompson, "Electoral Structure and State Legislative Representation: A Research Note," *Journal of Politics* 54 (February 1992): 246–256.

Chapter 1

1. It is true that the typology may also be thought of as two continua of behaviors rather than behaviors falling within discrete categories. I rely on the typology usage for ease and clarity of explanation. It is, in this sense, a heuristic device.

2. Barbara Ehrenreich, "Sorry, Sister, This Is Not the Revolution," *Time Magazine Special Issue, Women: The Road Ahead* 136 (Fall 1990): 15.

3. Gloria Steinem as quoted in Ehrenreich, "Sorry, Sister," 15.

4. Rebecca E. Klatch, *Women of the New Right* (Philadelphia: Temple University Press, 1987).

5. Elizabeth H. Wolgast, *The Grammar of Justice* (Ithaca, N.Y.: Cornell University Press, 1987).

6. See Rosemarie Tong, *Feminist Thought: A Comprehensive Introduction* (Boulder: Westview Press, 1989).

7. Mary Lou Kendrigan, "Introduction: An Understanding of Equality: The Public Policy Consequences" (Paper presented at the annual meeting of the American Political Science Association, Chicago, September 3–6, 1987; hereafter, "Understanding of Equality").

8. The states were Arizona, California, Georgia, Illinois, Iowa, Mississippi, Nebraska, North Carolina, Pennsylvania, South Dakota, Vermont, and Washington. Information about why these states were chosen and other aspects of research design and execution are included in Chapter 3.

9. "Verbatim: Women in the Foreign Service," *Washington Post,* May 26, 1992.

10. Eleanor Clift with Debra Rosenberg, "First Lady Culture Clash," *Newsweek,* June 8, 1992, 24.

11. Although there clearly needs to be some collective agreement about the merit of those proposals if they are to become law. This, however, is a separate issue.

12. Martha Minow, "Feminist Reason: Getting It and Losing It," *Journal of Legal Education* 38 (March/June 1988): 48.

13. Richard M. Battistoni, "Feminist Voices, Equality, and the U.S. Constitution" (Paper presented at the annual meeting of the American Political Science Association, Washington, D.C., September 1–4, 1988).

14. *Bradwell v. Illinois,* 83 U.S. 130 (1873).

15. *Minor v. Happersett,* 88 U.S. 627 (1875).

16. *Muller v. Oregon,* 208 U.S. 412 (1908).

17. *Goesart v. Cleary,* 335 U.S. 464 (1948).

18. *Hoyt v. Florida,* 368 U.S. 57 (1961).

19. Ibid.

20. Not all cases from 1971 on have resulted in the equal treatment of women and men. There have been some exceptions such as definitions of statutory rape (*Michael M. v. Superior Court of Sonoma County,* 450 U.S. 464 [1981]), and the decision to prevent women in the military from being assigned to combat duty (*Roskter v. Goldberg,* 453 U.S. 57, 101 S. Ct. 2646 [1981]).

21. Susan Welch et al., *American Government.* 3d ed. (Saint Paul, Minn.: West, 1990).

22. *Reed v. Reed,* 404 U.S. 71 (1971).

23. *General Electric Co. v. Gilbert,* 429 U.S. 125 (1976).

24. Minow, "Feminist Reason," 53.

25. Since this time, the United States Supreme Court has grappled with whether pregnant women ought to get preferential treatment compared with disabled male workers or whether they ought to be treated exactly equally because the policy of nondiscrimination advocated by the Pregnancy Discrimination Act did not solve all of women's pregnancy-related employment problems. Over the course of several decisions, the Court has still not set a consistent policy. Cases including the 1987 decision in *California Federal Savings and Loan v. Guerra,* 479 U.S. 272 (1987), and the 1987 decision in *Miller-Wohl Company v. Commissioner of Labor and Industry,* 479 U.S. (1987), suggest that the Court has had difficulty making a determinative decision, in part, because legislators across the United States have not done so, nor have women activists themselves. See Susan Gluck Mezey, *In*

Pursuit of Equality: Women, Public Policy, and the Federal Courts (New York: St. Martin's Press, 1992), 115–132.

26. See Eleanor Flexner, *Century of Struggle: The Woman's Rights Movement in the United States,* rev. ed. (Cambridge, Mass.: Belknap Press, 1980), and Christie Farnham, ed., *The Impact of Feminist Research in the Academy* (Bloomington: Indiana University Press, 1987).

27. "Constitutional Argument" by Susan B. Anthony, 1873, in Sheila Ruth, *Issues in Feminism: An Introduction to Women's Studies* (Mountain View, Calif.: Mayfield, 1990), 472.

28. See Emily Stoper and Roberta Ann Johnson, "The Weaker Sex and the Better Half: The Idea of Women's Moral Superiority in the American Feminist Movement," *Polity* 10 (Winter 1977): 192–217; Carol M. Mueller, "The Empowerment of Women: Polling and the Women's Voting Bloc," in Mueller, *Politics of the Gender Gap,* Anne N. Costain, "Women's Claims as a Special Interest," in Mueller, *Politics of the Gender Gap,* and Deborah L. Rhode, "The Woman's Point of View," *Journal of Legal Education* 38 (March/June 1988): 39–46.

29. McDonagh's work on legislative support for suffrage found that such votes were correlated with support for social justice, not issues such as temperance. Eileen Lorenzi McDonagh, "The Significance of the Nineteenth Amendment: A New Look at Civil Rights, Social Welfare, and Woman Suffrage Alignments in the Progressive Era," *Women & Politics* 10 (1990): 59–74.

30. Sara M. Evans, *Born for Liberty: A History of Women in America* (New York: Free Press, 1989), 154.

31. As quoted in Susan Cary Nicholas, Alice M. Price, and Rachel Rubin, *Rights and Wrongs: Women's Struggle for Legal Equality,* 2d ed. (New York: Feminist Press, 1986), 12.

32. See Flexner, *Century of Struggle*; Barbara Sinclair Deckard, *The Women's Movement* (New York: Harper and Row, 1975); Farnham, *Impact of Feminist Research;* and Carol M. Mueller, "Nurturance and Mastery: Competing Qualifications for Women's Access to High Public Office," in Gwen Moore and Glenna Spitze, eds., *Women and Politics: Activism, Attitudes, and Officeholding,* Research in Politics and Society, vol. 2 (Greenwich, Conn.: JAI Press, 1986).

33. Quoted in Flexner, *Century of Struggle,* 151.

34. See Kristen Luker, *Motherhood and the Politics of Abortion* (Berkeley and Los Angeles: University of California Press, 1984), and Klatch, *Women of the New Right.*

35. As quoted in Klatch, *Women of the New Right,* 145.

36. See Flexner, *Century of Struggle;* Farnham, *Impact of Feminist Research;* and Costain, "Women's Claims as a Special Interest."

37. See Simone de Beauvoir, *The Second Sex* (original ed., New York: Knopf, 1952, reprint ed., Random House, 1974); David L. Kirp, Mark G. Yudof, and Marlene Strong Franks, *Gender Justice* (Chicago: University of Chicago Press, 1986); Norma Basch, "Equality of Rights and Feminist Politics," *Law and Society*

Review 21 (1988): 783–787; and Trudy Steuernagel, "American Feminism and the Fear of Difference" (Paper presented at the annual meeting of the American Political Science Association, Washington, D.C., September 2–4, 1988).

38. Kendrigan, "Understanding of Equality."

39. Christine Di Stefano, "Postmodernism/Postfeminism?: The Case of the Incredible Shrinking Woman" (Paper presented at the annual meeting of the American Political Science Association, Chicago, September 3–6, 1987); Janet Sayers, *Biological Politics* (London: Tavistock, 1982); and Vicky Randall, *Women and Politics* (London: Macmillan, 1982).

40. As quoted in Carol Anne Douglas, *Love and Politics: Radical Feminist and Lesbian Theories* (San Francisco: ism press, 1990), 261.

41. See Dorothy McBride Stetson, "Work and Family in Comparative Perspective: Parental Leave in France and the United States" (Paper presented at the annual meeting of the American Political Science Association, Washington, D.C., September 1–4, 1988); and Elizabeth Holtzman and Shirley Williams, "Women in the Political World: Observations," *Daedalus* 116 (Fall 1987): 199–210. In addition, not all feminists advocate reforms to the existing system. Some denounce "liberal feminists" for allowing fundamental subordination of women to continue by just tinkering with policy at the margins. Such critics consist of Marxist feminists and socialist feminists, both of whom advocate a change in the underlying economic system that they see as intrinsic to women's lesser status. See Alison M. Jaggar, *Feminist Politics and Human Nature* (reprint, Totowa, N.J.: Rowman and Littlefield Publishers, 1988); and Tong, *Feminist Thought,* 1989, 1st publication 1983 by Harvester Press Limited.

42. See Carl N. Degler, "On Rereading 'The Woman in America,'" *Daedalus* 116 (Fall 1987): 199–210.

43. Minow, "Feminist Reason," 49.

44. The 1990 elections were, for a time, also touted as the year of the woman. Voters were said to have tired of the posturing and avoiding employed by men and of the few solutions to pressing problems being implemented. With the nation mired in months of fruitless budget politics, savings and loan scandals, and an impending recession, columnist after columnist wrote that voters saw women as more honest, more forthright, and better problem solvers. Pundits looked to women to win big. The pundits, however, did not count on U.S. involvement in the Persian Gulf. Once our attention was directed toward Saudi Arabia, Kuwait, and Iraq, other issues temporarily faded from view, and politics as usual won the day. Commentators no longer even discussed how women's bid for office would affect the political landscape.

Chapter 2

1. Sigrídur Dúna Kristmundsdóttir as quoted in Joanne Edgar, "Iceland's Feminists: Power at the Top of the World," *Ms.,* December 1987, 32.

2. Ibid., 3.

3. Joanne Edgar, "Political Miracle in Iceland?" *Ms.*, August 1988, 32.

4. For those interested in variables correlated with the presence or absence of women in legislatures, see Albert J. Nelson, *Emerging Influentials in State Legislatures: Women, Blacks, and Hispanics* (New York: Praeger, 1991).

5. Women legislators are compared with their male colleagues throughout this book for one overriding reason: we cannot tell whether they work toward changing standard modes of operation or whether they bring new policies to the legislative arena unless we determine what the status quo looks like. For our purposes, the collective attitudes and behaviors of male legislators constitute the status quo.

6. Irene Diamond, *Sex Roles in the State House* (New Haven: Yale University Press, 1977), 37.

7. Ibid.

8. Diamond, *Sex Roles,* 38.

9. Ibid.

10. See Jeane Kirkpatrick, *Political Woman* (New York: Basic Books, 1974).

11. See Diamond, *Sex Roles.*

12. See Marilyn Johnson et al., *Profile of Women Holding Office II* (New Brunswick, N.J.: Center for the American Woman and Politics, 1978).

13. Ibid.

14. Kirkpatrick, *Political Woman,* 163.

15. See Johnson et al., *Profile of Women.* Also note that in one study, Kirkpatrick's, she finds that the majority of women in her survey consider themselves effective legislators. However, Kirkpatrick asked no questions that compared women with men, so these findings do not help us evaluate relative levels of effectiveness.

16. Quoted in Diamond, *Sex Roles,* 99.

17. Ibid.

18. Quoted in Kirkpatrick, *Political Woman,* 160.

19. For a fuller discussion of this point, see Madeleine Kunin, "Lessons from One Woman's Career," *Journal of State Government* 60 (September/October 1987): 209–212.

20. Johnson et al., *Profile of Women.*

21. Diamond, *Sex Roles,* 89–90.

22. Kirkpatrick, *Political Woman,* 133.

23. Kirkpatrick, *Political Woman;* Diamond, *Sex Roles;* Johnson et al., *Profile of Women.*

24. Johnson et al., *Profile of Women.*

25. Ibid.

26. Eleanor C. Main, Gerard S. Gryski, and Beth Schapiro, "Different Perspectives: Southern State Legislators' Attitudes About Women in Politics," *Social Science Journal* 21 (January 1984): 21–28.

27. Diamond, *Sex Roles,* 105.

28. Diamond, *Sex Roles;* Denise Antolini, "Women in Local Government: An Overview," in Janet A. Flammang, ed., *Political Women: Current Roles in State and Local Government,* Sage Yearbooks in Women's Policy Studies, vol 8 (Beverly Hills: Sage, 1984), 23–40; Janet A. Flammang, "Female Officials in the Feminist Capital: The Case of Santa Clara County," *Western Political Quarterly* 38 (March 1985): 94–118; Debra W. Stewart, ed., *Women in Local Politics* (Metuchen, N.J.: Scarecrow Press, 1980); and Sharyne Merritt, "Sex Differences in Role Behavior and Policy Orientations of Suburban Officeholders: The Effect of Women's Employment," in Stewart, *Women in Local Politics,* 115–129.

29. Sue Thomas, "The Effects of Race and Gender on Constituency Service," *Western Political Quarterly* 45 (March 1992): 169–180.

30. These findings are statistically significant. Further, when demographic and other controls were applied, the relationships remained significant at the .05 level.

31. Kirkpatrick, *Political Woman;* Diamond, *Sex Roles.*

32. Diamond, *Sex Roles;* Johnson et al., *Profile of Women.*

33. Ehrenreich, "Sorry, Sister," 15.

34. Sara E. Rix, ed., *The American Woman, 1987–88 A Report in Depth* (New York: W. W. Norton, 1987), 241.

35. Ibid., 279.

36. Ibid., 279–280.

37. Ibid., 281–282.

38. Rebecca Tillet and Debbie Krafchek, eds., "Factsheet on Women's Political Progress," (Washington, D.C.: American Council of Life Insurance and National Women's Political Caucus, June 1991); and Virginia Sapiro, *Women, Political Action, and Political Participation* (Washington, D.C.: American Political Science Association, 1988).

39. Center for the American Woman and Politics, 1991 Fact Sheet.

40. See Diane Gillespie and Cassia Spohn, "Adolescents' Attitudes toward Women in Politics: A Follow-up Study, *Women & Politics* 10 (1990): 1–16.

41. The original material presented in this chapter and the next has appeared in a different form in Sue Thomas and Susan Welch, "The Impact of Gender on Activities and Priorities of State Legislators," *Western Political Quarterly* 44 (June 1991): 445–456; and Susan Welch and Sue Thomas, "Do Women in Public Office Make a Difference?" in Debra L. Dodson, ed., *Gender and Policymaking: Studies of Women in Office* (New Brunswick, N.J.: Center for the American Woman and Politics, 1991, 13–20.

42. Diversity in political culture was a major criterion for selection, with chosen states representing major political cultures. Political culture is a concept used by political scientists to explain how states differ in terms of predominant political, social, and cultural influences. The study was designed to incorporate all three major political cultures because the women and men surveyed in the states may feel differently about the political world or may have a different impact on the system depending on which culture they inhabit. Daniel Elazar, the political scientist

famous for tracing the political cultures of all fifty states, identifies three major cultures. These are the traditionalistic, the moralistic, and the individualistic. For a fuller description, see Daniel J. Elazar, *American Federalism: A View from the States,* 3d ed. (New York: Harper and Row, 1984).

43. Nebraska is the only state in the nation with a one-house legislature, the Unicameral. Lower houses were chosen because, on average, more women hold these offices than upper house-positions.

44. The response rate for each state was as follows:

State	%
Arizona:	59
California:	43
Georgia:	53
Illinois:	48
Iowa:	57
Mississippi:	22
Nebraska:	64
North Carolina:	53
Pennsylvania:	40
South Dakota	52
Vermont	49
Washington:	78

45. Gender-based differences in response rates were as follows:

	Male (%)	Female (%)
Arizona:	62	53
California:	37	58
Georgia:	43	65
Illinois:	37	65
Iowa:	38	89
Mississippi:	18	50
Nebraska:	70	44
North Carolina:	41	70
Pennsylvania:	43	36
South Dakota:	60	38
Vermont:	43	56
Washington:	63	93
Overall	46	63

46. Darcy, Welch, and Clark, *Women, Elections, and Representation.*
47. Duke, "Paying Their Dues."

48. Rix, *American Woman,* 79.

49. For more information, see Steven L. Willborn, *A Comparable Worth Primer* (Lexington, Mass.: D. C. Heath, 1986).

50. One study, which surveyed state legislators across the nation in 1981, provides information about the gradual gains in background discussed here. It also shows that women make little progress on the homefront. See Susan J. Carroll and Wendy S. Strimling with the assistance of John J. Cohen and Barbara Geiger-Parker, *Women's Routes to Elective Office: A Comparison with Men's* (New Brunswick, N.J.: Center for the American Woman and Politics, 1983).

51. Relatedly, Blair and Stanley find that women legislators respond to these circumstances by eliminating, to the extent possible, stereotypically female social conduct. Diane D. Blair and Jeanie R. Stanley, "Personal Relationships and Legislative Power: Male and Female Perceptions," Legislative Studies Quarterly 16 (November 1991): 495–507.

52. Regression equations controlling for state, ideology, family income, religion, educational level, occupation, constituency type, and state were also run on these data, and differences remained strong and significant.

53. These comparisons are statistically significant.

54. Quoted in A. G. Block, "The Top Six," *California Journal* 19 (July 1988): 281.

55. Ibid.

56. Kirkpatrick, *Political Woman.*

57. Edmond Costantini, "Political Women and Political Ambition: Closing the Gender Gap," *American Journal of Political Science* 34 (August 1990): 741–770.

58. One recent study sheds light on why some gap still remains. It appears that women are more influenced by the perceived strength of their current political position than men. Male councilmembers are more self-motivated and single-minded; they will run for higher office as ambition dictates, rather than because of a very high vote margin in the last election. This means, of course, that women feel less confident about and pursue higher office less frequently than their male colleagues. See Timothy Bledsoe and Mary Herring Munro, "Victims of Circumstances: Women in Pursuit of Political Office in America," *American Political Science Review* 84 (March 1990): 213–224.

59. In addition to comparing percentages, comparison of mean levels of activity by women and men shows little difference. Similarly, multivariate analysis using Ordinary Least Squares (OLS) regression showed no statistical differences between the sexes. Here again, control variables included state, ideology, family income, constituency type, age, education levels, religion, and occupational category.

Chapter 3

1. The case was later decided by the U.S. Supreme Court (*Phillips v. Martin Marietta* Corporation, 400 U.S. 542 [1971]) in favor of the women, and it consti-

tutes an important precedent in equal protection for women in employment situations. Hope Chamberlin, *A Minority of Members: Women in the U.S. Congress* (New York: Praeger, 1973), 312.

2. Ann Richards on November 6, 1990, as quoted in Tillet and Krafchek, "Factsheet on Women's Political Progress," 1.

3. Diamond, *Sex Roles*.

4. Johnson et al., *Profile of Women*.

5. Freida Gehlen, "Women Members of Congress: A Distinctive Role," in Marianne Githens and Jewell Prestage, eds., *A Portrait of Marginality: The Political Behavior of the American Woman* (New York: McKay, 1977), 304–319.

6. Shelah G. Leader, "The Policy Impact of Elected Women Officials," in Joseph Cooper and Louis Maisels, eds., *The Impact of the Electoral Process* (Beverly Hills: Sage, 1977), 265–284.

7. Pippa Norris, "Women in Congress: A Policy Difference?" *Politics* 6, no. 1 (Spring 1986): 34–40; Kathleen A. Frankovic, "Sex and Voting in the U.S. House of Representatives, 1961–1975," *American Politics Quarterly* 5 (July 1977): 315–331; and Susan Welch, "Are Women More Liberal than Men in the U.S. Congress?" *Legislative Studies Quarterly* 10 (February 1985): 125–134. Only Sue Thomas, "Voting Patterns in the California Assembly: The Role of Gender," *Women & Politics* 9 (1990): 43–56, found that in one state, California, women state legislators were not more liberal than their male counterparts, although they were more supportive of women's issues. This appears to have been true because both the women and men in that state were fairly liberal—a ceiling effect was operating.

8. Emmy E. Werner, "Women in the State Legislatures," *Western Political Quarterly* 21 (March 1968): 40–50. See also Rita Mae Kelly et al., "Gender and Behavior Styles of State Level Administrators" (Paper presented to the American Political Science Association, Chicago, September 3–6, 1987), for similar information on state-level administrators; Janet M. Martin, "Recruitment of Women to the President's Cabinet" (Paper presented at the annual meeting of the American Political Science Association, Chicago, September 3–6, 1987), on women in the presidential cabinet; Georgia Duerst-Lahti and Cathy Marie Johnson, "Gender and Style in Bureaucracy," *Women & Politics* 10 (1990): 67–120; and Katherine Meyer, "The Influence of Gender on Work Activities and Attitudes of Senior Civil Servants in the United States, Canada, and Great Britain," in Moore and Spitze, *Women and Politics,* on senior civil servants.

9. Virginia Sapiro, "Research Frontier Essay: When Are Interests Interesting? The Problem of Political Representation of Women," *American Political Science Review* 75 (September 1981): 711.

10. Diamond, *Sex Roles*, 45.

11. Susan Gluck Mezey, "Support for Women's Rights Policy: An Analysis of Local Politicians," *American Politics Quarterly* 6 (October 1978): 496.

12. Johnson et al., *Profile of Women*.

13. Susan J. Carroll, "Looking Back at the 1980s and Forward to the 1990s," *CAWP News & Notes* (Center for the American Woman and Politics) 7 (Summer 1990): 11.

14. A recent study of state legislators across the nation reports similar findings. See Dodson, *Gender and Policymaking*.

15. Ronald B. Rapoport, Walter J. Stone, and Alan I. Abramowitz, "Sex and the Caucus Participant: The Gender Gap and Presidential Nominations," *American Journal of Political Science* 34 (August 1990): 725–740.

16. Debra L. Dodson and Susan J. Carroll, *Reshaping the Agenda: Women in State Legislatures* (New Brunswick, N.J.: Center for the American Woman and Politics, 1991). See also Debra L. Dodson, "Are Parties Gender-Neutral?" (Paper presented at the annual meeting of the Midwest Political Science Association, Chicago, April 13–15, 1989), for information about attitudes broken down by parties.

17. Welch, "Are Women More Liberal," 125–134; Norris, "Women in Congress," 34–40.

18. The NWPC voting survey included issues of child care, minimum wage, the Civil Rights Act of 1990, family planning funds, various appropriations measures related to abortion funding, and in the Senate, the Souter nomination. The NWPC study included information on the votes of each legislator. Calculations of percentages by sex and by party were performed by the author.

19. These findings hold up under multivariate analysis.

20. Again, these findings are replicated with techniques of multivariate analysis. Differences between women and men in health and welfare assignments, chair positions on health and welfare committees, business assignments, and chair positions on business committees were statistically significant. No other assignments or chair positions achieved either statistical or substantive significance.

21. Susan J. Carroll and Ella Taylor, "Gender Differences in the Committee Assignments of State Legislators: Preferences or Discrimination?" (Paper presented at the annual meeting of the Midwest Political Science Association, Chicago, April 13–16, 1989). Also, Susan J. Carroll, and Ella Taylor, "Gender Differences in Policy Priorities of U.S. State Legislators" (Paper presented at the annual meeting of the American Political Science Association, Atlanta, August 31–September 3, 1989).

22. Costantini, "Political Women and Political Ambition," 763. In order to further evaluate the finding that women were more tied to their party (as seen in the analysis of 1988 survey data), readers should know that gender differences on the representation of party question no longer achieved statistical significance after adding controls during multivariate analysis.

23. Another study of women legislators in Arizona and California found that women representatives were more likely than men to consider women a very important reelection constituency. These women representatives also felt uniquely qualified to handle the concerns of female constituents. See Beth Reingold, "Concepts

of Representation among Female and Male State Legislators'' (Paper presented at the annual meeting of the American Political Science Association, Washington, D.C., August 29–September 1, 1991).

24. Readers will note that the gender differences in pride in accomplishment of those accomplishments listed first, while considerable, do not attain statistical significance. However, of those accomplishments listed second, the same pattern results and those differences are statistically significant. Furthermore, statistical significance was achieved for the variables concerning pride in accomplishments concerning women and concerning business when multivariate controls were applied.

25. G. E. Anderson, "Women in Congress," *Commonweal*, March 13, 1929, 532–34, as quoted in Irwin N. Gertzog, *Congressional Women: Their Recruitment, Treatment, and Behavior* (New York: Praeger, 1984), 158.

26. Geraldine Ferraro, "Women as Candidates," *Harvard Political Review* 7 (1979): 21–24, as quoted in Gertzog, *Congressional Women*, 160.

27. Fifty-six women legislators were interviewed as well as ten staff members between August 1988 and May 1989. The interviews also focused upon the impact of the percentage of women in the legislature and how that affected the behavior of women and men. These findings are reported in Chapter 4.

28. We chose as the definition of women's legislative issues those that embrace both feminist and traditional concerns of women for several reasons. The first is that feminist women's issues such as the ERA and reproductive rights are not necessarily the only ones of concern to women. Yet these are the measures usually used in studies of women elites. It may be a better measure to use issues that remove the bias of only those who refer to themselves as feminists. Indeed, it is perhaps the more mainstream issues that provide an indication of policy responsiveness to the general population rather than a small, specific one.

29. Examining the first priority state legislators list among their five also reveals interesting things about the kinds of priorities that emerge for women and men. Women have an average of 0.05 more bills dealing with women, and children and families among their single top priority than do men. This finding is statistically significant at the .10 level. Additionally, women legislators in seven out of twelve states conform to this pattern.

30. Center for the American Woman and Politics, Eagleton Institute, Rutgers University, New Brunswick, N.J., *Women State Legislators: Report from a Conference*, June 17–20, 1982, 13.

31. Carroll, "Looking Back," 9–12; Carroll and Taylor, "Gender Differences in Policy Priorities."

32. Debra L. Dodson, "A Comparison of the Impact of Women and Men's Attitudes on Their Legislative Behavior: Is What They Say What They Do?" (Paper presented at the annual meeting of the American Political Science Association, Atlanta, August 31–September 3, 1989). My research also finds that women of all

ideological viewpoints support women's legislation more than do their male counterparts. While it is true that liberal women support more women's legislation than
do moderate or conservative women, the gender differences within the categories
are compelling.

33. Carroll, "Looking Back," 9–12; and Carroll and Taylor, "Gender Differences in the Committee Assignments." Additionally, a study of women state legislators in Massachusetts found that twenty-eight out of the thirty women interviewed
felt that "if it were not for them, most of the legislation that affects women would
not have been on the legislative agenda." See Debra Gross, "Taking Another Look
at Descriptive Representation: The Case of Women Legislators" (Paper presented
at the annual meeting of the American Political Science Association, Atlanta,
August 31–September 3, 1989), 10.

34. Michelle A. Saint-Germain, "Does Their Difference Make a Difference?
The Impact of Women on Public Policy in the Arizona Legislature," *Social Science
Quarterly* 70 (December 1989): 956–968. In addition to evidence of gender differences in policy priorities among legislators on the state level, research is beginning
to track these kinds of differences on the local level as well. Janet Boles recently
reported that local women officeholders in Milwaukee reported more activity on
women's issues generally and were involved in a broader range of women's issues
than were their male counterparts. The local women placed greater importance on
such issues than men and were more likely to have provided leadership on them.
See Janet K. Boles, "Local Elected Women and Policymaking: Movement Delegates or Feminist Trustees?" (Paper presented at the annual meeting of the American Political Science Association, Washington, D.C., August 29–September 1,
1991). See also Janet K. Boles, "Advancing the Women's Agenda within Local
Legislatures: The Role of Female Elected Officials," in Dodson, *Gender and
Policymaking,* 39–48.

35. Lyn Kathlene, Susan E. Clarke, and Barbara A. Fox, "Ways Women Politicians Are Making a Difference," in Dodson, *Gender and Policymaking,* 31–38.

Chapter 4

1. Rosabeth Moss Kanter, *Men and Women of the Corporation* (New York:
Basic Books, 1977), 283–284, as quoted in Janice D. Yoder, "Rethinking Tokenism: Looking beyond Numbers," *Gender and Society* 5 (June 1991): 178.

2. See Robert A. Baron and Donn Byrne, *Social Psychology: Understanding
Human Interaction,* 4th ed. (Boston: Allyn and Bacon, 1984), 248–263.

3. For information on the effects of rewards and sanctions, see Leon Festinger,
"A Theory of Social Comparison Processes," *Human Relations* 7 (1954): 117–140;
and James Dittes and Harold Kelley, "Effects of Different Conditions of Acceptance upon Conformity to Group Norms," *Journal of Abnormal and Social Psychology* 53 (1956): 100–107.

4. See, for example, Leon Festinger, *A Theory of Cognitive Dissonance* (Stan-

ford, Calif.: Stanford University Press, 1957). See also Philip Meyer, "If Hitler Asked You to Electrocute a Stranger, Would You?" in Richard Greenbaum and Harvey A. Tilker, eds., *The Challenge of Psychology* (Englewood Cliffs, N.J.: Prentice-Hall, 1972), 457–465; Edward E. Sampson, "Status Congruence and Cognitive Consistency," in Carl W. Backman and Paul F. Secord, *Problems in Social Psychology: Selected Readings* (New York: McGraw-Hill, 1966), 218–226; and Harold B. Gerard, "Conformity and Commitment to the Group," in Backman and Secord, *Problems in Social Psychology*, 245–247.

5. Relatedly, minority status within an organization (whether or not one is a minority in the wider society) may serve to highlight the distance between the dominant and minority groups and cause members of the minority to perceive a constant reminder of a responsibility to help one's brethren. Such experience may lead them to be especially attentive to instances in which lightening the load for those similarly situated is possible.

6. Rosabeth Moss Kanter, "Some Effects of Proportions on Group Life: Skewed Sex Ratios and Response to Token Women," *American Journal of Sociology* 82 (March 1977): 965.

7. Kanter, *Men and Women of the Corporation*, and Cynthia Fuchs Epstein, *Deceptive Distinctions: Sex, Gender, and The Social Order*, (New Haven: Yale University Press, 1988).

8. A recent study of socialization of national convention delegates reveals interesting findings regarding how socialization is necessary to sustain certain types of political involvement but not others. See Debra L. Dodson, "Socialization of Party Activists: National Convention Delegates, 1972–1981, *American Journal of Political Science* 34 (November 1990): 1119–1141.

9. See Richard Fenno, *Congressmen in Committee* (Boston: Little, Brown, 1973). He discusses the three goals of every member of Congress: reelection, good public policy, and influence within the legislative chamber.

10. Donald Matthews, *U.S. Senators and Their World* (New York: Random House, 1960); Barbara Sinclair, *The Transformation of the U.S. Senate* (Baltimore: Johns Hopkins University Press, 1989); and John Hibbing and Sue Thomas, "The Modern United States Senate: What Is Accorded Respect?" *Journal of Politics* 52 (February 1990): 126–145.

11. Flammang, "Female Officials in the Feminist Capital," 94–118.

12. Quoted in Ibid., 113.

13. Rosemary Breslin and Joshua Hammer, *Gerry! A Woman Making History* (New York: Pinnacle Books, 1984), 81.

14. The types of bills investigated include those dealing with issues of abortion, children, education, family, health, sex, and welfare. Saint-Germain, "Does Their Difference Make a Difference?" 956–968.

15. Mary Fainsod Katzenstein, "Feminism within American Institutions: Unobtrusive Mobilization in the 1980s," *Signs* 16 (Autumn 1990): 54.

16. The research findings presented below appear in somewhat different form in

Sue Thomas, "The Impact of Women on State Legislative Policies," *Journal of Politics* 53 (November 1991): 958–976.

17. Legislators were asked in the mail survey to list their top five priority bills of the last complete legislative session. Eight coding categories differentiate bills dealing with women's issues, children's and family issues; budget and tax issues; crime; education and medical issues; business and economic issues; energy, environment, and public land use issues; and welfare issues.

18. The reader may wonder why so many states fall into the middle category while only two or three states compose the high and low categories. The reason is simply that so few states fall significantly above and below the average, there was little to choose from. The problem was compounded by the need to have regional balance and diversity in political culture in each category. In short, the problem here is the same one faced by all studies of women officeholders. We simply do not have the range and diversity that would be ideal.

19. See Virginia Sapiro, "The Gender Bias of American Social Policy," *Political Science Quarterly* 101 (1986): 221–238, for fuller analysis of this point.

20. Flammang, "Female Officials in the Feminist Capital," 94–118.

21. See Roger W. Cobb and Charles D. Elder, *Participation in American Politics: The Dynamics of Agenda Building* (Boston: Allyn and Bacon, 1972).

22. States in the middle category display no clear trend, as might be expected, given that the range of percentages of women is so limited. A possible alternate explanation, that political culture accounts for tendencies to give priority to bills dealing with women or the family, appears incorrect. In short, political culture is not a credible predictor of whether women legislators placed priority on bills in those areas more often than did men.

23. Nor are gender differences related to political culture or region. The only three states in which women's mean level of priority bills did not exceed men's were California, Washington, and North Carolina, two western states and one southern. The first two states are in the middle category with regard to percentage of women, and the final state is in the high category. Finally, California and Washington are considered to be within the moralistic political culture, and North Carolina is traditionalistic.

24. Political culture is a concept used by political scientists to explain how states differ in terms of predominant political, social, and cultural influences. Daniel Elazar, the political scientist famous for tracing the political cultures of all fifty states, identifies three major cultures. These are the traditionalistic, the moralistic, and the individualistic. For a fuller description, see Elazar, *American Federalism.*

25. In a related study, Berkman and O'Connor find that the percentage of women in state legislatures is related to the level of abortion policy. Michael B. Berkman and Robert E. O'Connor, "Do Women Legislators Matter? Female Legislators and State Abortion Policy," *American Politics Quarterly* 21 (January 1993): 102–124.

26. Notice that neither political culture nor region of the country can account for the pattern noted here.

27. *National NOW Times,* May/June 1987.

28. *California Journal,* January 1988.

29. Quoted in Kay Mills, "Maxine Waters: The Sassy Legislator Who Knows There's More Than One Way to Make a Political Statement," *Governing* (March 1988): 30.

Chapter 5

1. Responses were significant at the .0000 level.

2. On a scale in which 0 equals not selecting this option and 1 equals choosing it, the average score for women respondents was .59, and the average score for men was .23. This analysis is significant at the .0000 level.

3. Center for the American Woman and Politics, Eagleton Institute of Politics, Rutgers University, New Brunswick, N.J., *Women State Legislators: Report from a Conference,* June 17–20, 1982, 13.

4. Geraldine Ferraro in the afterward of Dorothy W. Cantor and Toni Bernay with Jean Stoess, *Women in Power: The Secrets of Leadership* (Boston: Houghton Mifflin, 1992), 288.

5. Iva Ellen Deutchman, "The Politics of Empowerment," *Women & Politics* 11 (1991): 5.

6. Cantor, Bernay, and Stoess, *Women in Power,* 40.

7. Ibid.

8. Ibid.

9. Cantor, Bernay, and Stoess, *Women in Power,* 56.

10. Flammang, "Female Officials in the Feminist Capital," 108.

11. Flammang, Janet A., "Feminist Theory: The Question of Power," in *Current Perspectives in Social Theory,* vol. 4, edited by S. B. Menall. Greenwich, Conn. JAI Press, 1983.

12. Dodson and Carroll, *Reshaping the Agenda,* 79.

13. Ibid., 83–84.

14. Quoted in Ibid., 84.

15. Madeleine Kunin, "Why Move On?" *CAWP News & Notes* (Center for the American Woman and Politics) 7 (Summer 1990): 15.

16. In Janet Rosenberg, Harry Perlstadt, and William R. F. Phillips, "Politics, Feminism, and Women's Professional Orientations: A Case Study of Women Lawyers," *Women & Politics* 10 (1990): 40. They find that it is not only women legislators who have trouble altering the norms and standards by which their work is done; another example of the same phenomenon exists with women lawyers. "They challenge the legitimacy of sex-based status distributions, but not the legitimacy of norms governing patterns of work or the allocations of rewards. . . . [They] are interested in changing the position of players, but not the rules of the professional game."

17. For a discussion of the goals of members of Congress, see Fenno, *Congressmen in Committees*.

18. Roger H. Davidson, "The Legislative Reorganization Act of 1946," *Legislative Studies Quarterly* 15 (August 1990): 357–373.

19. Ibid.

20. Ibid.

21. Davidson, "Legislative Reorganization Act," 367.

22. Ibid., 357.

23. Ibid., 371.

24. Ibid., 358.

25. Walter Kravitz, "The Legislative Reorganization Act of 1970," *Legislative Studies Quarterly* 15 (August 1990): 375–399.

26. Ibid.

27. Ibid.

28. See Stephen Smith and Christopher Deering, *Committees in Congress* (Washington, D.C.: Congressional Quarterly Press, 1984); and Roger H. Davidson and Walter J. Oleszek, *Congress and Its Members*, 3d ed. (Washington, D.C.: Congressional Quarterly Press, 1990).

29. Ibid.

30. Ibid. See also Janet Hook, "Big Reorganizations in 1946 and 1970 Were Exceptions to the Rule of Stasis," *Congressional Quarterly Weekly Report* (June 6, 1992): 1582–1583.

31. Smith and Dearing, *Committees in Congress;* Davidson and Oleszek, *Congress and Its Members*.

32. In Chapter 4, I introduced a discussion of norms to examine the circumstances under which members of minority groups are constrained from introducing their singular priorities and stylistic preferences into the institutional environment and those under which minority members are accorded more freedom to do so. The focus here is on the evolution of institutionwide norms, standards, and folkways.

33. See Matthews, *U.S. Senators and Their World*, for an excellent discussion of the norms of the 1950s.

34. Sinclair, *Transformation of the U.S. Senate*.

35. Ibid.

36. The Congress is faced with another prospect for procedural reform of the sort enacted in 1946 and again in 1970. Senators David Boren (D-OK) and Pete Domenici (R-NM) and Representatives Lee Hamilton (D-IN) and Willis Gradison (R-OH) joined together in the 102d Congress to introduce Senate Concurrent Resolution 57. It proposed a joint committee to study the following suggestions: restoration of parallel jurisdictions of the committees in the House of Representatives and the Senate; imposition of a germaneness rule in the Senate; reduction in the number of committees and subcommittees in both chambers; campaign finance reform; and reduction in congressional staffing. These members of Congress warned that if legislators do not reform an inefficient and frequently ineffective institution, then

the public will do it for them in the form of widespread support for challengers to sitting members. See David L. Boren, "Major Repairs for Congress," *Washington Post,* August 8, 1991. In addition to this reform proposal, based on its predecessors in 1946 and 1970, others are being introduced, mostly as a response to the stalemate and scandals of 1992. For more information, see Janet Hook, "Extensive Reform Proposals Cook on the Front Burner," *Congressional Quarterly Weekly Report* (June 6, 1992): 1579–1585.

37. See, for example, Hibbing and Thomas, "Modern United States Senate."

38. Jean Marie Brough, Republican floor leader in the Washington House of representatives in 1987; quoted in "Women in Politics Study Their Impact," *St. Louis Post Dispatch,* November 22, 1987, by Margaret Wolf Freivogel.

39. Kay Lehman Schlozman, "Representing Women in Washington: Sisterhood and Pressure Politics," in Louise A. Tilley and Patricia Gurin, eds., *Women, Politics, and Change* (New York: Russell Sage, 1990), 375–376.

40. Kenneth R. Mladenka, "Blacks and Hispanics in Urban Politics," *American Political Science Review* 83 (March 1989): 185.

41. See Darcy, Welch, and Clark, *Women, Elections, and Representation:* and Carroll, *Women as Candidates.*

42. The 1992 elections have just concluded. The patterns of incremental increases of women in state legislatures continued, and women's share of seats rose from 18 to 20 percent. Interestingly, previous patterns relating to women's share of seats in the U.S. Congress were shattered this year. Women now constitute 10 percent of Congress, or 10.8 percent of the House and 6 percent of the Senate. Widespread anti-incumbent sentiment stemming from the House banking and post office scandals; the savings and loan scandal; the recession; and the perceived deadlock between Congress and the president (and, no doubt, a host of other reasons) resulted in record retirements from the House and substantial losses in the primary and general elections. Perhaps most important, as a result of redistricting, a large number of open seats were available for which women candidates competed and won. Even this rather dramatic and much emphasized addition of women to the U.S. Conrgess does not come close to parity in representation, nor does it signal the near-term possibility.

43. Katzenstein, "Feminism within American Institutions," 37.

44. Lyn Kathlene, "The Impact of Gender Differences on Public Policy Formation," Discussion Paper No. 24, Center for Public Policy Research, University of Colorado at Boulder, September 1987.

45. Sue Tolleson Rinehart, "Do Women Leaders Make a Difference? Substance, Style, and Perceptions," in Dodson, *Gender and Policymaking,* 92–102

46. Dodson and Carroll, *Reshaping the Agenda,* 31.

47. Ibid., 49.

48. Ibid., 49.

49. Breslin and Hammer, *Gerry!,* 87.

Chapter 6

1. Ehrenreich, "Sorry, Sisters," 15.

2. It is true that creating categories such as political integrationists and political reformists is, in some ways, reductionistic and therefore does not do justice to the viewpoints of those so classified. However, I stand by this analysis not only because it is a good heuristic device but because it accurately depicts the fact that while individual commentators most certainly see the situation in far more complexity than I have allowed, much of their argumentation as well as much of the research and writing on political women uses the either-or nature of these stark claims as a starting assumption for analysis or a basis for arriving at conclusions as to women's impact.

3. For discussion about how candidates, campaign managers, and polling and media consultants view the perceptions of voters about the honesty and integrity of women candidates, see Celinda Lake, "Challenging the Credibility Gap," *Notes from Emily,* published by Enily's List, June 1991, 1, 4–5. For discussion about voters' perceptions of characteristics and issue attitudes of women candidates, see Darcy, Welch, and Clark, *Women, Elections, and Representation.*

4. This is illustrated by the 1992 U.S. Senate candidacy of Lynn Yeakel. Although she based her campaign on the paucity of women in the U.S. Senate and her plans to focus on legislation of interest to women, her opponent, Arlen Specter, prevailed.

5. It is important to remember that this analysis of the current behavior of women legislators and its variability over time is being cast in a collective perspective. I have not been in the business of explaining why a particular woman legislator acts or reacts as she does, nor have I been arguing that every female representative conforms to the general patterns under analysis. The patterns and the explanations for them refer to collective behavior and not each individual decision making up the whole.

6. See Flexner, *Century of Struggle;* Evans, *Born for Liberty;* Deckard, *Women's Movement;* Aileen Kraditor, *The Ideas of the Woman Suffrage Movement, 1890–1920* (New York: Columbia University Press, 1965).

7. See Flexner, *Century of Struggle;* Evans, *Born for Liberty;* Deckard, *Women's Movement;* Kraditor, *The Ideas of the Woman Suffrage Movement.*

8. See Flexner, *Century of Struggle;* Evans, *Born for Liberty;* Deckard, *Women's Movement;* Kraditor, *The Ideas of the Woman Suffrage Movement.*

9. C. Dreifus, "Women in Politics: An Interview with Edith Green," *Social Policy* 2 (1972): 16–22, as quoted in Gertzog, *Congressional Women,* 117.

10. Darcy, Welch, and Clark, *Women, Elections, and Representation.*

11. Ibid.; Carroll, *Women as Candidates.*

12. Quoted in Gross, "Taking Another Look at Descriptive Representation."

13. Kathlene, "Impact of Gender Differences."

14. Lyn Kathlene, "Gendered Approaches to Policy Formation in the Colorado

Legislature'' (Paper presented at the annual meeting of the Midwest Political Science Association, Chicago, April 18–20, 1991).

15. After the 1992 elections, in which women's representation in the U.S. Senate rose from two to six, the leadership decided to install a women's restroom off the Senate chambers. Shortly therafter, a seventh, Kay Bailey Hutchison (R-Tex), was added by special election.

16. Carol Steinbach of the *National Journal*, as quoted in Neal R. Pierce, ''Women's-Rights Battles Shifting to State Arenas,'' in the *Lincoln Journal-Star*, August 16, 1987.

17. Marcia Manning Lee, ''Why Few Women Hold Public Office: Democracy and Sexual Roles,'' *Political Science Quarterly* 91 (1976): 297–314.

18. James G. March and John P. Olsen, *Rediscovering Institutions* (New York: Free Press, 1989), as quoted in Charlene Wear Simmons, ''Thoughts on Legislative Ethics Reform and Representation,'' *PS: Political Science and Politics* 24 (June 1991): 194.

Chapter 7

1. Richard D. Manning, ''How Three Women Took Over Missoula County and the 'Gender Factor' Became an Edge,'' *Governing* (May 1988): 44.

2. Stevens and Dussault quoted in Ibid., 49.

3. Ibid.

4. Quoted in Manning, *Three Women*, 46.

5. Ibid., 44–46, 50.

6. Ibid.

7. Geraldine Ferraro in the afterword of Cantor, Bernay, and Stoess, *Women in Power*, 28.

8. This refers to Lyn Kathlene's definitions of contextualist and instrumentalist. See Kathlene, ''Impact of Gender Differences.''

9. This might also have something to do with women reaching a critical mass where male representatives recognize that they have to systematically court women's votes in order to pass their own (men's) legislative priorities—for example, horse trading between the sexes.

10. Carroll and Taylor, ''Gender Differences in Policy Priorities of U.S. State Legislators,'' 19–20.

11. Anne Phillips, *Engendering Democracy* (University Park: Pennsylvania State University Press, 1991), 21–22.

12. A postelection study of female Democratic candidates for Congress in 1990 as well as their campaign managers and polling and media consultants showed that the special challenges women faced appeared in three areas: ''Are they competent and qualified enough to do the job?'' ''Are they tough enough to handle the job?'' and, ''Are they going to be able to mount a winning campaign?'' See Lake, ''Challenging the Credibility Gap,'' 1, 4, 5.

13. Lake, ''Challenging the Credibility Gap,'' 1, 4, 5.

Appendix A

Means for Attitude Issues by Gender and by State

	Job	Politics	Profession	Appointment	Effect	Women run
AZ	†	*	†	†	†	*
CA	†	*	†	†	†	*
GA	†	*	†	†	†	*
IL	†		†	†	†	*
IA	†	*	†	†	†	*
MS					†	*
NE	†	*	†	†	†	*
NC	†	*		†	†	*
PA	†		†	†		*
SD		*	†	†	†	*
VT	†	*	†	†	†	*
WA	†	*	†	†	†	*

* = Female state legislators believe it is harder for women to obtain a job or political office, feel women are more effective once in office, would like to see more women run for office, and are prouder of particular achievements. These findings are statistically significant.

† = Female state legislators believe that these things are harder, etc., but not at a statistically significant level.

Appendix B

Means for Activity Variables by Gender and by State

	Floor	Committee	Bargain	Lobby	Bargaining Difficulty
AZ				*	†
CA					
GA					†
IL			†		†
IA		*			†
MS			†		
NE		*			
NC	*		†	*	
PA			†		†
SD				*	
VT			†		
WA	*		†		

* = Women are more active on the floor, in committee, bargaining with colleagues, and lobbying. They report more difficulty bargaining than men in their states, and each of these findings is statistically significant.

† = Women are more active, etc., but not at a statistically significant level.

Appendix C

MAIL QUESTIONNAIRE

The purpose of this survey is to gain insight into the workings of state legislatures. Again, we assure complete confidentiality of answers.

The first set of questions deals with your views about
performing some aspects of your job.

1. In your view, what is the main duty of a legislator? (Check the one you believe to be the main duty.)

    ——————— 1. To get bills passed
    ——————— 2. To aid in the process by working on committees
    ——————— 3. To provide constituency services
    ——————— 4. Other (please list) ———————————————

There are many interests demanding attention from you as a legislator. How important is representing each of the following interests to you? (Please circle answer in each category.)

	Very Important	Somewhat Important	Not Very	See No Separate Interest
2. The Elderly	1	2	3	4
3. Business	1	2	3	4
4. Labor	1	2	3	4
5. Women	1	2	3	4
6. Your Party	1	2	3	4
7. Racial Minorities	1	2	3	4

Please indicate, as best you can, the frequency with which you do the following in an *average week* of a *legislative session*. (Please circle answer in each category.)

	Never	Once or Twice	3–10 Times	More than 10 Times
8. Speak on the floor in a week where there are many hours of floor debate	1	2	3	4
9. Speak in committee in a week of committee hearings	1	2	3	4
10. Bargain with other legislators to win support for your bills	1	2	3	4
11. Meet with lobbyists	1	2	3	4

12. Do you find it difficult to bargain with other legislators for their votes?

    _____ 1. Frequently
    _____ 2. Occasionally
    _____ 3. Most of the time
    _____ 4. Never

We are interested in your top five priority bills in the last complete legislative session. (List bills by content area and circle if yes for each category)

	Passed by Legislature	Signed By Gov.	Was a Priority for Leadership	Had Strong Opposition
Example: _____	1	2	3	4
13. Bill 1 _____	1	2	3	4
14. Bill 2 _____	1	2	3	4
15. Bill 3 _____	1	2	3	4
16. Bill 4 _____	1	2	3	4
17. Bill 5 _____	1	2	3	4

18. What was the total number of bills you introduced in the last complete legislative session? _____

   19. How many were passed into law? _____

20. List one or two of the accomplishments you are proudest of during your tenure as a state legislator.

_____

_____

The next set of questions deals with your views about the role of women in society.

Do you think women have it easier or harder than men in the following ways:

	Easier	Same	Harder
21. Getting a job suitable to their education and training	1	2	3
22. Getting ahead in elective politics	1	2	3
23. Being accepted as a member of a profession such as law or medicine	1	2	3
24. Getting appointed to public office	1	2	3

25. In your legislature, how do you rate the effectiveness of women members compared with men?

_____ 1. Women more effective

_____ 2. Women less effective

_____ 3. Same

26. If women more effective, why? (Check as many as apply)

_____ 1. Women are more persuasive

_____ 2. Women are better at achieving consensus

_____ 3. Women receive special treatment

_____ 4. Women work harder

_____ 5. Women are less interested in being in the limelight and more interested in getting the job done behind the scenes

_____ 6. Other (list) _____

27. If women less effective, why? (Check as many as apply)

_____ 1. Lack of seniority

_____ 2. Lack of experience

_____ 3. Not suited for politics

_____ 4. Discrimination against them

_____ 5. Do not work as hard

_____ 6. Other (List) _____

28. Are you particularly interested in seeing more women run for political office?

_____ 1. YES   _____ 2. NO

29. If yes, why (Check as many as apply)

_____ 1. Need for balance reflecting proportions in society

_____ 2. The more women in the legislature, the more likely it is that women's goals will be met

_____ 3. The more women, the more likely it is that the process will change

_____ 4. Other (list) _____

30. If no, why? (Check as many as apply

_____ 1. Should not be concerned with any specific numerical goals based on sex

_____ 2. It does not matter which sex is elected

_____ 3. Other (List) _____

***The final set of questions deals with information about
your position and your demographic group.
Please check correct answer or fill in the blank.***

31. What year were you first elected to the legislature? _____

32. Have you served continuously since then?

       _____ 1. Yes   _____ 2. No

    33. *If no,* in what years were you absent? _____

34. Do you plan to run for a higher office in the next five years?

       _____ 1. Yes
       _____ 2. No
       _____ 3. Not yet decided

35. What is the size of the largest community in your district? _____

36. Would you say your constituency is:

       _____ 1. Rural
       _____ 2. Urban
       _____ 3. Suburban
       _____ 4. Mixed

    37. *If mixed,* please specify _____

38. Of which committees are you a member?

       1. _____
       2. _____
       3. _____
       4. _____
       5. _____

39. Are you currently a committee or subcommittee chair or a ranking member?

       _____ 1. Yes   _____ 2. No

    40. *If yes,* what position(s) do you hold? _____

41. Do you hold any other leadership positions, such as speaker, speaker pro tempore, whip, caucus chair, etc.?

       _____ 1. Yes   _____ 2. No

42. *If yes,* which position(s)? _____

43. In politics, do you consider yourself:

_____ 1. Very liberal

_____ 2. Liberal

_____ 3. Middle of the road

_____ 4. Conservative

_____ 5. Very conservative

44. What is your party identification?

_____ 1. Democrat

_____ 2. Republican

_____ 3. Other

_____ 4. None

45. What is your marital status?

_____ 1. Married

_____ 2. Divorced/separated

_____ 3. Single

_____ 4. Widowed

46. How many children do you have?

_____ 1. None

_____ 2. One

_____ 3. Two

_____ 4. Three

_____ 5. More than 3

47. What is your highest level of education?

_____ 1. High School

_____ 2. Some college

_____ 3. Technical school

_____ 4. College degree

_____ 5. Graduate or professional school

48. What year were you born? _____

49. What was your age when you were elected to your first office? _____

50. What category does your combined family income fit into:

_____ $20,000 OR LESS

_____ $21,000–35,000

_____ $36,000–50,000

_____ $51,000–65,000
_____ $66,000–80,000
_____ $81,000–95,000
_____ $95,000 AND ABOVE

51. What is your religious affiliation:

_____ 1. Protestant
_____ 2. Catholic
_____ 3. Jewish
_____ 4. Other
_____ 5. None

52. Have you held any prior political office?

_____ 1. Yes   _____ 2. No

53. *If yes,* which one(s)?

_____

_____

54. What is your present or prior occupation? _____

55. If you have any additional comments or concerns that will help us better understand your views about being a legislator, please write them in the space below.

Thank you for your assistance.

Appendix D

Interview Questions

The first set of questions deals with legislative priorities.

1. How do you choose your legislative priorities?

2. Do women focus on different legislative priorities than men? Are women as active in pursuing legislative responsibilities as men?

3. Would having more women in this legislature make you feel like you and other women might pursue a different legislative agenda or make a difference in how the legislature was run?

Now we will move on to a set of questions dealing with some specific issues areas.

4. Do you think there is an adequate amount of legislation passed dealing with the following topics:
   a. child and day care
   b. care of the elderly
   c. children's services
   d. teen pregnancy
   e. domestic violence
   f. homelessness of women and children
   g. parental leave
   h. prerelease programs for women prisoners
   i. un- or underemployment of women/job segregation and lower wages

5. Do you participate in the meetings of the women's caucus in your state?
   a. Is the caucus bipartisan?
   b. Is there an annual agenda?
   c. How extensive is your involvement?
   d. How effective do you think the women's caucus is?
   e. Would you say bills pass that might not if it weren't for the backing of the caucus? Examples?
   f. Do most women participate? Any men?

6. Do women's groups of either end of the ideological continuum approach you to sponsor legislation? Which ones? How often?

The next several questions deal with factors governing success of women in politics.

7. Are the women in leadership (either committee, party, or house) effective? Why or why not? Do women need more experience or seniority to achieve these positions than men?

8. Have you ever felt that you were directed toward committee assignments that are presumed to be interests of women or directed away from certain posts because you are a woman? Which? How did you respond?

9. Are there any "rules of the game" in your legislature that apply particularly to women?

10. Are women legislators as ambitious as men?

11. Are the male legislators sensitive to the concerns of females in politics or females in society? Why do you say this?

12. Are there any problems specific to women in elective politics? Any advantages?

13. Do you participate in any events or actions focused on getting more women elected to political office? If so, what are they? Have you received support from women's PACs?

Bibliography

Andersen, Kristi. "Working Women and Political Participation, 1952–1972." *American Journal of Political Science* 19 (August 1975): 439–453.

Anderson, Margaret L. "From the Editor." *Gender and Society* 6 (June 1992): 165.

Antolini, Denise. "Women in Local Government: An Overview." In *Political Women: Current Roles in State and Local Government*, vol. 8, Sage Yearbooks in Woman's Policy Studies, edited by Janet A. Flammang, 23–40. Beverly Hills: Sage, 1984.

Baron, Robert A., and Donn Byrne. *Social Psychology: Understanding Human Interaction*. 4th ed. Boston: Allyn and Bacon, 1984.

Basch, Norma. "Equality of Rights and Feminist Politics." *Law and Society Review* 21 (1988): 783–787.

Battistoni, Richard M. "Feminist Voices, Equality, and the U.S. Constitution." Paper presented at the annual meeting of the American Political Science Association, Washington, D.C., September 1–4, 1988.

Baxter, Sandra, and Marjorie Lansing. *Women and Politics: The Invisible Majority*. Ann Arbor: University of Michigan Press, 1980.

Beckwith, Karen. *American Women and Political Participation: The Impacts of Work, Generation, and Feminism*. New York: Greenwood Press, 1986.

Berkman, Michael B., and Robert E. O'Connor. "Do Women Legislators Matter? Female Legislators and State Abortion Policy." *American Politics Quarterly* 21 (January 1993): 102–124.

Blair, Diane D., and Jeanie R. Stanley. "Personal Relationships and Legislative Power: Male and Female Perceptions." *Legislative Studies Quarterly* 16 (November 1991): 495–507.

Bledsoe, Timothy, and Mary Herring Munro. "Victims of Circumstances: Women in Pursuit of Political Office in America." *American Political Science Review* 84 (March 1990): 213–224.

Block, A. G. "The Top Six." *California Journal* 19 (July 1988): 280–288.

Boles, Janet K. "Advancing the Women's Agenda within Local Legislatures: The Role of Female Elected Officials." In *Gender and Policymaking: Studies of Women in Office*, edited by Debra L. Dodson, 39–48. New Brunswick, N.J.: Center for the American Woman and Politics, 1991.

Boles, Janet K. "Local Elected Women and Policymaking: Movement Delegates or Feminist Trustees?" Paper presented at the annual meeting of the American Political Science Association, Washington, D.C., August 29–September 1, 1991.

Boren, David L. "Major Repairs for Congress." *Washington Post,* August 8, 1991.

Breslin, Rosemary, and Joshua Hammer. *Gerry! A Woman Making History.* New York: Pinnacle Books, 1984.

Bullock, Charles, and Susan MacManus. "Municipal Electoral Structure and the Election of Councilwomen." *Journal of Politics* 53 (February 1991): 75–89.

Burrell, Barbara C. "Women's Candidacies and the Role of Gender in Open Seat Primaries for the U.S. House of Representatives, 1968–1990." Paper presented at the annual meeting of the Midwest Political Science Association, Chicago, April 18–20, 1991.

Cantor, Dorothy W., and Toni Bernay, with Jean Stoess. *Women in Power: The Secrets of Leadership.* Boston: Houghton Mifflin, 1992.

Carroll, Susan J. "Looking Back at the 1980s and Forward to the 1990s." *CAWP News & Notes* (Center for the American Woman and Politics) 7 (Summer 1990): 9–12.

Carroll, Susan J. *Women as Candidates in American Politics.* Bloomington: Indiana University Press, 1985.

Carroll, Susan J., and Wendy S. Strimling, with the assistance of John J. Cohen and Barbara Geiger-Parker. *Women's Routes to Elective Office: A Comparison with Men's.* New Brunswick, N.J.: Center for the American Woman and Politics, 1983.

Carroll, Susan J., and Ella Taylor. "Gender Differences in the Committee Assignments of State Legislators: Preferences or Discrimination?" Paper presented at the Midwest Political Science Association, Chicago, April 13–16, 1989.

Carroll, Susan J., and Ella Taylor. "Gender Differences in Policy Priorities of U.S. State Legislators." Paper presented at the American Political Science Association, Atlanta, August 31–September 3, 1989.

Center for the American Woman and Politics. Woman State Legislators: Report from a Conference. New Brunswick, N.J. Center for the American Woman and Politics, June 17–20, 1982.

Center for the American Woman and Politics. Eagleton Institute. *Women in Legislative Leadership: Report from a Conference.* New Brunswick, N.J., November 14–17, 1985.

Chamberlin, Hope. *A Minority of Members: Women in the U.S. Congress.* New York: Praeger, 1973.

Clift, Eleanor, with Debra Rosenberg. "First Lady Culture Clash." *Newsweek,* June 8, 1992, 24.

Cobb, Roger W., and Charles D. Elder. *Participation in American Politics: The Dynamics of Agenda-Building.* Boston: Allyn and Bacon, 1972.

Conover, Pamela Johnston. "Feminism and the Gender Gap." *Journal of Politics* 50, No. 4 (1988): 985–1010.

Conover, Pamela Johnston. "Group Identification and Group Sympathy: Their Political Implications." Paper presented at the annual meeting of the Midwest Political Science Association, Chicago, April 10–12, 1986.

Conover, Pamela Johnston. "The Influence of Group Identifications of Political Perceptions and Evaluations." *Journal of Politics* 46 (August 1984): 760–785.

Cook, Elizabeth Adell, and Clyde Wilcox. "Feminism and the Gender Gap—A Second Look." *Journal of Politics* 54 (November 1991): 1112–1122.

Costain, Anne N. "Women's Claims as a Special Interest." In Carol M. Mueller, ed., *The Politics of the Gender Gap: The Social Constriction of Political Influence* (Newbury Park, CA: Sage, 1988): 150–172.

Costantini, Edmond. "Political Women and Political Ambition: Closing the Gender Gap." *American Journal of Political Science* 34 (August 1990): 741–770.

Darcy, R., Susan Welch, and Janet Clark. *Women, Elections, and Representation.* New York: Longman, 1987.

Davidson, Roger H. "The Legislative Reorganization Act of 1946." *Legislative Studies Quarterly* 15 (August 1990): 357–373.

Davidson, Roger H., and Walter J. Oleszek. *Congress and Its Members.* 3d ed. Washington, D.C.: Congressional Quarterly Press, 1990.

de Beauvior, Simone. *The Second Sex.* 1952 (Knopf). Reprint. New York: Random House, 1974.

Deckard, Barbara Sinclair. *The Women's Movement.* New York: Harper & Row, 1975.

Degler, Carl N. "On Rereading 'The Woman in America.'" *Daedalus* 116 (Fall 1987): 199–210.

Deutchman, Iva Ellen. "The Politics of Empowerment." *Woman & Politics* 11 (1991): 1–18.

Diamond, Irene. *Sex Roles in the State House.* New Haven: Yale University Press, 1977.

Di Stefano, Christine. "Postmodernism/Postfeminism?: The Case of the Incredible Shrinking Woman." Paper Presented at the annual meeting of the American Political Science Association, Chicago, September 3–6, 1987.

Dittes, James, and Harold Kelley. "Effects of Different Conditions of Acceptance upon Conformity to Group Norms." *Journal of Abnormal and Social Psychology* 53 (1956): 100–107.

Dodson, Debra L. "Are Parties Gender-Neutral?" Paper presented at the annual meeting of the Midwest Political Science Association, Chicago, April 13–15, 1989.

Dodson, Debra L. "A Comparison of the Impact of Women and Men's Attitudes on Their Legislative Behavior: Is What They Say What They Do?" Paper presented at the annual meeting of the American Political Science Association, Atlanta, August 31–September 3, 1989.

Dodson, Debra L. "Socialization of Party Activists: National Convention Delegates, 1972–1981." *American Journal of Political Science* 34 (November 1990): 1119–1141.

Dodson, Debra L., ed. *Gender and Policymaking: Studies of Women in Office.* New Brunswick, N.J.: Center for the American Woman and Politics, 1991.

Dodson, Debra L., and Susan J. Carroll. *Reshaping the Agenda: Women in State Legislatures.* New Brunswick, N.J.: Center for the American Woman and Politics, 1991.

Douglas, Carol Anne. *Love and Politics: Radical Feminist and Lesbian Theories.* San Francisco: ism press, 1990.

Dreifus, C. "Women in Politics: An Interview with Edith Green." *Social Policy* 2 (1972): 16–22.

Duerst-Lahti, Georgia, and Cathy Marie Johnson. "Gender and Style in Bureaucracy." *Women & Politics* 10 (1990): 67–120.

Duke, Lois L. "Paying Their Dues: Women as Candidates in the U.S. House of Representatives." Paper presented at the annual meeting of the American Political Science Association, Chicago, September 3–6, 1987.

Duke, Lois L. *Women in Politics: Outsiders or Insiders?* Englewood Cliffs, N.J.: Prentice-Hall, 1993.

Ehrenreich, Barbara. "Sorry, Sister, This Is Not the Revolution." *Time* Magazine Special Issue, *Women: The Road Ahead* 136 (Fall 1990): 15.

Elazar, Daniel J. *American Federalism: A View from the States.* 3d ed. New York: Harper and Row, 1984.

Epstein, Cynthia Fuchs. *Deceptive Distinctions: Sex, Gender, and the Social Order.* New Haven: Yale University Press, 1988.

Evans, Sara M. *Born for Liberty: A History of Women in America.* New York: Free Press, 1989.

Farnham, Christie, ed. *The Impact of Feminist Research in the Academy.* Bloomington: Indiana University Press, 1987.

Fenno, Richard. *Congressmen in Committees.* Boston: Little, Brown, 1973.

Festinger, Leon. *A Theory of Cognitive Dissonance.* Stanford, Calif.: Stanford University Press, 1957.

Festinger, Leon. "A Theory of Social Comparison Processes." *Human Relations* 7 (1954): 117–140.

Flammang, Janet A., ed. *Political Women: Current Roles in State and Local Government,* Sage Yearbooks in Women's Policy Studies, vol. 8 (Beverly Hills: Sage, 1984).

Flammang, Janet A. "Female Officials in the Feminist Capital: The Case of Santa Clara County." *Western Political Quarterly* 38 (March 1985): 94–118.

Flammang, Janet A. "Feminist Theory: The Question of Power." In *Current Perspectives in Social Theory*, vol. 4, edited by S. B. McNall. Greenwich, Conn.: JAI Press, 1983, 37–84.

Flexner, Eleanor. *Century of Struggle: The Woman's Rights Movement in the United States*. Rev. ed. Cambridge, Mass.: Belknap Press, 1980.

Fowlkes, Diane L. "Women in Georgia Electoral Politics: 1970–1978." *Social Science Journal* 21 (January 1984): 43–55.

Frankovic, Kathleen A. "Sex and Voting in the U.S. House of Representatives, 1961–1975." *American Politics Quarterly* 5 (July 1977): 315–331.

Gehlen, Freida. "Women Members of Congress: A Distinctive Role." In *A Portrait of Marginality: The Political Behavior of the American Woman*, edited by Marianne Githens and Jewell Prestage, 304–319. New York: McKay, 1977.

Gerard, Harold B. "Conformity and Commitment to the Group." In *Problems in Social Psychology: Selected Readings*, edited by Carl W. Backman and Paul F. Secord, 245–247. New York: McGraw-Hill, 1966.

Gertzog, Irwin N. *Congressional Women: Their Recruitment, Treatment, and Behavior*. New York: Praeger, 1984.

Gillespie, Diane, and Cassia Spohn. "'Adolescents' Attitudes toward Women in Politics: A Follow-up Study." *Women & Politics* 10 (1990): 1–16.

Gross, Debra. "Taking Another Look at Descriptive Representation: The Case of Women Legislators." Paper presented at the annual meeting of the American Political Science Association, Atlanta, August 31–September 3, 1989.

Gurin, Patricia. "Women's Gender Consciousness." *Public Opinion Quarterly* 49 (Summer 1985): 143–163.

Hibbing, John, and Sue Thomas. "The Modern United States Senate: What Is Accorded Respect?" *Journal of Politics* 52 (February 1990): 126–145.

Holtzman, Elizabeth, and Shirley Williams. "Women in the Political World: Observations." *Daedalus* 116 (Fall 1987): 199–210.

Hook, Janet. "Big Reorganizations in 1946 and 1970 Were Exceptions to the Rule of Stasis." *Congressional Quarterly* (June 6, 1992): 1582–1583.

Hook, Janet. "Extensive Reform Proposals Cook on the Front Burner." *Congressional Quarterly Weekly Report* (June 6, 1992): 1579–1585.

Jaggar, Alison M. *Feminist Politics and Human Nature*. 1983 (Harvester Press Limited). Reprint. Totowa, N.J.: Rowman and Littlefield Publishers, 1988.

Johnson, Marilyn, and Susan Carroll, with Kathy Stanwyck and Lynn Korenblit. *Profile of Women Holding Office II*. New Brunswick, N.J.: Center for the American Woman and Politics, 1978.

Kanter, Rosabeth Moss. *Men and Women of the Corporation*. New York: Basic Books, 1977.

Kanter, Rosabeth Moss. "Some Effects of Proportions on Group Life: Skewed Sex

Ratios and Response to Token Women." *American Journal of Sociology* 82 (March 1977): 965–990.

Kathlene, Lyn. "Gendered Approaches to Policy Formation in the Colorado Legislature." Paper presented at the annual meeting of the Midwest Political Science Association, Chicago, April 18–20, 1991.

Kathlene, Lyn. "The Impact of Gender Differences on Public Policy Formation." Discussion Paper No. 24, Center for Public Policy Research, University of Colorado at Boulder, September 1987.

Kathlene, Lyn, Susan E. Clarke, and Barbara A. Fox. "Ways Women Politicians Are Making A Difference." In *Gender and Policymaking: Studies of Women in Office,* edited by Debra L. Dodson, 31–38. New Brunswick, N.J.: Center for the American Woman and Politics, 1991.

Katzenstein, Mary Fainsod. "Feminism within American Institutions: Unobtrusive Mobilization in the 1980s." *Signs* 16 (Autumn 1990): 27–54.

Kelly, Rita Mae, Mary McBrayer Hale, and Jayne Burgess, with assistance from Brian C. McNeil. "Gender and Behavior Styles of State Level Administrators." Paper presented at the annual meeting of the American Political Science Association, Chicago, September 3–6, 1987.

Kendrigan, Mary Lou. "Introduction: An Understanding of Equality: The Public Policy Consequences." Paper presented at the annual meeting of the American Political Science Association, Chicago, September 3–6, 1987.

Kirkpatrick, Jeane. *Political Woman.* New York: Basic Books, 1974.

Kirp, David L., Mark G. Yudof, and Marlene Strong Franks. *Gender Justice.* Chicago: University of Chicago Press, 1986.

Klatch, Rebecca E. *Women of the New Right.* Philadelphia: Temple University Press, 1987.

Klein, Ethel. *Gender Politics: From Consciousness to Mass Politics.* Cambridge: Harvard University Press, 1984.

Kraditor, Aileen. *The Ideas of the Woman Suffrage Movement, 1890–1920.* New York: Columbia University Press, 1965.

Kravitz, Walter. "The Legislative Reorganization Act of 1970." *Legislative Studies Quarterly* 15 (August 1990): 375–399.

Kunin, Madeleine. "Lessons from One Woman's Career." *Journal of State Government* 60 (September/October, 1987): 209–212.

Kunin, Madeleine. "Why Move On?" *CAWP News & Notes* (Center for the American Woman and Politics) 7 (Summer 1990): 15.

Leader, Shelah G. "The Policy Impact of Elected Women Officials." In *The Impact of the Electoral Process,* edited by Joseph Cooper and Louis Maisels, 265–284. Beverly Hills: Sage, 1977.

Lee, Marcia Manning. "Why Few Women Hold Public Office: Democracy and Sexual Roles." *Political Science Quarterly* 91 (1976): 297–314.

Luker, Kristen. *Motherhood and the Politics of Abortion.* Berkeley and Los Angeles: University of California Press, 1984.

McDonagh, Eileen Lorenzi. "The Significance of the Nineteenth Amendment: A New Look at Civil Rights, Social Welfare, and Woman Suffrage Alignments in the Progressive Era." *Women & Politics* 10 (1990): 59–94.

Main, Eleanor C., Gerard S. Gryski, and Beth Schapiro. "Different Perspectives: Southern State Legislators' Attitudes about Women in Politics." *Social Science Journal* 21 (January 1984): 21–28.

Manning, Richard D. "How Three Women Took Over Missoula County and the 'Gender Factor' Became an Edge." *Governing* (May 1988): 44–50.

March, James G., and John P. Olsen. *Rediscovering Institutions*. New York: Free Press, 1989.

Martin, Janet M. "Recruitment of Women to the President's Cabinet." Paper presented at the annual meeting of the American Political Science Association, Chicago, September 3–6, 1987.

Matthews, Donald. *U.S. Senators and Their World*. New York: Random House, 1960.

Merritt, Sharyne. "Sex Differences in Role Behavior and Policy Orientations of Suburban Officeholders: The Effect of Women's Employment." In *Women in Local Politics*, edited by Debra W. Stewart, 115–129. Metuchen, N.J.: Scarecrow Press, 1980.

Meyer, Katherine. "The Influence of Gender on Work Activities and Attitudes of Senior Civil Servants in the United States, Canada, and Great Britain." In *Women and Politics: Activism, Attitudes, and Officeholding*, edited by Gwen Moore and Glenna Spitze, 211–232. Research in Politics and Society, vol. 2. Greenwich: Conn.: JAI Press, 1986.

Meyer, Philip. "If Hitler Asked You to Electrocute a Stranger, Would You?" In *The Challenge of Psychology*, edited by Richard Greenbaum and Harvey A. Tilker, 457–465. Englewood Cliffs, N.J.: Prentice-Hall, 1972.

Mezey, Susan Gluck. *In Pursuit of Equality: Women, Public Policy, and the Federal Courts*. New York: St. Martin's Press, 1992.

Mezey, Susan Gluck. "Support for Women's Rights Policy: An Analysis of Local Politicians." *American Politics Quarterly* 6 (October 1978): 485–497.

Mills, Kay. "Maxine Waters: The Sassy Legislator Who Knows There's More Than One Way to Make a Political Statement." *Governing* (March 1988): 26–33.

Minow, Martha. "Feminist Reason: Getting It and Losing It." *Journal of Legal Education* 38 (March/June 1988): 47–60.

Mladenka, Kenneth R. "Blacks and Hispanics in Urban Politics." *American Political Science Review* 83 (March 1989): 165–192.

Moncrief, Gary F., and Joel A. Thompson. "Electoral Structure and State Legislative Representation: A Research Note." *Journal of Politics* 54 (February 1992): 246–256.

Mueller, Carol M. "The Empowerment of Women: Polling and the Women's Voting Bloc." In *The Politics of the Gender Gap: The Social Construction of*

Political Influence, edited by Carol M. Mueller, 16–36. Newbury Park, Calif.: Sage, 1988.

Mueller, Carol M. "Nurturance and Mastery: Competing Qualifications for Women's Access to High Public Office." In *Women and Politics: Activism, Attitudes, and Officeholding,* edited by Gwen Moore and Glenna Spitze, 211–232. Research in Politics and Society, vol. 2. Greenwich, Conn.: JAI Press, 1986.

Mueller, Carol M., ed. *The Politics of the Gender Gap: The Social Construction of Political Influence.* Newbury Park, Calif.: Sage, 1988.

Nelson, Albert J. *Emerging Influentials in State Legislatures: Women, Blacks, and Hispanics.* New York: Praeger, 1991.

Nicholas, Susan Cary, Alice M. Price, and Rachel Rubin. *Rights and Wrongs: Women's Struggle for Legal Equality.* 2d ed. New York: Feminist Press, 1986.

Norris, Pippa. "Women in Congress: A Policy Difference?" *Politics* 6, no. 1 (Spring 1986): 34–40.

Phillips, Anne. *Engendering Democracy.* University Park: Pennsylvania State University Press, 1991.

Randall, Vicky. *Women and Politics.* London: Macmillan, 1982.

Rapoport, Ronald B., Walter J. Stone, and Alan I. Abramowitz. "Sex and the Caucus Participant: The Gender Gap and Presidential Nominations." *American Journal of Political Science* 34 (August 1990): 725–740.

Reingold, Beth. "Concepts of Representation among Female and Male State Legislators." Paper presented at the annual meeting of the American Political Science Association, Washington, D.C., August 29–September 1, 1991.

Rhode, Deborah L. "The Woman's Point of View." *Journal of Legal Education* 38 (March/June 1988): 39–46.

Rix, Sara E., ed. *The American Woman, 1987–1988: A Report in Depth.* New York: W. W. Norton, 1987.

Rosenberg, Janet, Harry Perlstadt, and William R. F. Phillips. "Politics, Feminism, and Women's Professional Orientations: A Case Study of Women Lawyers." *Women and Politics* 10 (1990): 19–48.

Ruth, Sheila. *Issues in Feminism: An Introduction to Women's Studies.* Mountain View, Calif.: Mayfield, 1990.

Saint-Germain, Michelle A. "Does Their Difference Make a Difference? The Impact of Women on Public Policy in the Arizona Legislature." *Social Science Quarterly* 70 (December 1989): 956–968.

Sampson, Edward E. "Status Congruence and Cognitive Consistency." In *Problems in Social Psychology: Selected Readings,* edited by Carl W. Backman and Paul F. Secord, 218–226. New York: McGraw-Hill, 1966.

Sapiro, Virginia. "The Gender Bias of American Social Policy." *Political Science Quarterly* 101 (1986): 221–238.

Sapiro, Virginia. *The Political Integration of Women: Roles, Socialization, and Politics.* Urbana: University of Illinois Press, 1983.

Sapiro, Virginia. "Research Frontier Essay: When Are Interests Interesting? The Problem of Political Representation of Women." *American Political Science Review* 75 (September 1981): 701–716.

Sapiro, Virginia. *Women, Political Action, and Political Participation.* Washington, D.C.: American Political Science Association, 1988.

Sayers, Janet. *Biological Politics.* London: Tavistock, 1982.

Schlozman, Kay Lehman. "Representing Women in Washington: Sisterhood and Pressure Politics." In *Women, Politics, and Change,* edited by Louis A. Tilley and Patricia Gurin, 339–382. New York: Russell Sage, 1990.

Sinclair, Barbara. *The Transformation of the U.S. Senate.* Baltimore: Johns Hopkins University Press, 1989.

Smith, Stephen, and Christopher Deering. *Committees in Congress.* Washington, D.C.: Congressional Quarterly Press, 1984.

Stetson, Dorothy McBride. "Work and Family in Comparative Perspective: Parental Leave in France and the United States." Paper presented at the annual meeting of the American Political Science Association, Washington, D.C., September 1–4, 1988.

Steuernagel, Trudy. "American Feminism and the Fear of Difference." Paper presented at the annual meeting of the American Political Science Association, Washington, D.C., September 2–4, 1988.

Stewart, Debra W., ed. *Women in Local Politics.* Metuchen, N.J.: Scarecrow Press, 1980.

Stoper, Emily, and Roberta Ann Johnson. "The Weaker Sex and the Better Half: The Idea of Women's Moral Superiority in the American Feminist Movement." *Polity* 10 (Winter 1977): 192–217.

Thomas, Sue. "The Effects of Race and Gender on Constituency Service." *Western Political Quarterly* 45 (March 1992): 169–180.

Thomas, Sue. "The Impact of Women on State Legislative Policies." *Journal of Politics* 53 (November 1991): 958–976.

Thomas, Sue. "Voting Patterns in the California Assembly: The Role of Gender." *Women & Politics* 9 (1990): 43–56.

Thomas, Sue, and Susan Welch. "The Impact of Gender on Activities and Priorities of State Legislators." *Western Political Quarterly* 44 (June 1991): 445–456.

Tillet, Rebecca, and Debbie Krafchek, eds. "Factsheet on Women's Political Progress." Washington, D.C.: American Council of Life Insurance and National Women's Political Caucus, June 1991.

Tolleson Rinehart, Sue. "Do Women Leaders Make a Difference? Substance, Style, and Perceptions." In *Gender and Policymaking: Studies of Women in Office,* edited by Debra L. Dodson, 91–102. New Brunswick, N.J.: Center for the American Woman and Politics, 1991.

Tolleson Rinehart, Sue. *Gender Consciousness and Politics.* New York: Routledge, Chapman and Hall, 1992.

Tong, Rosemarie. *Feminist Thought: A Comprehensive Introduction.* Boulder: Westview Press, 1989.

Welch, Susan. "Are Women More Liberal than Men in the U.S. Congress?" *Legislative Studies Quarterly* 10 (February 1985): 125–134.

Welch, Susan, John Gruhl, Michael Steinman, and John C. Comer. *American Government.* St. Paul, Minn.: West, 1986.

Welch, Susan, and Sue Thomas. "Do Women in Public Office Make a Difference?" In *Gender and Policymaking: Studies of Women in Office,* edited by Debra L. Dodson, 13–20. New Brunswick, N.J.: Center for the American Woman and Politics, 1991.

Werner, Emmy E. "Women in the State Legislatures." *Western Political Quarterly* 21 (March 1968): 40–50.

Willborn, Steven L. *A Comparable Worth Primer.* Lexington, Mass.: D. C. Heath, 1986.

Wolgast, Elizabeth H. *The Grammar of Justice.* Ithaca, N.Y.: Cornell University Press, 1987.

Yoder, Janice D. "Rethinking Tokenism: Looking beyond Numbers." *Gender and Society* 5 (June 1991): 178–192.

Index

201